# The Vulnerable Child

# The Vulnerable Child

## Volume 2

*Edited by*

**Theodore B. Cohen, M.D.,**
**M. Hossein Etezady, M.D.,**
**and Bernard L. Pacella, M.D.**

INTERNATIONAL UNIVERSITIES PRESS, INC.
Madison                                    Connecticut

**Library of Congress Cataloging-in-Publication Data**
(Revised for volume 2)

The Vulnerable child.

Includes bibliographical references and index.
1. Child psychopathology—Etiology. 2. Child psychopathology—Risk factors. 3. Child analysis—Case studies. I. Cohen, Theodore B. II. Etezady, M. Hossein. III. Pacella, Bernard L. [DNLM: 1. Mental Disorders—in infancy & childhood. 2. Psychoanalytic Therapy—in infancy & childhood. 3. Child Development. 4. Psychoanalytic Theory. 5. Child of Impaired Parents. 6. Mothers—in adolescence. 7. Child Abuse—Psychology WS 350.5 V991]
RJ499.V85 1993      618.92'89      93-33421

ISBN 0-8236-6755-3 (v. 1)
ISBN 0-8236-6756-1 (v. 2)

Manufactured in the United States of America

# Table of Contents

# Contributors

**Thomas F. Barrett, Ph.D.,** Director, Hanna Perkins Therapeutic School and Cleveland Center for Research in Child Development.

**Peter Blos Jr., M.D.,** Training Analyst, Supervising Analyst for child, adolescent, and adult cases, and Chair of the Child Analysis Committee, Michigan Psychoanalytic Institute; Lecturer, Department of Psychiatry, University Of Michigan Medical Center; former president, the Association for Child Psychoanalysis; in private practice, child, adolescent and adult psychoanalysis and psychiatry, Ann Arbor, Michigan.

**Erma Brenner,** Creator of Small House Program; Consultant, Parents' and Children's Program, New York Psychoanalytic Institute; Consultant, Rockland State Children's Hospital; Consultant, Children's Psychiatric Hospital of Queens.

**Ira Brenner, M.D.,** Training and Supervising Analyst, Philadelphia Psychoanalytic Institute; Clinical Assistant Professor, Department of Psychiatry, University of Pennsylvania; Attending Psychiatrist, Institute of Pennsylvania Hospital; participant and interviewer/researcher of the International Study of Organized Persecution of Children, Sands Point, New York; in private practice, Philadelphia, Pennsylvania; author of numerous publications on Psychic Trauma.

**Theodore B. Cohen, M.D., P.C.,** Clinical Professor of Psychiatry and Human Behavior, Jefferson Medical School, Philadelphia; Chairman of the Vulnerable Child Discussion Group, American Psychoanalytic Association; and of the Vulnerable Child Workshop, Association for Child Psychoanalysis; in private practice as a child, adolescent, and adult psychoanalyst, Narberth, Pennsylvania.

**Anne McDonald Culp, Ph.D.,** Associate Professor, Department of Family Relations and Child Development, Stillwater, Oklahoma.

**Alice Eberhart-Wright, M.A.**, Director, Preschool Day Treatment Center, Menninger Clinic, Topeka, Kansas.

**M. Hossein Etezady, M.D.**, Faculty, Philadelphia Psychoanalytic Institute; Assistant Clinical Professor, Medical College of Pennsylvania; former Clinical Director of Psychiatric Services, Paoli Memorial Hospital, Paoli, Pennsylvania; former President, Regional Council of Child and Adolescent Psychiatry; in private practice of adult, child, and adolescent psychiatry and psychoanalysis.

**Jo Ann B. Fineman, M.D.**, Associate Clinical Professor in Child Psychiatry, University of New Mexico, School of Medicine; former Faculty, Boston Psychoanalytic Institute and Southern California Psychoanalytic Institute; in private practice of child, adolescent, and adult psychiatry and psychoanalysis, Albuquerque, New Mexico.

**Eleanor Galenson, M.D.**, Clinical Professor of Psychiatry, Mount Sinai School of Medicine, New York; Faculty, Columbia Psychoanalytic Institute; member of New York Psychoanalytic Institute and Society; in private practice, infant, child, and adult psychiatry and adult psychoanalysis, New York, New York.

**Jules Glenn, M.D.**, Clinical Professor of Psychiatry and Training and Supervising Analyst Emeritus, Psychoanalytic Institute, New York University Medical Center; in private practice as a child, adolescent, and adult psychoanalyst and psychotherapist, Great Neck, New York.

**Leon Hoffman, M.D.**, Faculty, The New York Psychoanalytic Institute and Cornell University School of Medicine; certified in adult, adolescent, and child psychoanalysis by the American Psychoanalytic Association and in adult, adolescent, and child psychiatry by the American Board of Psychiatry and Neurology.

**Laura Hubbs-Tait, Ph.D.**, Associate Professor and John and Sue Tayor Professor of Human Environmental Sciences, Department of Family Relations and Child Development, Oklahoma State University, Stillwater, Oklahoma.

**Judith S. Kestenberg, M.D.**, Clinical Professor of Psychiatry and Analyst, New York University, New York; co-founder, Child Development Research, Sands Point, New York; Co-Director (from 1972–1990), Center for Parents and Children, Roslyn Heights, New York; Co-Project Director, International Study of Organized Persecution of Children; in private practice, Sands Point, New York and New York City; author of numerous articles on the child survivors of the Holocaust.

**Margaret Morgan Lawrence, M.D.**, former chief of the Developmental Psychiatry Service for Infants, Young Children, and their Families in the Division of Child Psychiatry, Harlem Hospital Center; former Associate Clinical Professor of Psychiatry, Columbia College of Physicians and Surgeons, New York City; founder and former director of the Child Development Center of the Rockland County Community Mental Health Board; in the private practice of child psychiatry and psychoanalysis, Rockland County, New York.

**Kato van Leeuwen, M.D.**, Clinical Assistant Professor, UCLA; Training and Supervising Analyst, the Southern California Psychoanalytic Institute; Chair, Emeritus, the Child and Adolescent Analysis Section of the Southern California Psychoanalytic Institute.

**Joy D. Osofsky, Ph.D.**, Professor of Pediatrics and Psychiatry, Louisiana State University Medical Center, New Orleans; Adjunct Professor of Psychology, University of New Orleans; Faculty, New Orleans Institute for Psychoanalysis.

**Shirley R. Rashkis, M.D.**, Senior Attending Medical Staff, The Institute of Pennsylvania Hospital; Clinical Assistant Clinical Professor, Department of Mental Health Sciences, Hahnemann University.

**Bertram A. Ruttenberg, M.D.**, Honorary Professor of Psychiatry and Human Behavior, Thomas Jefferson University, Philadelphia; Medical Director, Center for Autistic Children, Philadelphia; in private practice of psychiatry and psychoanalysis.

**Isaiah A. Share, M.S., M.D.**, Associate Clinical Professor of Psychiatry, Thomas Jefferson University, Philadelphia; Senior Attending Physician, The Institute of Pennsylvania Hospital; Faculty, Institute of the Philadelphia Association for Psychoanalysis.

**Marguerite A. Smith, Ph.D.**, Faculty, Department of Psychiatry (Child Psychiatry), Boston University Medical Center.

**Lucile M. Ware, M.D.**, Child Psychiatrist and Psychoanalyst, Menninger Clinic, Topeka, Kansas; Faculty, Topeka Institute for Psychoanalysis, Topeka, Kansas.

# Introduction

A listing of the topics discussed by the Vulnerable Child Discussion Group over the past thirty years reads like a compendium of psychoanalytic development and psychoanalytic luminaries. Topics covered have included aggression, speech development, issues of prevention, attachment and bonding, divorce, conflict, failure to thrive, paternity, affect development, transsexualism, parent loss, abuse and neglect, separation-individuation, invulnerability, developmental arrest, sadomasochism, the effects of blindness, depressed mothers, internalization, handicaps and chronic illness, body image, sexual abuse, narcissism, early intervention, single parenthood, termination, internal structures, reconstituted families, resilience, character formation, violence, neuropsychiatric disorders, absent fathers, early stages of ego development, child abuse, and the law. Analysts and child analysts of every persuasion have been presenters: Eleanor Galenson, Judith Kestenberg, and Paulina Kernberg as well as Sally Provence have supported the group and presented regularly. Hossein Etezady and Alex Burland have prepared detailed summaries of the group's discussions over the years, but the success of the group and the vigor of its influence must be largely attributed to Ted Cohen, who has planned and orchestrated its presentations and discussions over the past twenty years, and acted as mentor and guide to the organization and its members.

This, the second volume of papers derived from the Vulnerable Child Discussion Group, opens with a section on Narcissism and Hostile Aggression, ranging from the theoretical discussions of the first couple of papers to reports on experiences of Holocaust survivors, Indians in the Southwest, and the distressed children who found the magic of play in Erma Brenner's Small House. The first paper, by M. H. Etezady, "Narcissism: Primary-Secondary, Fundamental, or Obsolete?" reminds us that "Narcissism as a metapsychological concept was first introduced by Freud in the language of his earlier prestructural theory (Freud, 1914)" (this volume, p. 3). The author sees primary and secondary narcissism as sequential phases "of the same unitary and gradually transitioning developmental process," as opposed to the view of Temeles (1993) and others whose developmental view of narcissism questions the validity of Freud's primary and secondary narcissism.

Etezady's paper is followed by "A Developmental Approach to Narcissism," by Isaiah A. Share, Shirley R. Rashkis, and Bertram A. Ruttenberg who discuss the ontogenesis and function of narcissism in normal development in light of new data revealing the infant to be a "functioning, receptive, responding individual . . . aware in many senses of their surroundings and seeming to effectively interchange with their caregivers." They note that "Narcissism is more readily comprehended as a developmental concept if it is considered as contributing to an ongoing resynthesis of affects and thinking about the self." They end by saying that "those affective-cognitive inputs from stable self representations or self schemata . . . are a major factor to be reckoned with in therapeutic efforts to modify behavior whether by psychotherapy or other interventions."

Leon Hoffman discusses Etezady and Share, Rashkis, and Ruttenbergs' papers. Pointing out that "Psychic determinism is one of the basic postulates of psychoanalytic theory," he discusses what narcissism is, how narcissism relates to object relations, and the differences between healthy and pathological forms of narcissism. He asks what vicissitudes narcissism encounters, and whether narcissism develops along a single or double track. In his discussion of aggression, which rounds out the paper, he notes his agreement with Kernberg's statement that a general integration of the developmental schemata of libido and aggression has not yet been done adequately. He points out that "An adequate theoretical understanding of the vicissitudes of aggression would greatly further our understanding of narcissism."

Judith S. Kestenberg and Ira Brenner's paper on "Narcissism in the Service of Survival" briefly reviews Freud's theory of narcissism and amplifies his idea that primary narcissism may persist throughout life. They go on to formulate the experiences of Holocaust survivors obtained by means of interviews and memoirs. They postulate that under such extraordinary life-threatening conditions, there is a redistribution of narcissistic libido which provides for additional resilience. They note that the Nazis, intending to deprive the Jews of dignity, spirit, and the will to live and learn, denied them air, warmth, food, and life-sustaining people such as parents, spouses, and children. Under the circumstances, the libidinization of the self contributed to the wish to live.

Eleanor Galenson in her paper on "The Influence of Hostile Aggression on the Development of Expressive Language," proposes, based on her own research and clinical data from both normal and pathological infants, that "conflicts over oral aggressive impulses which normally emerge during the last quarter of the first year may be intensified by anal phase conflicts over sphincter control and the accompanying anxiety during the second year." Galenson's hypothesis regarding the dynamic relationship between oral and anal aggression clarifies many of the "puzzling features of distortions in language development, particularly the delay in the emergence of speech."

Jo Ann B. Fineman has been acting as child psychiatry consultant and program supervisor for two Indian tribes who live in the desert of the Southwest. The average income is $5000, the infant mortality rate is 66 percent higher than that of the surrounding area, children suffer from fetal alcohol syndrome and fetal alcohol effect at levels higher than those of nearby communities, and there is a high incidence of death from car accidents and suicide. In many instances, "children have experienced extreme trauma in their early years: desertion, violent abuse, and the death of major caregivers." Fineman's own focus of interest over the seven-year period has been the "relationship between catastrophic early loss, later aggressive and violent manifestations, self-destructive acts and fantasies, and affective object attachments." She describes in her clinical case study a family group caught in "internal and external forces which result in the sequence of loss, abuse, and object attachment pathology." She suggests that analysts can gain "further understanding of the relationship between early loss, the internalization of the aggressive and sadistic lost parent, and the resulting latent fixation on the sadistic treatment of objects," and thereby begin to understand the forces which lead inevitably to violent acts.

Erma Brenner describes an innovative program of imaginative play which she developed for emotionally disturbed students at the New York-Cornell Medical Center, Westchester Division. The children were enrolled in school at the day hospital because "they were too difficult and disruptive to be maintained in the regular public school system." The children had histories of sexual abuse, violence, physical abuse, overcrowded housing conditions, parents addicted to alcohol or other drugs, inadequate or psychotic parents, one or other parent in the prison system, and outright abandonment. The program was named the Small House because the only space for it was a small classroom. It was furnished with child size furniture and an array of toys, and the children came to the Small House to play one on one with an adult volunteer. Originally created as a place for pleasurable imaginative play for children who in most cases had never learned how to play, the Small House soon became as well a place for successful crisis intervention. In this capacity it offered the company of a sympathetic adult to a child too disruptive to remain in the classroom, and served as a more supportive environment for the child to regain some measure of control, than the usual quiet room where he or she would be alone.

The next section, on Child Analysis on the Mental Health Scene, starts off with a paper by Peter Blos, Jr., who, after reflecting on his own career in order to provide historical focus to the subject, says that analysts should consider what has been retained from the thirty- or forty-year period which might be called the golden age of psychoanalysis. He notes that there has been an upsurge during the 1980s and 1990s in research and intervention in the life of the infant, and the importance of infant experience in clinical analysis, that is, the infant't mental capacities for memory and the influence of this memory on

later development, and "the possibility of reconstructing something of this experience in an analysis." He also notes the importance of psychoanalytic thinking in the development of the
Head Start program and the Early Assessment program. Dr.
Blos fears that mental health care for children will not fare well
under the new national health care plan, finding the concept
of short-term mental health care intervention misleading, in
that it suggests that people have helped children in some real
and lasting way when they have merely alleviated symptoms.
He goes on to note some of the losses in the field of child
mental health: the child guidance clinic, whether run by a hospital, social agency, school, or otherwise has largely disappeared. Residential treatment for children and adolescents and
work with delinquents has become a thing of the past. Funding
for research of a dynamic and clinical nature has almost disappeared. He finds that fantasy, and its importance to the developing child and adolescent, is largely being overlooked today.
He notes areas of importance to be: services to the birth to 4-
year-old population; case studies, clinical vignettes, and theory
building, pointing out, however, that it has been a long time
since the fields of child psychiatry, pediatrics, psychology, social
work, and education have "considered psychoanalytic observations to be of scientific interest and validity." He urges analysts
to become politically active, pointing out that the struggle for
the national health plan calls for effort, energy, and attention.

Jules Glenn, in his discussion of Peter Blos, Jr.'s paper,
notes the important contributions to "sensible child rearing
practices" which have derived from psychoanalysis. He goes
on to say that "our society has produced conditions of fear,
overstimulation, failures of conscience and deprivation that interfere with sublimation." Children and adults in impoverished
inner city neighborhoods and other like areas live in constant
terror of injury and death to themselves and their loved ones,
"a terror that fosters denial and identification with aggressors."
He goes on to list such things as poor housing, unemployment,
low income, and homelessness, which, whilst they have always
been with us, are now more "malignant and insoluble" than
before. Lack of government support for decent day care, un-
derfunding of Head Start do not help children thrive. He

underlines the importance of informing politicians that "medication without supplemental health care has quite limited benefits," and that psychoanalysis, psychotherapy, guidance, and environmental change can bring about real change.

Thomas F. Barrett further develops the themes outlined by Blos and Glenn in his discussion of an innovative program of applied child analysis developed by the TRW corporation and the Cleveland Center for Research in Child Development whereby four child analysts from the Cleveland Center were paired with four TRW sites, and then combined with a TRW representative to identify potential day care centers and child analysts or child development specialists in each of the respective communities. The author worked with day care facilities in a Detroit suburb sponsored by the community education department. Dr. Barrett notes that $1 invested in young children can save anywhere from $4 to $6 in later expenses, and ends by saying that "it would be hard to imagine a better application or investment of our child analysis resources and expertise than in this area of day care consultation."

In his discussion of Thomas Barrett's paper Jules Glenn notes that it would be a mistake to think that day care centers necessarily advance development "when parents work and when children have no primary parenting for long hours."

Part III on adolescent mothers and children with constitutional deficits, begins with a paper by Margaret Morgan Lawrence on developmental psychiatry for infants, young children, and their families in an inner city setting. An inner city hospital in Harlem, New York City, is the setting in which a mental health clinical-educational team provided consultation, evaluation, psychoanalytic psychotherapy, therapeutic education, and remediation for a population principally of young African-American families living on a poverty level. "The children are plagued with constitutional deficits, poor nurturing, and traumata, all related to poverty. Psychoanalytic principles pervaded the action in all aspects of the program. The author notes that, "Essential to the action was the mutual identification and mutual responsibility of the dynamically oriented, racially integrated team. . . . Our expectation is that the tools of analysis can apply to the children and families of poverty. As Winnicott said (1971), "Psychotherapy has to do with two people playing together" (p. 38).

Osofsky, Hubbs-Tait, Eberhart-Wright, Culp, and Ware describe a longitudinal study of 180 adolescent mothers and their infants in Topeka, Kansas, 69 of whom were followed for the first 4½ years of life. "The purpose of the research component of the project was to learn about the social and emotional development of adolescent mothers and their children." Intervention strategies were developed to help the young mothers move forward with their lives despite parenthood at a very young age. In addition, strategies were developed to help the infant and child's development. The researchers set out to find whether there was a relationship between "the child's external experience of conflict in his or her early life and later internalizations and representations in stories told through standardized play narratives." One mother-child dyad is described in some detail to "illustrate how observations made as part of a research study using standard play narratives helped to identify vulnerability in a child over the first 44 months of life."

In their paper, "Some Effects of Lost Adolescence: The Child Mothers and Their Babies," Jo Ann B. Fineman and Marguerite A. Smith attempt to understand the psychodynamics of adolescent parenthood. They note that while their study took place before the era of AIDS and crack, the self-same dynamics between mother, infant, and grandmother still pertain, albeit complicated by neurological compromises at birth, and the effects on infants of crack and AIDS. They offered individual, mother-child focused intervention via both clinic and home visit contacts. They note that such studies lost funding by the end of the 1970s. In the six years of the program they followed 167 families in which the mothers and infants had been identified as being at risk across a spectrum from the child having had difficulties at birth to the mother's situation being the risk factor. The paper ends with a discussion of the characteristics of attachment behaviors within the baby–mother–grandmother triad.

Two papers on child sexual abuse by Kato van Leeuwen make up the section on child abuse. The first paper discusses

"Resistances in the Treatment of a Sexually Molested 6-Year-Old Girl," while the second paper discusses changes in psychoanalytic perspective and countertransference denial in cases of child sexual abuse.

The book concludes with a description of the current status of children in the United States by Theodore B. Cohen. Whilst acknowledging that the Clinton administration has at least attempted to fund programs that help children, Dr. Cohen finds the overall situation to be appalling. The United States ranks twenty-first in infant mortality (9 deaths per 1000 births), with nearly a quarter of infants and toddlers, 3 million children, living in poverty. American children are among the least likely to be immunized in the industrialized world: Boston with a 58 percent immunization rate was the highest; Houston the lowest with 11 percent. The situation of American women, the mainstay of the family, and in an era of high divorce rates, too often the sole support of their families is extremely difficult. In 1989 American women were paid only 66 percent of their male counterpart's earnings. The child care situation is at a crisis point: there is a massive shortage of preschools in the country. Dr. Cohen notes that a Harvard Graduate School of Education report says that 4 million children now attend 80,000 preschools nationwide, and that there is a long waiting list for preschools in the inner cities. Working class families in which both parents work are hit particularly hard, since their earnings are likely to be too high for them to qualify for subsidies for Head Start and other preschool programs. Adolescents are committing suicide and being murdered at increasing rates, and the HIV rate is going up faster than in any other segment of the population.

While we are living today in a period of the "quick fix" with the emphasis being on treating symptoms rather than underlying causes, on a perception of cost effectiveness as being tied to brief treatments or medication, this should be seen by child analysts as the time when political activism is not only essential but a matter of survival for the children who need our help. Child analysts must be more aggressive in presenting their views in a world in which so many children and young people live devastated lives of poverty and violence, without the most basic health care, without meaningful education, in dangerous neighborhoods, in appalling housing, and this in the richest country in the world. There are some specific targets we should organize ourselves around. Peter Blos, Jr., has pointed out that the child guidance clinic is a thing of the past; that there is no longer any remedial work being done with delinquents; residential treatment of troubled children has all but disappeared; the fields of pediatrics, child psychiatry, psychology, social work, and education do not look to psychoanalysis for help in solving problems. Surely these trends can be reversed by a systematic approach at both an organizational and a personal level.

## REFERENCES

Freud, S. (1914), On narcissism: An introduction. *Standard Edition*, 14:69–102. London: Hogarth Press, 1957.

Temeles, M. (1993), A developmental line for narcissism, the path to self-love and object-love. In: *The Vulnerable Child*, Vol. 1, ed. T. B. Cohen, M. H. Etezady, & B. L. Pacella. Madison, CT: International Universities Press.

Winnicott, D. W. (1971), *Playing and Reality*. New York: Tavistock Publications/Methuen, 1982.

# PART I:

# Narcissism and Hostile Aggression

# 1.

# Narcissism: Primary-Secondary, Fundamental, or Obsolete?

M. H. ETEZADY, M.D.

Narcissism as a metapsychological concept was first introduced by Freud in the language of his earlier prestructural theory (Freud, 1914). Since then, both our theory and language have undergone a veritable course of metamorphosis. Consequently, vestiges of earlier notions tend to evoke confusion or controversy when viewed in the light of later findings based on clinical experience and observational data. Pulver (1970) has addressed the difficulties inherent in the use of the term in such a multitude of divergent contexts and references. In a developmental view of narcissism, Temeles (1993) has questioned the validity and usefulness of Freud's designation of primary and secondary narcissism. This view regards narcissism as a unitary line of development evolving during the course of development and maturation. A distinction between a primary versus a secondary narcissism in this point of view is considered unjustifiable.

Opposing this assertion, I will attempt to describe Freud's designation of primary versus secondary narcissism in our contemporary language. Far from obsolete, in my view such distinction is fundamental in conceptualizing internalization and self-regulation.

In today's language, we might say that primary narcissism refers to the libidinal cathexis of the subject, that is, the bodily self (York, 1991), and its internal components and states. This neonatal phase coincides with the period that Mahler (reluctantly) calls the normal autistic phase. As described by Spitz (1965), Mahler, Pine, and Bergman (1975), and others, during this period perceptions are global. External impingements are not differentiated from those that originate from within. Reactions are based on sensorimotor reflex (Piaget, 1954). The infant experiences himself as the source of all gratification. Gratifying interactions with the caregiver stimulate and gradually integrate the surface sensations. The libidinal cathexis is drawn from the core to the rind and from the body itself toward the caregiver. The mother actively woos this shift from the center to the surface and from the subject toward the object.

With the dawning awareness of the mother as a beacon of orientation, the infant begins to seek the mother with directed intentionality and specific recognition in an expanded realm of subjective experience, sharing in the maternal omnipotence through an illusion of symbiotic "dual unity."

With advancing development of the ego and enhancement from incremental doses of tolerable frustration, the illusion of unity with the mother gives way to the process of differentiation. The advent of stranger anxiety by 8–9 months is a telling indication that the child is becoming aware of his separateness and the vulnerability of his infantile omnipotence.

Before the establishment of self and object constancy, mental representations of the self are more or less fused with those of the object. Homeostasis cohesion and a background of safety (Sandler, 1960) are initially achieved in the context of mother–child interaction of the symbiotic phase and early self-object experiences (Kohut, 1978) in a state of complete dependency. Internalization of these experiences lead to increasing autonomy and *relative* independence.

In distinction from primary narcissism, secondary narcissism can be thought of as the libidinal cathexis of self representation *subsequent* to the formation of ego boundaries when self and object representations are adequately differentiated and more or less stable. During the extended period of separation-individuation, this transition from a primary to a secondary mode of narcissism proceeds along a continuum toward self and object constancy. The second year of life is *the* crucial developmental period for this transition. Beginning in the third year, stabilization and consolidation in attainment of self and object constancy continue through subsequent development in oedipal, latency, adolescent, and adulthood periods. Failure of differentiation and various degrees of selfobject fusion may persist due to developmental arrest, fixation or regression, as in instances of pathology. It may also be reactivated adoptively or creatively through regression in the service of the ego.

Secondary narcissism was originally defined by Freud as withdrawal of object libido and its reinvestment into the ego (self). This was to be accomplished through identification and introjection. Hartmann (1950), Jacobson (1964), Mahler et al. (1975), Kernberg (1975), and others have elaborated on this process and the advent of internalization and structure formation. Representations of interaction with the object world are internalized through libidinal cathexis of part-objects and their subsequent introjection (primary identification). Repeated recycling and "metabolism" of these introjects promotes self and object differentiation, structure formation, and increasing integration. This eventually enables the individual to relinquish complete dependence on the primary object and to function with relative independence.

Disruptions in "selfobject functions," depending on their severity, duration, and phase of development, may result in fixation or regression, and can lead to persistence or reactivation of archaic introjects, compensatory megalomanic or hallucinatory restitutive phenomena characteristic of primary narcissism and primary process.

The notion of healthy narcissism implies the capacity to maintain a sense of well-being and positive self regard in order to sustain self and object constancy and to preserve a "background of safety" (Sandler, 1960) and confident expectation. This complex capacity involves constitutional, environmental, and structural elements. It is rooted in the quality of early object relations and is mediated through the synthetic and executive functions of the ego. Narcissistic vulnerability can result from problems involving any, or a combination, of these elements.[1]

---

[1] A partial listing of these conditions includes but is not limited to peculiarities of temperament, overactivity, passivity, irritability, special sensitivities,

From a developmental perspective, the distinction between primary versus secondary narcissism resembles that between primary versus secondary process thinking. Primary process thinking, similar to primary narcissism, is the primitive mode operating before the establishment of ego boundaries, reality principle, and the differentiation of inner from the outer, self from the object, or wish from fantasy. It is not influenced by the constraints of time, place, or person. Secondary process thinking, not unlike secondary narcissism, develops as a by-product of development through the process of self-object differentiation, consolidation of ego boundaries, establishment of reality principle and compromise formation, along with relinquishment of magical thinking and infantile omnipotence.

Primary and secondary process thinking (similar to primary and secondary narcissism) operate in relative rather than absolute terms. They may exist side by side, and may be evoked in the service of the ego adaptively or creatively. They may be operative in normal states, such as sleep, dreams, jokes, problem solving, and parapraxes; as well as in pathological circumstances, such as psychoses, hypochondriasis, drug-induced states, etc.

It is in the context of normality versus pathology that primary versus secondary narcissism as theoretical constructs can be particularly useful. The two are distinct in quality and mode of function. They originate in different stages of development and are characterized by distinct epigenetic and clinical features.

Freud's original definition of narcissism predates the advent of "dual instinct theory" and, therefore, makes no allowance for the role of aggression in the vicissitudes of narcissism

---

birth defects, prenatal and postnatal detriments, birth injuries, major surgical procedures and hospitalization during infancy and childhood, sensory and/ or motor disorders, genetic and metabolic disorders, deafness, blindness, twinship, constitutional and neurological factors affecting drive endowment and drive development, organically based ego deficits, cognitive impairment, parental absence, parental psychopathology, parental illness or loss, parental divorce, separation, significant chronic marital discord, parental addiction, violence and abuse or neglect, a "poor fit" between the caregiver and the child, neurotic conflict affecting object relations due to guilt or symptomatic regression.

and its self-regulatory attributes. Spitz, Jacobson, Mahler, Kernberg, and others have described the early phases of ego development, internalization, and structure formation which precede eventual establishment of the capacity for relative autonomy and self-regulation. According to this view, the constituents of the early pleasure ego are confined to purely pleasurable experiences associated with libidinal drive derivatives and their inherently positive affective quality. Such experiences are deposited in the pleasure ego indistinguishable from their undifferentiated self-object matrix. The derivatives of the aggressive drive, their negative affective charge, and their *bad* undifferentiated self-object matrix are defensively split off and projected in order to protect the fragile pleasure ego from the destructive effects of aggression. The pleasurable experiences associated with the *good* self-object introjects are perceived as internal, while the bad self-object introjects and their negative aggressive charge are experienced as nonself (vertical split). This form of splitting and primitive mechanisms of defense are later replaced by more mature mechanisms effected predominantly through repression.

Self and object differentiation on the one hand, and, on the other hand, the fusion of libido and aggression (i.e., integration of good and bad) proceed incrementally through the course of separation-individuation, and in particular during the critical subphase of rapprochement. Normally, by about the end of the third year, the beginnings of self and object constancy have been established. Under optimal conditions, maintaining a state of self-experience colored by a positive affective tone becomes a matter of homeostasis under the executive province of ego functions. This ideal circumstance is approximated through relative dominance of pleasurable and libidinally derived experiences initially made possible through modulation of aggression by the caregiver. In the absence of libidinal availability of the caregiver, adequate modulation of aggression and resulting libidinization of selfobject experiences cannot take place (Barrett, chapter 8). The emerging sense of self is negative, painful, and intolerable. Splitting and other primitive defenses cannot be relinquished. The development of the ego, superego, and ego ideal remain arrested. Archaic selfobject states and narcissistic structures and their function, characteristic of primary narcissism, persist.

## CONCLUSION

Primary and secondary narcissism are sequential phases of the same unitary and gradually transitioning developmental process. Primary narcissism is operative predominantly during the preobjectal phase and before self and object representations are adequately differentiated. Through the process of identification and internalization, the libidinally cathected primary object and its attributes are introjected. The primary object is thus relinquished, and the object libido is invested in its mental representations; that is, it is withdrawn into the ego (self). This process of internalization and progressive structure formation involves development of secondary narcissism which serves to preserve a sense of well-being, cohesion, and self-esteem during the course of future development. While these functions were originally provided by the caregiver, they are later internally regulated through the synthetic and executive functions of the ego according to the principles of compromise formation. Like primary and secondary process thinking, primary and secondary narcissism are the two poles of the same continuum, but differ in quality. Optimal balance between the drives with a relative preponderance of libido over aggression is essential for establishment of self and object constancy and healthy narcissism. Maternal libidinal availability is crucial in libidinalization of experience, modulation of aggression, drive fusion, separation-individuation, and emergence of healthy narcissism, namely, the ability to maintain an affectively positive sense of self.

## REFERENCES

Freud, S. (1914), On narcissism: An introduction. *Standard Edition*, 14:69–102. London: Hogarth Press, 1957.
Hartmann, H. (1950), Comments on the psychoanalytic theory of the ego. In: *Essays on Ego Psychology*. New York: International Universities Press, 1964, pp. 113–141.

Jacobson, E. (1964), *The Self and the Object World*. New York: International Universities Press.

Kernberg, O. (1975), *Borderline Conditions and Pathological Narcissism*. New York: Jason Aronson.

Kohut, H. (1978), The psychoanalytic treatment of narcissistic personality disorders: Outline of a systematic approach. In: *The Search for the Self*, ed. P. Ornstein. New York: International Universities Press, pp. 477–509.

Mahler, M., Pine, F., & Bergman, A. (1975), *The Psychological Birth of the Human Infant*. New York: Basic Books.

Piaget, J. (1954), *The Construction of Reality*. New York: Basic Books.

Pulver, S. (1970), Narcissism. *J. Amer. Psychoanal. Assn.*, 18:319–341.

Ruttenberg, B. (1990), Study group on narcissism. Association for Child Psychoanalysis. Typescript.

Sandler, J. (1960), The background of safety. *Internat. J. Psycho-Anal.*, 41:352–356.

Spitz, R. A. (1965), *The First Year of Life*. New York: International Universities Press.

Temeles, M. (1993), A developmental line for narcissism, the path to self-love and object-love. In: *The Vulnerable Child*, Vol. 1, ed. T. B. Cohen, M. H. Etezady, & B. L. Pacella. Madison, CT: International Universities Press.

York, C. (1991), Freud's "On Narcissism": A teaching text. In: *Freud's "On Narcissism: An Introduction,"* ed. J. Sandler, E. S. Person, & P. Fonagy. New Haven, CT: Yale University Press.

# 2.

# A Developmental Approach to Narcissism

## ISAIAH A. SHARE, SHIRLEY R. RASHKIS, BERTRAM A. RUTTENBERG

In his 1914 paper "On Narcissism: An Introduction" Freud first indicated the importance of this phenomenon in pathology, in everyday life, in love, and in normal development, and also presented it as an extension of libido theory. Despite a large number of clinical and theoretical expositions (Etchegoyen, 1991), however, significant aspects of narcissism, including clarity of definition and understanding of its function and developmental course, remain unsettled, vague, and elusive. This study explores some of the problems which have contributed to this state of affairs and which stand in the way of the emergence of a more effective clinical theory, and also presents a clarifying reconceptualization.

New research data about the infant, information which, in contrast to older views, reveals them to be functioning, receptive, responding individuals (Pulver, 1970; Compton, 1980; Brazelton, 1981), aware in many senses of their surroundings and seeming to effectively interchange with their caregivers, further focused our attention upon the ontogenesis and function of narcissism in normal development. In this context, we

This paper was first presented at an ACP Study Group on Narcissism: Drs. Theodore Cohen, Hossein Etezady, Bertram Ruttenberg, Shirley R. Rashkis, Isaiah A. Share, and Herman Staples, March 24, 1994.

11

regard the important role that narcissism plays in normal development as having been underestimated. Assertiveness, exploration and mastery are examples of adaptive behaviors which are
contingent upon adequate narcissism. The emphasis here will
be upon this adaptive potential as compared, for example, to
Kohut's views, which stress deficiency (Kohut and Wolf, 1978;
Ornstein, 1991), or other clinical approaches which emphasize
pathology.[2]

Freud initially defined narcissism as the libidinal cathexis
of the ego where the term *ego* refers to the self, to "das Ich"
(1914). This was later modified by Hartmann (1964) who substituted the word *self* for the term *ego*, and introduced the notion
of the self representation (York, 1991). Jacobson took the concept one step further by proposing instead that narcissism could
better be understood as the libidinal cathexis of the self representation (1954). Both the Hartmann and Jacobson modifications of the definition bring to mind qualities of force, direction,
and object, operating intrapsychically, features which are generally associated with drive theory. In the following year, 1915,
with the papers on metapsychology, particularly "Instincts and
Their Vicissitudes" (1915), Freud began to consider narcissism
more in cognitive and affective terms. As David Smith (1985)
observes, "Looking at 'Instincts and Their Vicissitudes' as a

---

[2]Freud reflected upon narcissism with great curiosity and creativity. A
brilliant ad hoc theorist, he boldly moved concepts about in response to
clinical evidence. An example is his discussion of the influence of organic
disease upon the distribution of libido (1914), where "Closer observation
teaches us that he [the sick person] also withdraws *libidinal* interest from his
love objects: so long as he suffers he ceases to love . . . We should then say:
the sick man withdraws his libidinal cathexes back upon his own ego, and
sends them out again when he recovers" (p. 82). Freud observes further how
"a lover's feelings, however strong, are banished by bodily ailments, and
suddenly replaced by complete indifference" (pp. 82–83). Here, the essentially clearly drawn clinical observations of the individual's response to pain
and discomfort are followed by theoretical conclusions about the distribution
of libido, conclusions which follow closely on the data. Yet, despite this demonstration of the possibility of clinical data gathering regarding narcissism,
Freud felt that there were "special difficulties" in the way of its direct study.
These difficulties, which may well have also reflected his conflicts with Adler
and Jung (ego instincts versus sexual instincts, Jung's introversion of the
libido), mandated to him that further understanding must derive from studies
of psychopathology as well as from organic disease and normal data.

whole, one must conclude that there has been a subtle yet pervasive terminology shift. Freud begins to consider narcissism more in cognitive terms, that is, in terms of the infant's primitive conceptions of the origin and sources of pleasurable experiences" (p. 492). It is a key hypothesis of the present paper that an approach to narcissism in these terms, in cognitive and affective dimensions, provides a more comprehensive account of the phenomena that we ascribe to it than does drive theory alone.

In the 1914 paper, Freud developed his operational ideas about narcissism in an economic mode, conceptualizing the principles and pathways for distribution of fixed quantities of libido. In our view, he was seeking in this essay to present narcissism as a quantitative system in contrast to what had heretofore been an exclusively drive oriented paradigm, and he was recognizing difficulties in correlating such ideas with clinical findings. He was also considering the relationship of narcissism to ego formation and to aspects of mental functioning, and, for clinical and theoretical reasons, felt it necessary to account for the "narcissistic attitude" which was present in those "who suffered with narcissism to a perverse degree" (1914) and in neurotics in whom "this kind of narcissistic attitude . . . constituted one of the limits in their susceptibility to (analytic) influence" (1914). He was led to conclude that "it seemed probable that an allocation of the libido such as deserved to be described as narcissism might be present far more extensively, and that it might claim a place in the regular course of human sexual development" (1914, p. 73).

Although Freud emphasized qualitative features and later even dispensed with the quantitative model, it was nevertheless via this model that the perception has evolved that narcissism does not fully follow a drive paradigm but operates as a different sort of motivational force. Sandler, Person, and Fonagy (1991) refer to the 1914 essay as "opening up our understanding of motivation as stemming from something other than instinctual gratification" (p. ix). We would add that narcissism seems to operate by a different set of rules than do the libidinal and aggressive drives. Clinical observations demonstrate that narcissistic gratification is not regularly followed by a drop in

urgency as seems to occur with drive impelled affects and behaviors nor, to the observer, do there appear to be comparable
amplitudinal shifts in levels of these urges as seem to occur
with primarily appetitive phenomena. In our view, for example,
the reservoir concept which envisages a steady state fluid pressure acting on an unyielding barrier, probably represents an
attempt by Freud to deal with this conceptual difficulty.

Another conceptual issue concerns the evolution of thinking about the relation of narcissism to ego development. In his
early work Freud held the view that ego development cannot
be present from birth as are autoerotic instinctual drives (1914)
and that "a new psychical action" had to be added to autoerotism for narcissism to be created. Freud's three requirements
in defining an autoerotic behavior or "infantile sexual manifes-
tation" included attachment to a major somatic function, a high
degree of erogeneity, and lack of an object (1905). He commented that in the infant, sucking, with its easily observed excitement and pleasurable relaxation, obviously satisfied these
criteria. Subsequently, Freud (1915) modified his views and
shifted the emergence of ego (i.e., the self [das Ich]) to an
earlier time in development and proposed that the ego is present from the beginning of psychological life; he simultaneously
began considering narcissistic phenomena more in affective
and cognitive terms (Freud, 1905; Smith 1985). Later theorizing, clinical studies, and observations (Hartmann, 1964; Pulver,
1970; Stern, 1985; York, 1991) confirmed that, in fact, infantile
responses are predicated to a significant degree on inborn ego
apparatuses and ego functioning. In neurophysiological terms,
the newborn's reflexively activated central nervous system can
be viewed as accommodating inputs from an enteroceptive core
and proprioceptive rind and from peripheral audiovisual apparatuses, and as responding with tension reduction. The baby's
internal shift to pleasurable affects and pleasure seeking and
intrapsychically sourced feelings of well-being as well as repre-
sentational abilities, probably begins developing in the first few
months.

Stern describes the young infant as purposefully seeking
and affectively responding in an interpersonal exchange. Clinically reproducible, verifiable examples are the recognition of

his mother's milk by the third day, the cross-modal information processing of the 3-week-old, and the complicated gaze behavior of the 2-month-old (Stern, 1985; Temeles, 1989). Such data and additional observations point to an emphasis on cognitive and motor development in the first 2 months, followed by a definite surge of observable social and affective behaviors after that time. Accordingly, Stern's findings in particular may represent the record of the beginning of the infant's internalized object representation and experiencing of the relationship with the primary caregiver(s). Kernberg, in "A Contemporary Reading of Narcissism" (1991), finds very questionable the concept of autoerotism and of a self or ego (as self) "predating the psychic experience of the actual relation of the infant with the primary object" (p. 133). His emphasis, like that of Stern and others (1991), is upon the importance of object relations *and* affects in the development of the infant's early responses and reactions. As has been suggested and as will be further elucidated, a cognitive–affective understanding of narcissism offers a better explanation for the distinctive nondrive aspects of its normal functioning than do other formulations. This view was heralded by Joffe and Sandler (1968) in their paper "Some Conceptual Problems Involved in the Consideration of Disorders of Narcissism."

The above cited observations of the perceptible shift toward increased affective responsiveness and evolving ego functioning, and the very discernible social changes in infant (and caregiver) beginning as early as the third month of life, also put to rest the questions of primary and secondary narcissism. The argument had been that there is a primary narcissism for the first few months of life coexisting with a relatively nonaffective body ego, such that neonatal behaviors aimed at discharging body tensions are at once autoerotic and yet without internal psychological significance. It was posited that this changes to a secondary narcissism which is largely a function of the later developing object relationship, but the observations reported above make it necessary in our view to posit only one narcissism.

There is considerable confusion in the psychoanalytic literature regarding the appropriate uses of the word *narcissism* and multiple meanings are regularly attached to the term. The current revision of *Psychoanalytic Terms and Concepts*, the glossary published by the American Psychoanalytic Association (Moore and Fine, 1990) states, "in psychoanalytic literature *narcissistic* thus came to be applied to many things: a sexual perversion, a developmental stage, a type of libido or its object, a type or mode of object choice, a mode of relating to the environment, an attitude, self-esteem, and a personality type, which may be relatively normal, neurotic, psychotic or borderline." In ordinary social or professional parlance narcissism or narcissistic can also simultaneously connote several meanings, often deprecatory (Gay, 1988, pp. 338–342). Also, the self psychologists have their own specific ideas about the development of narcissism and narcissistic libido and object libido and about what are called "narcissistic structures," such as mirroring and idealizing transferences, the grandiose self, and the selfobject, all terms which have their own definitions (Kohut, 1971).

A major associated issue has been the widespread pejorative view of narcissism which is based upon a presumed association with pathology (Joffe and Sandler, 1968; Ornstein, 1991), contributing, in our opinion, to a disinclination to assign it a role in normal or normal neurotic mental functioning. This view is often subtly introduced on the pretext of seeking to be scientific or "objective" about clinical observations and envisages psychopathological significance in narcissistic phenomena. For example, descriptive phrases such as "self-centered" and "self-serving" are processed critically, and as a result that which is narcissistic becomes axiomatic with pathology. Also, as Ornstein (1991) points out, the idea of narcissism as basically normal had been stated clearly from 1914 on, but that its position in the so-called single axis theory of libido development (from autoerotism through narcissism to object love) caused it to be regarded as something to be overcome, that is, as pathological, or at the very least, as a harbinger of pathology.[3]

---

[3]On another associated level, there has been little progress made in our understanding of the possible role of narcissistic clinical phenomena in neurosis and as aspects of what we ordinarily understand to be unconscious defensive operations. Again, returning to Kohut, for example, it appears that his clinical data regarding the mirror and idealizing transferences and his inferences regarding the bipolar self and its dependence on the selfobject, address

Pulver (1970) noted that the application of Freud's economic formulation to diverse psychic phenomena led to concepts about narcissism which are broad, vague, and difficult to delineate. He observed that when specific developmental complexities are finally unraveled, as in tracing a line of development in the infant from birth to the cathexis of or identification with an early object, narcissism as a term becomes too general and lacking in explanatory power to describe what actually seems to occur. These considerations are especially important when attempts are made to relate normal developmental aspects of narcissism to its role in pathological conditions, as, for example, in narcissistic and borderline personalities and various psychoses. These issues are of special significance because the best sources of our knowledge of development are early infant observations, both systematic and anecdotal, as well as retrospectively reconstructed information from the psychoanalytic situation. To use different or conflicting measures of narcissism when interpreting such information would tend to generate confusing conclusions; by contrast, there is an obvious need for a widely and consensually understood interpretive framework for such data. Since Pulver's 1970 paper there have been many changes in this field, exemplified particularly by the more extensive use clinically of developmental formulations, by the development and more precise use of object relations theories and ideas, and by an exponential increase in research involving early infant observation. As a result, there are available today many carefully executed developmental and observational studies of infants and children, essentially prospective, which can serve as sources of information about narcissistic phenomena and many more observations of narcissistic responses of individuals in psychoanalytic treatment, essentially retrospective observations, which can provide a view of these phenomena in process. Definitional and terminological problems and confusions continue, however, which

---

problems regarding narcissism in a quantitative mode to the relative exclusion of conflict as a primary force (1971). In such a developmental scheme the analysis of defenses would be of secondary importance when issues of narcissism present themselves in the clinical situation and therefore would lead, in our view, to an incomplete psychoanalytic process.

limit our abilities to understand and communicate complex aspects of affect and behavior in our patients.

As previously noted, the increase in new research data about the newborn further focused our attention on the desirability of exploring the developmental roots of narcissism. In pursuing this goal we found that *self* as a construct provides a useful context in which to consider the meaning of narcissism in relation to affective experience and to overall mental functioning. Emde, Biringen, Clyman, and Oppenheim (1991), taking a functional perspective, discuss self "as an organizing mental process and a regulator of experience" (see also Beres, 1981). From a similarly functional viewpoint Spiegel (1959) brings together the cognitive and the affective, and states that the self offers a frame of reference for inner experience along with a sense of continuity in time. Facilitated by what he postulates to be an inherent ego ability to compare and compute, the self, in a schematic way, is seen as being assembled from the resulting "constancy" of a small group of self representations which are derived from the pooling and averaging of mental representations of separate states of tension and discharge. "This constant frame of reference (the self) thus acts as a steadying flywheel to overcome the disturbing discontinuity of intermittent self-representations" (Spiegel, 1959, p. 97).

It seems apparent that a range of different affects, experiences, and postulated self representations are relevant to the conceptualization of self. Emde (1983) as well as Dare and Holder (1981) have focused on the organization and continuity of affective experience. Emde (1983) refers to the "affective core" as guaranteeing continuity of experience across development in spite of the many ways we change. Following Spiegel's metaphor of the "steadying fly wheel," we regard self as including the affects and associated experiences which are encoded into relatively stable self representations. A psychoanalytic glossary definition of self schemata (Moore and Fine, 1990) is "enduring cognitive structures that actively organize mental processes and code how one consciously and unconsciously perceives oneself." Keeping in mind Jacobson's earlier definition of narcissism as the libidinal cathexis of the self representation, we hypothesize that the more stable self representations or self schemata, which are directly relevant to narcissism, figure in the cognitive-affective mental processing of current and recalled past self experiences and influence the affects associated with these experiences.

Having thus considered the concept of self, we can now turn to a closer examination of our formulations about narcissism. Dare and Holder (1981) define narcissism as "the positively colored affective qualities associated with self experience which subsequently become an integral part of the self-representation that derives from such experiences" (p. 329). This definition is of particular significance because it operationally connects the concepts of self and narcissism, and also designates past experiences and the attendant affects as one of the important resources in establishing self representations. Using this conceptualization, we would infer the mental operation of a computing, registering, and comparing process, functioning over time, which utilizes cognitive and affective memory traces deriving from those aspects of the self representation relevant to narcissism, as being a central feature of narcissism.

The cognitive and affective aspects of the self representations which are relevant to narcissism are thought to be established early on, and could, by tracking current affective shifts, introduce a motivational dimension into thinking and behavior, which the reservoir analogy, for example, simply cannot accommodate. The overall motivational quality that is associated with narcissism could very well result from the operation of this type of inner process. It is noteworthy that the ability to unconsciously and automatically internalize and compute affective inputs is conceptually similar to the automatic type of skill acquisition in "procedural learning" which has been described (Emde, Biringen, Clyman, and Oppenheim, 1991; Clyman, 1991). (There are obvious psychobiological implications in these ideas.) The early affects and self experience which figure in the self representation are also important elements of the longitudinal development of narcissism. Some of the affects and experiences which it is suggested are encoded as memory traces of the self schemata, could continue over time to influence the affective investment in new self perceptions and self representations. For example, this conception can account for the commonly observed stability as well as inconsistency in self-assessment which occurs in everyone because it provides for variation of inputs from the self representation into one's operant thinking.

In this context, what we understand to be healthy or normal narcissism would seem to be largely dependent upon a confluence of factors present at birth. These include genetic endowment, appropriate maturation of the central nervous system and other systems, and adequate caregivers. While babies may vary in the level of intrapsychically sourced feelings, because of these developmental influences their affective responses in conjunction with their inborn adaptive faculties can provide the conditions to evoke affection (and useful attention to needs) from others. These early affective investments in the caregivers also have significant self-protective functions, an important characteristic, we feel, of narcissism.

While many features of normal narcissism may have genetic and maturational bases, the phenomenon is uniquely nurtured by interaction with the caregiver and sustained by object relations from infancy onward. Also, while appreciating narcissism as a continuing important component of normal psychobiologic development, we must recognize that our current state of knowledge requires that we can only hypothesize concerning individual differences in evoking and maintaining positive feelings about the self and about the relative role of maturational achievements and mastery in sustaining these attitudes.

## SUMMARY

The positive affects and subjective experience which are encoded in stable self representations and which may affect thinking, feeling, and behavior, are the elements of normal narcissism as the concept is developed in this paper. Viewed in this way narcissism has relevance to the drives and to mental functioning.

While we do not know the relationship of the early affects to the drives as they are developing and differentiating, once fully operant the drives influence self experience and hence the affective qualities of the self representations. In turn, over time the affects involved in the self representation have a role in how the drives are expressed.

The libidinal cathexes of past self experience as reflected and recorded in the self representations have potential motivational, affective, and cognitive relevance to the processing of current thinking about the present and past. From this perspective narcissism figures significantly in self-observation, self-assessment, and in the modulation of aggression.

Narcissism is more readily comprehended as a developmental concept if it is considered as contributing to an ongoing resynthesis of affects and thinking about the self. The suggested "computing" of cognitive and affecting memory traces deriving from aspects of self representation relevant to narcissism provides for the continual reworking of feelings about the self. This system would operate to influence or modify the impact of other inputs, including those physically external to the individual. However stored and retrieved, the cognitive impressions and related affects about oneself would influence one's response to current experience and to the review of past experience. Accordingly, the residuals of past feeling states may generate a panoply of initiatives and responses; for example, thoughts, fantasies, and behaviors which are important to coping and adaptation. Those affective–cognitive inputs from stable self representations or self schemata which are referred to above are a major factor to be reckoned with in therapeutic efforts to modify behavior whether by psychoanalysis, psychotherapy, or other interventions.

## REFERENCES

Beres, D. (1981), Self, identity and narcissism. *Psychoanal. Quart.*, 50:515–533.

Brazelton, T. B. (1981), The first four developmental stages in attachment of parent and infant. Paper presented at the 12th Annual Mahler Symposium, Philadelphia, PA.

Clyman, R. B. (1991), The procedural organization of emotions: A contribution from cognitive science to the psychoanalytic theory of therapeutic action. *J. Amer. Psychoanal. Assn.* (suppl.), 39:349–383.

Compton, A. (1980), The current status of the psychoanalytic theory of instinctual drives, I. *Psychoanal. Quart.*, 50:363–392.

Dare, C., & Holder, A. (1981), Developmental aspects of the interaction be-
    tween narcissism, self-esteem, and object relations. *Internat. J. Psycho-
    Anal.*, 62:323–337.
Emde, R. N. (1983), The pre-representational self and its affective core.
    *The Psychoanalytic Study of the Child*, 38:165–192. New Haven, CT: Yale
    University Press.
——— Biringen, Z., Clyman, R. B., & Oppenheim, D. (1991), The moral self
    of infancy: Affective core and procedural knowledge. *Developmental
    Rev.*, 11:251–270.
Etchegoyen, R. H. (1991), On narcissism: An introduction: Text and context.
    In: *Freud's "On Narcissism: An Introduction,"* ed. J. Sandler, E. S. Person,
    & P. Fonagy. New Haven, CT: Yale University Press, pp. 54–74.
Freud, S. (1905), Three essays on the theory of sexuality. *Standard Edition*,
    7:125–243. London: Hogarth Press, 1953.
——— (1914), On narcissism: An introduction. *Standard Edition*, 14:69–102.
    London: Hogarth Press, 1957.
——— (1915), Instincts and their vicissitudes. *Standard Edition*, 14:111–140.
    London: Hogarth Press, 1953.
Gay, P. (1988), *Freud: A Life for Our Time*. New York: W. W. Norton.
Hartmann, H. (1964), The mutual influences in the development of the ego
    and the id. In: *Essays on Ego Psychology*. New York: International Univer-
    sities Press, pp. 155–181.
Jacobson, E. (1954), The self and the object world: Vicissitudes of their infan-
    tile cathexis and their influence on ideational and affective develop-
    ment. *The Psychoanalytic Study of the Child*, 9:75–127. New York: Interna-
    tional Universities Press.
Joffe, W. G., & Sandler, J. (1968), Some conceptual problems involved in the
    consideration of disorders of narcissism. *J. Child Psychother.*, 2:56–66.
Kernberg, O. (1991), A contemporary reading of on narcissism: An introduc-
    tion. In: *Freud's "On Narcissism: An Introduction,"* ed J. Sandler, E. S.
    Person, & P. Fonagy. New Haven, CT: Yale University Press, pp.
    131–145.
Kohut, H. (1971), *The Analysis of the Self*. New York: International Universities
    Press.
——— Wolf, E. (1978), The disorders of the self and their treatment: An
    outline. *Internat. J. Psycho-Anal.*, 59:413–425.
Moore, B. E., & Fine, B. D. (1990), *Psychoanalytic Terms and Concepts*. New
    Haven, CT: American Psychoanalytic Association/Yale University
    Press.
Ornstein, P. H. (1991), From narcissism to ego psychology to self psychology.
    In: *Freud's "On Narcissism: An Introduction,"* ed. J. Sandler, E. S. Person,
    & P. Fonagy. New Haven, CT: Yale University Press, pp. 175–194.
Pulver, S. (1970), Narcissism: The term and the concept. *J. Amer. Psychoanal.
    Assn.*, 18:319–341.
Sandler, J., Person, E. S., & Fonagy, P., Eds. (1991), *Freud's "On Narcissism:
    An Introduction."* Introduction p. ix. New Haven, CT: Yale University
    Press.
Smith, D. L. (1985), Freud's developmental approach to narcissism: a concise
    review. *Internat. J. Psycho-Anal.*, 66:489–497.
Spiegel, L. A. (1959), The self and perception. *The Psychoanalytic Study of the
    Child*, 14:81–109. New York: International Universities Press.

Stern, D. (1985), *The Interpersonal World of the Infant*. New York: Basic Books.

Temeles, M. S. (1983), The infant: A socially competent individual. In: *Frontiers of Infant Psychiatry*, ed. J. O. Call, E. Galenson, & R. L. Tyson. New York: Basic Books.

———— (1989), Gaze behavior, smiling, and vocalization. Paper presented to ACP Study Group on Narcissism, February 1983.

Treurniet, N. (1991), Introduction to "On Narcissism." In: *Freud's "On Narcissism: An Introduction,"* ed. J. Sandler, E. S. Person, & P. Fonagy. New Haven, CT: Yale University Press, pp. 75–94.

York, E. C. (1991), Freud's "On Narcissism: A Teaching Text." In: *Freud's "On Narcissism: An Introduction,"* ed. J. Sander, E. S. Person, & P. Fonagy. New Haven, CT: Yale University Press, pp. 35–53.

# Discussion

## LEON HOFFMAN, M.D.

Narcissism is a concept whose use is ubiquitous in clinical situations. However, its role in theory is affected by, what seems to me, an inherent conundrum as a result of attempts to integrate analytic data with developmental schema. To use a metaphor from infant researchers, how do we integrate our cross-modal perceptions, that is, observational data from the prelinguistic period, with verbally mediated analytic data? Second, since the concept is difficult to specify, how can one generate abstractions which go beyond definitional restatements of the phenomena which one is trying to unravel?

I will structure my discussion of the two fascinating, and to me very instructive, papers, "A Developmental Approach to Narcissism" by Isaiah A. Share, Shirley R. Rashkis, and Bertram A. Ruttenberg and "Narcissism: Primary-Secondary, Fundamental, or Obsolete" by M. Hossein Etezady, along those lines. In addition, I will also refer to "A Developmental Line for Narcissism: The Path to Self-Love and Object-Love" by Margaret Stewart Temeles (1993). I will draw some comparisons between their ideas of narcissism and those of Freud. Finally, I will make some comments on the problem of aggression.

## WHAT IS NARCISSISM?

Share, Rashkis, and Ruttenberg state that definitional and terminological problems and confusions abound in the literature

---

This discussion took place at The Association for Child Psychoanalysis Vulnerable Child Workshop, March 18, 1994.

about the term. They emphasize, for example, that in the glossary of the American Psychoanalytic Association many mental phenomena are considered to be narcissistic (Moore and Fine, 1990). Narcissism is a sexual perversion, a developmental stage, a type of libido or its object, a type or mode of object choice, a mode of relating to the environment, an attitude, self-esteem, or a personality type which may be normal, neurotic, or psychotic. Share, Rashkis, and Ruttenberg add that the addition of developmental meanings to the term magnifies the vagueness.

Freud's elaboration of the libido theory and his development of the concept of narcissism in 1914 and 1915 was prompted by the need to counteract Jung's and Adler's defections (1905 [revisions made], 1914a, 1915). Freud's struggles with these two important defections led to a line of theorizing which began with narcissism and culminated in the structural theory. The first phase of analytic theorizing by Freud and his early followers had focused on the qualities of the id and rudimentary conceptions of the ego, mainly repressions (or defense). Adler and Jung spurred Freud to amplify on a variety of psychological functions which eventually were subsumed by his mature constructs, id, ego, and superego. In "On the History of the Psycho-Analytic Movement" (1914b), Freud stated that Adler's ideas, that all human behavior was a reaction to power and powerlessness, were a result of Adler's socialist background. Jung's concern with religious issues was a result of his theological background. Freud did acknowledge, however, that Adler made a contribution to the psychology of the ego and Jung to that of ethics. Freud's argument with them and need to distance himself from them was a result of their consideration that sexual drives were secondary phenomena. Essentially both Adler and Jung focused on the impact of external factors on the individual. Freud eventually incorporated their ideas into the intrapsychic tripartite model. The concept of narcissism offered an alternative to Jung's nonsexual libido and Adler's masculine protest. Freud stated that the development of the ego occurred as a departure from primary narcissism and subsequently the individual attempted to recover that primary narcissistic state by a displacement of the libido to an ego ideal.

## HOW DOES NARCISSISM RELATE TO OBJECT
## RELATIONS?

For Freud the concept of narcissism was intimately intertwined
with the concept of object libido, namely, it was connected to
drive issues as well as to object relations issues. Freud (1914a)
in essence maintained that object love and narcissistic love were
diametrically opposed to each other. Decrease in one led to an
increase in the other. For example, he conceptualized that in
schizophrenia secondary narcissism was a result of the withdrawal of libido from the outside world which secondarily directed itself toward the ego (self) leading to megalomania.
Kernberg (1991, p. 133) stresses the intimate relationship between libidinal investment of the self and libidinal investment
of the object in narcissism. Temeles (1993, pp. 17–18) stresses
that positive interactions with objects are essential for the generation of narcissistic supplies. In contrast to Freud's ideas, she
maintains that one's narcissism does not have a reciprocal relationship with object love. Narcissism is not depleted when there
are interactions with the object.

Clearly, the development of object relations goes hand in
hand with the development of a sense of self. But, how does
one define and conceptualize this idea of sense of self? Kernberg (1991, p. 132) states that Freud's das Ich (the I) had a
broad subjective connotation. However, there are contradic-
tions in the usage of terms which refer to oneself. For example,
following Mahler's stages, Etezady conceptualizes that the infant enters the realm of *subjective* experience when he or she
seeks the mother intentionally. In contrast, Temeles (1993, pp.
21–22) asserts that a young infant is his own *agent* and that the
sense of the infant as a *subject* predates the sense of the infant
as a *self*. Temeles describes a fourth stage in the development
of narcissism, which she calls "awareness of awareness: self-
centeredness," that is characterized by the emergence of *self-
awareness* and occurs after the consolidation of *subject constancy*
and object constancy (p. 23). She seems to imply that the constructs "subject constancy" and "self-awareness" are entities
which occur sequentially. I would contend that those two constructs, subject constancy and self-awareness, are inseparable

and can only be conceptualized in a linguistic self-reflective frame of reference and cannot be considered as external entities to be observed and studied with instruments like external objects.

The notion of subjectivity, as used in linguistics (Benveniste, 1971), is derived from the post-Enlightenment Western philosophical tradition of the presumption of man as *active* agent. Benveniste (1971) has argued that language is a noninstrumentalist capacity inherent to human existence. Language, for example, cannot be compared to an arrow or a wheel (i.e., instruments), which were invented by humans for their own use. In this frame of reference, in other words, one cannot hypothesize a prediscursive state in which a language is invented like an instrument. Benveniste (1971, pp. 223–225) states that: "It is speaking man whom we find in the world, a man speaking to another man, and language provides the very definition of man. It is in and through language that man constitutes as a *subject*, because language alone establishes the concept of 'ego' in reality, in *its* reality which is that of being."

In other words, from this point of view, subjectivity, the capacity of the speaker to posit him- or herself as a subject (awareness of awareness as posited by Temeles), is a fundamental property of language. In the polarity between I and you, neither term can be conceived without the other. When an I speaks to a you, the you responds as an I to that you.

The concept of narcissism involves a sense of oneself as a subject. Theoretical constructs (which themselves are language based) about the sense of oneself as a subject, only seem credible when one is considering the conscious linguistic productions (words or play) or the inferred unconscious fantasies (also linguistic productions). I would argue, therefore, with Temeles' (1993, p. 21) assertion that the newborn infant is his own agent as when he or she demonstrates essential bits of competence in the interactions with the environment. Such a theory, which constructs the prelinguistic infant as his or her own agent, poses philosophical and epistemological problems. Observations of differential motoric behavior by a young infant or newborn allow us to infer the development or presence of a variety of cognitive functions: perception, memory, recognition. Adults or older children can attempt to infer intention on the part of the newborn infant. However, the demonstration that the infant is capable of particular cognitive functions, which are indispensable to the development of later capacities, does not allow us to infer essentially linguistic constructs, such as intention. There is a discontinuity in development before and after the development of language. Gerald Edelman (1989) describes the similar discontinuity in evolutionary development. He states:

> Whatever their present relations, it is obvious that during evolution a great variety of brain states have historically preceded conscious states, which appeared rather late in evolutionary history. There was a long time in the history of the world when it was free of consciousness and certainly of thought. It is not likely that, prior to the emergence of language, there were any "selves" or "persons" inhabiting the world either. *Biological individuality is not simply equated with personhood* [p. 260; emphasis added].

## DIFFERENCES BETWEEN HEALTHY AND PATHOLOGICAL FORMS OF NARCISSISM

Share, Rashkis, and Ruttenberg address a critical dilemma: normal narcissism functions in a distinctive but difficult to define manner. They stress that the role of narcissism in normal development has been underestimated. Assertiveness, exploration, and mastery are examples of adaptive behaviors that are contingent upon adequate narcissism. Normal or healthy narcissism is dependent upon the genetic endowment, the maturation of central nervous system, and the quality of caregivers. The good enough caregiver helps the process of fusion between libido and aggression by modulating the infant's aggression through libidinal availability which results in a positive balance that favors the libidinal component of experience.

Etezady states that the notion of healthy narcissism implies the capacity to maintain a sense of well-being and positive self-regard in order to sustain self and object constancy and to preserve a background of safety (Sandler, 1987) and confident expectation. This complex capacity involves constitutional, environmental, and structural elements. Narcissism is rooted in the quality of early object relations and is mediated through the synthetic and executive functions of the ego.

Assessments which are made in terms of adaptation always require value judgments. Therefore, how can we understand a concept that at times is considered good and at other times bad? How can one psychoanalytically distinguish healthy narcissism from pathological narcissism? Is it a matter of quantity, quality, or reference to a particular interaction? Share, Rashkis, and Ruttenberg state that narcissism has had many pejorative connotations. Is the stress on "normal narcissism" a reversal to counteract the pejorative connotations?

It seems to me that there is an implicit equation between the idea of "adequate or healthy narcissism" and that of "adequate mental health." Have I misread Share, Rashkis, and Ruttenberg or is my inference correct that they consider narcissism to be equivalent to a global mental health construct? Although Kernberg (1991, p. 133) also stresses the concepts of normal and pathological narcissism, he points to Freud's idea of the "central function of the dialectic relationship in normality and pathology." Freud (1914a) contrasted normal from pathological object choice while simultaneously stressing the ubiquitous fluidity between normality and pathology in his discussion of the two types of object choice—anaclitic and narcissistic (p. 88). The idea that normal and pathological narcissism do not have distinct borders seems more consistent with psychoanalytic data.

## WHAT VICISSITUDES DOES NARCISSISM ENCOUNTER?

Share, Rashkis, and Ruttenberg emphasize a cognitive–affective understanding of narcissism. They point to various neonatal and infant studies which stress the early development of affects, cognition, and object relations. They define the self as "enduring cognitive structures that actively organize mental processes and code how one consciously and unconsciously perceives oneself." The self is, thus, an organizing mental process and a regulator of experience. Narcissism is involved in the cognitive impressions and related affects about oneself and can be conceptualized as the positively colored affective qualities associated with self experiences.

Share, Rashkis, and Ruttenberg following Clyman (1991) maintain that the development of these positively colored affective qualities can be compared to procedural learning, that is, automatic skill acquisition. (Declarative memory refers to memories and facts [conscious or unconscious] which can be recalled, whereas underlying automatic skills are conceptualized as evidence of procedural memories which cannot be recalled. Adequate procedural memory is observed in the presence of impaired declarative memory in patients with hippocampal lesions. These patients have clinical amnesia yet are able to acquire complex perceptual, motor, and cognitive skills.) Clyman (1991, pp. 363–364) states that young infants develop "affective procedures" which function comparably to procedural learning without declarative memory. However, Clyman does not address adequately how one can differentiate whether a complex reaction is secondary to an unconscious declarative memory or whether the reaction is secondary to an affective procedure.

## DOES NARCISSISM DEVELOP ALONG A SINGLE OR DOUBLE TRACK?

Etezady states that from a developmental perspective the distinction between primary and secondary narcissism resembles the distinction between primary and secondary process thinking. There is a qualitative difference between the early, primitive, preobjectal primary narcissism and secondary narcissism. Secondary narcissism occurs subsequent to the establishment of self and object differentiation and evolves through the internalization of optimal object relations. The primary object is relinquished and the object libido withdrawn into the ego (self). This process involves the development of secondary narcissism which serves to preserve a sense of well-being, cohesion, and self-esteem during future development. These functions, originally provided by caregiver, thus, are internally regulated through the synthetic and executive functions of the ego according to the principles of compromise formation. The postulated cognitive skill, "theory of the mind" (the capacity for a child to attribute meaning to another person's actions, beliefs, and feelings, Mayes and Cohen, 1994), may be helpful in understanding the shift in a child from a more "narcissistic" state to a more "object connected" state. Does this function apply to Etezady's idea about the shift from primary to secondary narcissism?

For Freud (1914a), secondary narcissism was a hypothesis attempting to organize actual clinical data. In contrast, the concept of primary narcissism was nebulous and did not seem grounded on clinical data. He hypothesized its existence because of, for example, the omnipotence of thought in children and primitive people.

## AGGRESSION

Etezady discussed how Freud did not properly consider the vicissitudes of aggression in narcissism since the theory of narcissism pre-dated the dual instinct theory. It is not clear to me how Share, Rashkis, and Ruttenberg and Etezady actually conceptualize the role of aggression vis-à-vis narcissism? Are assertiveness, exploration, and mastery examples of sublimated aggression? Freud always lacked an adequate theory of aggression, which evolved along a very circuitous route. Very late in his career, in "Civilization and Its Discontents," Freud (1930) stated: "I can no longer understand how we can have overlooked the ubiquity of non-erotic aggressivity and destructiveness and can have failed to give it its due place in our interpretation of life" (p. 120).

The difficulty with the development of a clinically useful theory of aggression seemed to have been tied to Freud's theoretical disputes. Stepansky (1977, pp. 112–142) discussed the impact of the conflict with Adler on Freud's ideas about aggression. In Little Hans, for example, Freud (1909) spelled out his ambivalent disagreement with Adler's idea of an aggressive instinct. On the one hand he maintained that Little Hans' analysis confirmed Adler's hypothesis that a patient's anxiety was caused by the repression of aggressive propensities. On the other hand, he decried the idea of such an instinct, preferring to conceptualize a pressing character for all instincts, that is, their capacity for initiating movement (pp. 140–141). When he acknowledged the need for an aggressive instinct in psychoanalytic theory, he differentiated *his* instinct from Alder's by calling it the destructive or death instinct (1909, p. 140fn.). He eventually stressed the role of defense against aggression in the development of Hans' phobia with his reformulation in "Inhibitions, Symptoms, and Anxiety" (1926, p. 102). In "Civilization and Its Discontents" (1930) Freud acknowledged Melanie Klein's influence in understanding the role of the suppressed retaliatory aggression toward a frustrating object in the formation of the superego (pp. 124–130).

In 1937 he wrote to Marie Bonaparte,

> I will try to answer your question [about aggression] . . . "Sublimation" is a concept that contains a judgment of value. . . . All activities that rearrange or effect changes are to a certain extent destructive and thus redirect a portion of the instinct from its original destructive goal. Even the sexual instinct we know cannot act without some measure of aggression. Therefore in the regular combination of the two instincts there is a partial sublimation of the destructive instinct.
>
> One may regard finally curiosity, the impulse to investigate, as a complete sublimation of the aggressive or destructive instinct [quoted in Jones, 1957, p. 464].

I agree with Kernberg's (1991, p. 134) statement that a general integration of the developmental schemata of libido and aggression has not yet been done adequately. An adequate theoretical understanding of the vicissitudes of aggression would greatly further our understanding of narcissism.

## CONCLUSION

Psychic determinism is one of the basic postulates of psychoanalytic theory. Therefore, psychoanalysts have always been very interested in studying development in order to investigate the complexities that contribute to the continuity in mental life. I would like to underscore Temeles' (1993, p. 18) statement that developmental schema have to be conceptualized as processes in which there are complex actions, interactions, and reactions. I think there may be disagreement with my idea that there may be a procrustean danger inherent in attempting to comprehensively synthesize developmental observations and the resultant theory with a theory derived from and useful to psychoanalytic treatment of children and adults. However, I do think that there would be agreement that developmental schema which attempt to draw very sharp demarcations, between normality and pathology or one developmental stage and another, oversimplify the complexities of mental life. Clearly, the theoretical knowledge derived from clinical psychoanalysis and that derived from developmental psychology ultimately cannot be inconsistent and can only be mutually enriching.

## REFERENCES

Benveniste, E. (1971), *Problems in General Linguistics*, tr. M. E. Meek. Miami Linguistics Series Number 8. Coral Gables, FL: University of Miami Press, pp. 223–230.

Clyman, R. B. (1991), The procedural organization of emotions: A contribution from cognitive science to the psychoanalytic theory of therapeutic action. *J. Amer. Psychoanal. Assn.*, 39(Suppl.):349–382.

Edelman, G. M. (1989), *The Remembered Present: A Biological Theory of Consciousness*. New York: Basic Books.

Freud, S. (1905), Three essays on the theory of sexuality. *Standard Edition*, 7:125–245. London: Hogarth Press, 1953.

—— (1909), Analysis of a phobia in a five-year-old boy. *Standard Edition*, 10:3–149. London: Hogarth Press, 1955.

—— (1914a), On narcissism: An introduction. *Standard Edition*, 14:67–102. London: Hogarth Press, 1957.

—— (1914b), On the history of the psycho-analytic movement. *Standard Edition*, 14:3–66. London: Hogarth Press, 1957.

—— (1915), Instincts and their vicissitudes. *Standard Edition*, 14:109–140. London: Hogarth Press, 1957.

—— (1926), Inhibitions, symptoms, and anxiety. *Standard Edition*, 20:77–174. London: Hogarth Press, 1959.

—— (1930), Civilization and its discontents. *Standard Edition*, 21:59–145. London: Hogarth Press, 1961.

Jones, E. (1957), *The Life and Work of Sigmund Freud. Volume 3, The Last Phase 1919–1939*. New York: Basic Books.

Kernberg, O. F. (1991), A contemporary reading of "On Narcissism." In: *Freud's "On Narcissism: An Introduction,"* ed. J. Sandler, E. S. Person, & P. Fonagy. New Haven, CT: Yale University Press, pp. 131–148.

Mayes, L. C., & Cohen, D. J. (1994), Experiencing self and others: Autism and psychoanalytic social development theory. *J. Amer. Psychoanal. Assn.*, 42:191–218.

Moore, B. E., & Fine, B. D., Eds. (1990), *Psychoanalytic Terms and Concepts*. New Haven, CT: Yale University Press.

Sandler, J. (1987), *From Safety to Superego. Selected Papers of Joseph Sandler.* New York: Guilford Press.

Stepansky, P. E. (1977), A History of Aggression in Freud, Vol. 10, ed. H. J. Schlesinger. *Psychological Issues*, Monograph 39. New York: International Universities Press, pp. 223–230.

Temeles, M. S. (1993), A developmental line for narcissism. The path to self-love and object-love. In: *The Vulnerable Child*, Vol. 1, ed. T. B. Cohen, M. H. Etezady, & B. L. Pacella. Madison, CT: International Universities Press, pp. 17–29.

# 3.

# Narcissism in the Service of Survival

## JUDITH S. KESTENBERG and IRA BRENNER

The children who were victims of Nazi persecution needed to find ways to survive and maintain their self-worth in the presence of overwhelming threats. Not only were their lives threatened, but their very rights to exist at all were denied. Teased, mocked, jeered, degraded, and seeing that their elders were similarly treated, they felt completely abandoned and in lack of protection by parents and state authorities. They lost the right to live because of their purported inferiority. They were starved, beaten, tortured, and experimented upon. The will to survive under these toxic conditions was interrelated with the belief that narcissistic investment in their body functions and the skill to maintain them, was a necessary prerequisite for the maintenance of the struggle for life, since the alternative was to give up and submit to death.

In this paper, we shall briefly summarize our views on narcissism and give examples from literature, interviews, and groups of child survivors on how primary and secondary narcissism, and even a tertiary narcissism served survival. We shall

An earlier version of this paper was presented at the "Vulnerable Child" discussion group chaired by Dr. Theodore Cohen, in Chicago, May 1987, at the annual Meetings of the American Psychoanalytic Association.

The material in this chapter is based on interviews with survivors of the Holocaust, who were children under the Nazis, conducted by members of the Jerome Riker International Study of Organized Persecution of Children.

also report on the pathological aspects of narcissism in child survivors.

On the basis of movement observation and interpretation it has been suggested (Kestenberg, 1967; Kestenberg and Borowitz, 1983) that primary narcissism persists throughout life and is interrelated with not only secondary narcissism, but also with relationships to objects (Jacobson, 1964; Kernberg, 1975; Bergmann, 1980). Kohut (1971, 1977), however, does not make this distinction between primary and secondary narcissism and he introduces the concept of the selfobject to bridge the gap between narcissism and object relationships.

The current theory of primary narcissism no longer refers to it as the libidinal cathexis of the ego, but rather of the self (Freud, 1914, 1916–1917, 1920, 1921, 1923; Hartmann, 1950; Guss Teichholz, 1978). Most authors concur with Freud that the original narcissism is later deposited in the ego ideal (Sandler, Holder, and Meers, 1963). Freud, however, occasionally contradicted himself over the issue of the persistence of primary narcissism after early infancy. He saw the beginnings of object relationships in the perception of changes in the external world after birth (1921), with narcissism "not necessarily disappearing" (1916–1917, p. 416), when object relationships started.

Regarding primary narcissism, Freud's notion that the narcissistic libido is derived from the soma (1920), implies that the body is its primary source. We concur with the view that a painful or diseased organ draws narcissistic libido to itself (1914, 1923), as if reviving it and curing it, and add that narcissistic investment in every vital part of the body guarantees survival and well-being. Primary narcissism has its developmental line, as various organs and zones gain prominence and are more cathected than others. Psychosexually, oral narcissism is followed by anal, urethral, inner-genital, and phallic narcissistic needs.

In addition, there are movement patterns present in every living tissue that act as conveyors of libido and aggression (in this paper we will only speak of libido). We will describe two such patterns, the first of which alternates rhythmically between growing and shrinking of body shape:

1. To take in vital external life and comfort-giving substances, such as oxygen, warmth, and nourishment (Balint's primary objects [1952]), the organism expands as it grows. To expel noxious substances accumulated in the body, it shrinks. These patterns of growing and shrinking are linked with affects of comfort and discomfort, with intake and output. They are part of the motor apparatus, underlying primary narcissism, which diminishes as we grow older, but never disappears as long as we are alive. We view primary narcissism as the psychic reflection of growth and maintenance of life whose early manifestations are seen in the smile of content, in the joy of grasping, turning, creeping, standing up, and walking or talking. While this "Funktionslust" persists, another source of narcissism is added which can be construed as a form of secondary narcissism. Self-love and self-admiration is heightened when the child feels loved, approved, and admired. This ability to thrive under another's adoring eye persists throughout life. The child, for example, seems to grow, to become bigger, when one claps for him. Freud said, "if a man has been his mother's undisputed darling, he retains throughout his life the triumphant feelings, the confidence of success which not seldom brings actual success along with it" (p. 156).

2. Another change of shape in which parts of the body are extended to reach pleasant stimuli and are withdrawn from unpleasant stimuli or when the stimulus loses its nourishing quality (usually exemplified in the ameba), underlies attraction and repulsion. This apparatus forms the basis for anaclitic relationships in which the object is sought for gratification, but is abandoned when no longer needed or when it is felt as unpleasant. This is the substrate of what Freud described as secondary narcissism.

We have to distinguish between primary narcissism with its sources in the body and two kinds of secondary narcissism: one that arises from withdrawal from the object, from lack of care or disappointments (if you don't love me, I won't love you and will love myself instead), and the other one where libido is drawn from the loving object (you love me and that makes me love myself so much more). How these can combine can be exemplified in the following story of a child survivor. Deprived of primary sources of care in camps, she had to stand up for herself and care for herself. She described the feeling of ecstasy when she could finally take a shower or when issued silverware, a comb, and blanket. The primary feeling of warmth, of having something nice with which to care for herself combined with the secondary narcissistic gratification, which stemmed from feeling loved and protected. It conjured up the image of her loving mother who had provided all these pleasures prior to her deportation when the young girl was 5 years old.

The primary sensory experiences associated with comfort are the biological basis for the investment of the body with primary narcissism. However, not only can the body or the whole self be invested with libido, but also the mental apparatus or parts of it, like the id, the ego, or the superego, can be selectively cathected. We need not say that we must substitute the concept of self-libido for ego-libido. The ego can be selectively invested with narcissism and in further differentiation, selected ego functions like memory or motor skills can be highly cathected, sometimes at the expense of others. Specifically, a redistribution of narcissistic libido may be necessary in order to maintain physical survival that is inspired by spiritual survival.

Drexel (1980), who was tortured in Mauthausen for his anti-Nazi political beliefs, wrote that he was forced to sing during his tortures. He used the songs as "an enlivening drug," which sparked his "vital spirits," lamed by anxiety and pain. When the libidinization of a wounded body can no longer be effective, libidinizing a creative experience may serve as sublimatory outlet for caring for one's wounds. Oftentimes, Drexel felt a dichotomy in himself: while his body was tied to the table and beaten, one part of him felt the intolerable pain and the threat to his life, as well as his desire to give up and die, but the other floated, "without sensation and [is] devoid of gravity, but in a strange spatial congruence with the martyred body" (p. 118). Here the delightful feeling of becoming master over gravity and over space is revived from the time of early childhood when conquering gravity and space were the primary narcissistic triumphs of the previously earth-bound and space-limited baby.

Drexel was kept in a dark cell by himself. He was afraid of the constricting darkness, which he equated with the loss of space. However, he could invest the darkness with a narcissistic fantasy in which the night simulated the wideness of infinite spaces large as "the ALL." His thoughts ceased to be oppressive and they flowed as if they were carried by waking dreams. This fantasy was sustained by the feeling of being cared for and protected. He felt "held by the invisible spirits and suspended on the wings of memories" (p. 11). Being carried and thus safe are the nonverbal memories which man, threatened by extinction, conjures up to feel born again into a safe, holding environment. Indeed, not many people survived the kind of torture Drexel was subjected to. He could not use physical resistance. It was his spiritual resistance which saved his body and soul. By retaining his dignity, a high self-esteem, and by regaining faith in his own ability to resist the pull toward death, he gained the will and the wherewithall to survive. In other circumstances and with other people, dignity was retained, but death could not be averted. Young girls and even children in the camps went to the gas chambers singing their national anthems.

Short respites from deprivation or torture could allow the persecuted to regain their narcissistic equilibrium by enjoying bodily care. When Drexel was able to rinse himself with water, he felt a well-being that reminded him of having been newly bathed and "a strong will to live flowed through my blood vessels" (p. 105).

Janka Herszeles (1946), an 11-year-old girl who was imprisoned in the Janowski camp in Lwow, described her experiences in a diary written when she was 12. Frozen, hungry, alone, and deprived of air in the crowded waiting room leading to the showers, she asked a man she knew to let her go to the showers first. She had just witnessed the beating of prisoners by the SS and was in a despondent mood, ready to give up. The shower restored her interest in life because it warmed and sheltered her for a while, but the man's kindness revived her as well.

It is remarkable that a tortured person can become aware of his inner organs when he feels his tortured breath and the frantic beating of his heart. Drexel declared his love for his heart, which he addressed as if it were a beloved child, "I held my breath and listened to its (the heart's) uneasy beats, and a strange, almost affectionate love pulled me towards this small courageous bundle-like organ and its secret and wonderful, soft and unerring force. You small wonderful being in my chest . . . I could trust you now. . . . You would not disappoint me" (p. 102). Is it possible that this investment of libido in an inner organ is a corollary to the withdrawal of libido from the external objects to the inside of the body, as if a fetus rather than one's own caring mother were endowed with love? How precious our parts of the body can become after an expectation that some limbs are injured and lost is exemplified in Drexel's discovery of lack of serious injury to his body which "filled me with a wild satisfaction" (p. 102).

Herszeles, too, described how she almost lost her desire to live and then discovered a will in herself that was akin to Drexel's wild satisfaction. She had witnessed an execution of a man who willingly put the noose around his neck and ascended the scaffold. She stuffed her ears, held her breath not to see, and not to hear, but to escape. She was interfering with her vital function, thus preventing herself from feeling alive. Some time later, she commented that she was not afraid of anyone's death and not of her own death. She had been afraid of a particular form of dying before, when she heard that children had been buried alive, and she dreaded the feeling of suffocation. Now, in the midst of murders, executions, and starvation, it occurred to her suddenly, "I wanted to live immensely and I felt as if something calls out in me, 'live, live.' I had no strength to inhibit it and I could not calm down" (p. 54). She resolved that she would not cooperate in her own death with resignation and humility like the condemned man did. She asked whether giving in to death could be considered heroism. Her answer was, "No, I have to live." At the same time, she acknowledged that she was all alone, had no one and nothing to live for. The here-and-now was all suffering, yet, she said to herself, "I prefer to suffer, to starve, only to live because I love life" (p. 55). Then she added that even though she would not escape, she would not undress for her own hanging. This belated resolve to resist death was not only due to an increase of primary and secondary narcissism, but also a link to her mother, whose parting words enjoined her to live, despite the great suffering she had to endure.

Not infrequently, the parting words of a loving parent restored the wish to live, even when the child's primary wish to live had been severely curtailed. Identifying with the mother, the child decided to care for herself as her mother or father did when they were alive. The parent seems to love the child from beyond the grave, and that imagined and remembered love increases narcissism enough to bolster the will to live. Even though Janka initially resented that her mother poisoned only herself, abandoning Janka and condemning her to suffering, she was able to use her mother's parting words as a sort of holding environment in which she could cling to life.

Not only parents, but surrogate parents can sustain a child's feelings of self-worth and his or her right to live. Approval from older people bolsters the child's ego ideal and its creative potential, another sign of creating life. Janka was not saved by accident. Her survival evolved from her participation in the camp's literary circle, where accomplished poets and writers gathered to recite their work (Borwicz, 1946). In excitement, Janka composed rhymeless poems (Maria Hochberg Marianska, 1946). Because they valued her creativity, the leaders of the underground in the camp decided to rescue her. She was escorted from Lwow to Krakow, where the 12-year-old wrote her diary in hiding. The libidinal investment in creative writing, an ego function, and the admiration she received from her adult audience, fostered her will to live and also induced others to save her. Living on through one's poetry may be seen as another form of survival, also.

Even Nazis in camp appreciated creativity. An 18-year-old woman poet who wrote in broken German, was assigned to a children's block and saved because the guard valued her poems (Klein, 1985). Sender (1986), an adolescent girl, wrote poems in a labor camp which became a source of morale for the rest of the inmates. Her ability to do so was instrumental in saving her life, despite having a severe infection. Thus, there were practical aspects to creativity which led to physical survival. But perhaps just as significant was the spiritual survival, which prompted adults and children to invest creative endeavor with narcissism and enhance the will to live, not only in themselves, but also in others. A sublimatory activity could effectively arouse the joy of life in the face of extreme physical deprivation. Many of these gifted people libidinized words and phrases, melodies or visual sensory experiences (Brenner, 1987) then or later reproduced in art, and treated them as treasures that belonged to them and to the group of people who shared their misery. Almost invariably, starved and deprived people would libidinize the memories of good food, of trees, of flowers once seen, and the faces of their loved ones, from whom they were separated. As one child survivor, a poet, said, "I feel in love with nature. That was my mother." Such a statement may reflect the universal wish for oneness, which becomes activated under these traumatic conditions.

The confrontation with death, therefore, has a profound effect upon the psyche (de Wind, 1968). A redistribution of narcissistic libido may occur naturally in the normal course of aging with the gradual awareness of the inevitability of one's death. The maintenance of self-esteem, self-worth, and the right to live all have to be reconciled with the ultimate narcissistic injury, the recognition of aging, leading to death. When one is forced to confront this normal developmental task prematurely, it is out of phase and requires a tremendous reorganization of psychic forces. In a sense, it is the antithesis of a fixation. Therefore, in the face of constant threats to survival and a lingering deterioration of the body way before old age, the employment of excessive narcissistic defenses may be fueled by a redistribution of narcissistic libido from nonessential cathexes of the self to the body, for certain essential bodily functions, and to the ego ideal, all of which may intensify and make effective the will to survive. We have tentatively agreed to call such narcissism tertiary, that is, a return to the overcathexis of the body, to life-saving ego functions, and to associated aspirations to live a long life.

In such extraordinary life-threatening situations, therefore, the ego and bodily functions which maintain self-preservation become invested with or "fueled" by tertiary narcissism. Invoking the reservoir analogy of narcissistic libido (Freud,

1923), we postulate that primary narcissism coalesces with secondary narcissism under such condition, which is forged into tertiary narcissism. Tertiary narcissism then provides for additional resilience which, in the case of child survivors, enabled them to endure until liberation.

The persistence, however, of this putative redistribution of narcissism might explain some of the sequelae of massive psychic trauma. Specifically with regard to child survivors, the extent to which the Holocaust experience affected and colored their psychological growth would be influenced not only by the nature of the trauma, their stage of development, and their permorbid mental health, but also by the continuation of such a narcissistic configuration. The fate of this narcissism, which was adaptive under such extreme conditions, remains an area of ongoing investigation.

Some forty years later, clinical observation from one source, the dynamic process which has developed in the context of a group for child survivors, is beginning to shed some light. The intense feeling of isolation and alienation which many felt, has been remedied by a very strong sense of belonging, of group loyalty, and of group pride. The establishment of a separate child survivors' organization which required a charter, a checking account, and officers, resulted in an air of legitimacy and permission to call themselves survivors. The heightened self-esteem which went along with being part of this group was infectious and has continued for more than six years now. The definition of child survivor, however, has become a very heated topic, on more than one occasion. Our criteria for the interviewing protocol was extremely liberal—allowing for those children who experienced any exposure to persecution while under the age of 13. One woman member of the group, however, insisted that only concentration camp survivors had really survived and that only they had earned the title of "survivor." She, incidentally, felt she had suffered the most and for the longest period of time, which seemed to give her an exalted status. She incurred the wrath of the other members who, feeling insulted and devalued, confronted her about the trauma that everyone had experienced.

Another child survivor, when first contacted about the group, remarked incredulously, "I thought I was the only child to survive!" Such myths are not uncommon, and again betray an underlying sense of being an exception. The consensus is that these children felt they were robbed of their childhood, and many felt that they did not have a home country. Though they also felt that they were scarred for life, an intense feeling of camraderie, hope, and enjoyment of the small pleasures of living is generated each time they meet.

On one occasion, this reaffirmation of life was dramatically lived out when the hostess for the evening lit a fire in her fireplace, forgetting to open the damper. (Though her unconscious motivation for forgetting is of great interest, the group reaction was significant also.) Within seconds, the room, which was packed with unsuspecting child survivors, filled up with dense smoke. Without panic, several people sprang into action, opening doors and windows, thereby "rescuing" everyone from what was becoming a gas chamber. The unspoken communication about protecting each other, and their seeming readiness for danger was quite striking. The survival value of group formulation was demonstrated quite clearly here, also it almost seemed that the group will to survive increased as each person recognized his value to the other. Thus, the group's narcissism increased in the face of danger which was successfully averted.

Many child survivors reported that they often sensed that it was a triumph to wake up alive each day, despite the meaningless of time and the dangers that lie ahead. Finding and having something to eat became a source of great pride and accomplishment. Appropriating a new piece of clothing such as a coat or a pair of shoes was similarly a sign of great resourcefulness, along with finding shelter, escaping by running fast, eluding guards, and acquiring false papers. In short, any behavior which prolonged survival for one's self or one's loved ones became necessary, not only for a sense of self-worth, but for life itself. In addition, a number of these survivors attribute their survival to certain highly valued traits or skills in themselves, which also reflect their primary narcissism. For example, having an Aryan appearance of blond hair and blue eyes is mentioned quite often. One woman recalled a harrowing train ride with her very Semitic looking parents whose false papers were being questioned. She felt that her looks confused the German officers who naturally assumed that she was not Jewish. She then felt a sense of omnipotence because she had saved herself and her parents. The pride she had had in her pretty face prior to the war took on a life and death significance during persecution. Similarly, a fluency in the German language was highly prized and had survival value. Another survivor credited his survival to the command of German so that he was able to translate and communicate with the Nazis. They, according to him, thought he was special, which made him feel protected.

Feeling protected is related to feeling loved, and interestingly, there is a dearth of literature on the effect on narcissism of being loved. Infant observation suggests that narcissism is heightened when a child is loved, approved of, and admired, which originates from the baby's tendency to incorporate the good that comes from the outside. This tendency continues throughout life, and being loved, the individual takes in libidinal supplies offered by the loving object. His body feels better when fed, cared for, and caressed. It then becomes more precious, owing to the good care which it has been given. Thus, the loving object's behavior is another source of secondary narcissism, which is antithetical to the first source of secondary narcissism, which arises from the lack of care or pain associated with object, such as narcissistic wounds due to disappointments, feelings of abandonment, and the like (Freud, 1914).

Another area worth mentioning is the seeming dilemma over ego-libido and self-libido. Narcissistic libido cathects not only the self, the body, and the wishes, but it also cathects the ego and the superego. As a result, these terms refer to different areas of narcissistic investment. Frequently, we may see uneven distribution with selective investment in certain attributes such as intellect or creativity. A redistribution of narcissistic libido might therefore be necessary in order to maintain not only physical, but spiritual survival.

Where an increase of narcissism does not enhance survival, we must speak of pathogenic narcissism as seen in the following two vignettes of child survivors who experienced themselves as having special powers:

Mrs. A, who was in Auschwitz at age 9, became convinced that she was invisible and therefore unknown to her Nazi captors. In so doing, she felt invulnerable and safe from danger. During the selection in which her mother and younger sisters were sent to the gas chambers she clung to her aunt who shielded her. Mrs. A then began to feel that as long as she were hidden and unknown to the Nazis, she could not get hurt. Indeed, when Auschwitz was evacuated prior to the arrival of the Russians, she refused to leave her barracks, hiding under a bed, crouched, and in a corner.

As a young woman following the war, she proceeded with her education showing exceptional intelligence and a literary talent. She, interestingly, had her tattoo surgically removed while in college in the United States, in order to try to erase her past and to assimilate. When confronted about her fantasy of being invisible and unknown to the Germans in Auschwitz, she became puzzled and bewildered. She could not remember having been tattooed, an act which clearly proved that she was not only known but had to be accounted for. In her mind, she survived as a sickly, malnourished, frightened young girl simply because "they" didn't know she was there. Prior to the war she was raised in a very affluent, sophisticated family, the first grandchild on both sides of the family. She was indulged and became the center of attention, not only because of her birth order but because of her intelligence and affability. She was healthy, proud, and felt very special. The degradation of her parents left her with an indelible scar which filled her with profound anxiety, sadness, despair, and guilt. As the family's fortune declined, so did their hopes for survival. Mrs. A soon learned that she could no longer count on her parents anymore. However, she felt as though she were nothing without them. One memorable event which reinflated her depleted sense of self-worth occurred on the train ride to Auschwitz.

Starved, dehydrated, overcrowded, and exhausted beyond belief, her father traded a gold cigarette case for a drink of water for her. Aside from the obvious value of the water, the narcissistic nourishment seemed to be of tremendous value for her also. Here again she felt how important and how worthy she was in her father's eyes as he gave away such a valuable possession for water for his special daughter. In recalling this event, she paused in her despair and mourning to take great delight in this extraordinary moment.

Another child survivor, referred to earlier, Mrs. B felt as though she were a powerful bundle of energy. As such, she felt safe, protected, and immune from danger. She had the distinction of being the smallest worker in a torpedo factory and was so nicknamed "the little one." Her Jewish identity was concealed because a Polish woman spontaneously adopted her in the camp which made her life somewhat less intolerable. She felt that her Aryan appearance and her special status of being the tiniest prisoner in the camp bestowed a special protection upon her. Prior to her assignment to this camp she had lived on a farm with an old, crippled Polish woman who let her tend the cow. This cow became imbued with the characteristics of her mother and at the age of 5 she lived with this image for almost a year. She would clutch the rope attached to the cow and take great pleasure in being licked on the cheek by its raspy tongue. In her cow's presence, she felt safe, protected, and warm. Having been traumatically separated from her parents when they were arrested and having never seen them again, she recreated sensory images of her mother which bridged the gap between them. For example, she would luxuriate over the thin, watery soup, keeping the spoon in her mouth for long periods of time, conjuring up the smell of her mother's chicken soup. At that time she would then feel protected and safe. Similarly, when feeding her cow or cuddling against it, she again recreated a sense of invulnerability.

When she was transported from the farm to the labor camp, she never saw her cow again and experienced another traumatic loss. When issued a rough, hairy blanket and a small steel comb, she was then able to regenerate her good feelings about herself and her sense of safety. The rough textured blanket reminded her of the cow's hide and the sharp toothed, scratchy comb was like its raspy tongue. In this manner she stimulated herself and activated the sensory memories of the cow which comforted her and gave her the illusion of being safely protected by her mother. The small steel comb became a highly prized possession which survived the war also. She kept it hidden in a safe place until after the survivors' reunion in Washington, DC in 1983. At that time, she dug up this relic and felt an emotional flooding as she reexperienced the pain, sadness, longing, and grief for her parents and her cow. In recalling this event, she conveyed a sense of strength, power, and energy.

In these vignettes we sense that the basic functions of nourishment are highly invested with narcissistic libido. With Mrs. A, her father's bartering gold for water intensified the pleasurable act of drinking. Starved and depleted, the miracle of water is further exalted by the father's demonstration of his love and devotion to her. Here the secondary narcissism associated with the father's reflection of his love is interwoven with the primary narcissism of filling her belly with life-sustaining water. Similarly with Mrs. B, the experience of eating soup was further intensified by the memory of mother's chicken soup and the loving protection of her presence. These moments in time during the periods of suffering and deprivation provided a basis of heightened narcissism which perhaps coalesced into a state of grandiosity and illusions of invincibility.

The fact that these children survived does not prove that their narcissism was adaptive, however, in that adults protected them as much as possible. In addition, the presence of mood instability along with the persistence of intense preoccupations with self-worth and survival itself, which at times interfered with daily functioning, suggests the presence of deep psychological scars in some child survivors.

In conclusion, it is important to realize that the Nazis intended to deprive Jews of their dignity, their spirit, and their pervasive will to live and learn (J. Kestenberg, M. Kestenberg, and Amighi, 1988). They deprived them of vital objects such as air, warmth, food, and of life-sustaining people like parents, spouses, and children. Under the circumstances, the libidinization of the self as a valuable, dignified person, who was loved and cherished by his or her own people, the libidinization of sensory experiences and satisfactions of the past, contributed to the raising of self-esteem and to the wish to live. These mechanisms prompted not only actions that would save the lone individual, but it also enhanced the desire of others to save the individual. The survival that led to the continuation of the heritage and to the perpetuation of genes in children was also experienced as a triumph over evil and a further justification for living.

To summarize, the heightened instinct for survival and a reclaimed sense of self-esteem seem to have persisted, as a result of the interweaving of primary, secondary, and tertiary narcissism which we presume to be operative in these remarkable individuals.

## REFERENCES

Balint, M. (1952), *Primary Love and Psychoanaytic Technique*. London: Hogarth Press/Psychoanalytic Institute, 1952.

Bergmann, M. (1980), On the intrapsychic function of falling in love. *Psychoanal. Quart.*, 49:56–77.

Borwicz, M. M. (1946), *Literatura w Obozie* (Literature in camp). Krakow Wojewodzka Zydowska Komisja Zydowska w Krakowie. No. 5.

Brenner, I. (1987), Multisensory bridges in response to object loss during the Holocaust. *Psychoanal. Rev.*, 75/4:573–588.

Drexel, J. (1980), *Rueckkehr Unerwuenscht* (Return not desirable). Joseph Drexel Reise nach Mauthausen der Widerstandskreis Ernst Niekisch, ed. W. R. Beyer DTV Dokumente. Muenchen: Deutsher Taschenbuch Verlag.

Freud, S. (1914), On Narcissism. *Standard Edition*, 14:69–100. London: Hogarth Press, 1957.

———— (1916–1917), Introductory Lectures. *Standard Edition*, 16:243–463. London: Hogarth Press, 1963.

———— (1920), Beyond the pleasure principle. *Standard Edition*, 8:3–66. London: Hogarth Press, 1955.

———— (1921), Group psychology and the analysis of the ego. *Standard Edition*, 8:67–144. London: Hogarth Press, 1955.

———— (1923), The ego and the id. *Standard Edition*, 19:3–66. London: Hogarth Press, 1961.

Jacobson, E. (1964), *The Self and the Object World*. New York: International Universities Press.

Hartmann, H. (1950), Comments on the psychoanalytic theory of the ego. In: *Essays on Ego Psychology*. New York: International Universities Press.

Herszeles, J. (1946), *Oczyna Dwunastoletniej Dziewczyny* (Through the eyes of a 12-year-old girl). *Wojewodzka Zydowska Komisja Historyczna*. Krakow, Poland: Wojewodzka.

Hochberg-Marianska, M. (1946), Preface. *Oczyma Dwunastoletniej Dziewczyny* (Through the eyes of a 12-year-old girl), J. Herszeles. Krakow, Poland: Wojewodzka Komisja Historyczyna.

Kernberg, O. (1975), *Borderline Conditions and Pathological Narcissism*. New York: Jason Aronson.

Kestenberg, J. (1967), Movement patterns in development. II Shape. *Psychoanal. Quart.*, 36:356–409.

———— Brenner, I. (1986), Children who survived the Holocaust. The role of rules and regulations on the development of the superego. *Internat. J. Psycho-Anal.*, 67:309–316.

———— Borowitz, E. (1983), Thoughts on the development of narcissism. Paper presented at the Symposium on Narcissism, sponsored by the New England Psychiatric Society, New Haven, CT.

———— Kestenberg, M., & Amighi, J. (1988), The Nazis' quest for death and the Jewish quest for life. In: *The Psychological Perspective of the Holocaust and Its Aftermath*, ed. R. L. Braham. New York: Social Science Monographs, pp. 13–44.

Klein, C. (1985), *Poems of the Holocaust*. Jerusalem: Gefen Publishing House.

Kohut, H. (1971), *The Analysis of the Self*. New York: International Universities Press.

———— (1977), *The Restoration of the Self*. New York: International Universities Press.

Sandler, J., Holder, A., & Meeris, D. (1963), The ego ideal and the ideal self. *The Psychoanlytic Study of the Child*, 18:139–158. New York: International Universities Press.

Sender, R. M. (1986), *The Cage*. New York: Macmillan.

Teicholz, J. G. (1978), A selective review of the psychoanalytic literature on theoretical conceptualizations of narcissism. *J. Amer. Psychoanal. Assn.*, 26:831–862.

Wind de, E. (1968), The confrontation with death. *Internat. J. Psycho-Anal.*, 49:302–305.

# 4.

# The Influence of Hostile Aggression on the Development of Expressive Language

## ELEANOR GALENSON, M.D.

Among the most frequent developmental deviations in infants who are at "psychological risk" is delay in the acquisition of expressive language, commonly known as speech. Data from psychoanalytically informed infant observation and treatment offer intriguing insight as to the role of disturbances in the libidinal and aggressive impulse balance during a critical period in the second year of life. Factors which contribute to this imbalance in some children and their parents will be described, and a direction for preventative and therapeutic intervention will be suggested.

Reports in the psychiatric and psychoanalytic literature of cases of "elective mutism" in children usually do not distinguish between those children who have *never attained* the use of expressive language and those suffering from an *inhibition* of expressive language which had already developed. Expressive language usually begins to emerge during the middle of the second year, following the period of receptive language acquisition. The infant not only comprehends the meanings of familiar words, but can now utilize *socially accepted* words to communicate his or her personal subjective experiences and share them with others.

51

While many factors undoubtedly influence this process of language acquisition (constitutional endowment, language exposure, the presence of siblings, etc.), a major influence appears to be the nature of the mother–child relationship. I will propose that it is the balance between libidinal and aggressive aspects of this relationship which affects the development of speech in a profound way.

A specific connection between speech and the sphincteric aspect of anality was first proposed by Greenacre (1969). She wrote:

> It may be significant that speech begins and is then elaborated during periods of special spurts of development of the body sphincters. The muscles of the mouth, pharynx and larynx which play such an important part in speech have rather complex sphincter-like activities. Clinically we know that the infant's speech may be much affected by the vicissitudes of sphincter control in other parts of the body. There may still be such a degree of plasticity in the body organization forming the basis of self-image that synchronous and similar body developments of early childhood affect each other through avenues of easy displacement [p. 361].

Yet another connection between speech and anal phase development was suggested by Stone's (1979) evolutionary view of the development of the aggressive drive. Stone proposed that transformation of oral aggression facilitates the emergence of speech; oral cannibalistic fantasies which accompany the onset of teething are gradually deployed from mouth and teeth to hand activities under normal circumstances, leaving the mouth free for the development of the function of speech. At the same time, oral rage is gradually replaced by bodily sensations relating to sphincter activity, and the struggle between retention and expulsion becomes an *internal* one, unlike the feeding interaction of the first year.

Both Greenacre and Stone emphasized the importance of drive activity during the first 2 years in regard to both its bodily expression and the incipient ego function of social communication. Data from psychoanalytically informed infant research and clinical experience offer support for their hypotheses. Direct infant observational research findings indicate that there is a decisive turn in the management of oral aggression between the eighth and tenth months. As oral aggression intensifies with the eruption of teeth, infants normally develop a greater adaptive capacity to cope with delay as well as a greater repertoire of active affectionate behavior toward their caretakers. But this developmental phase is also characterized by mother–infant interchanges which are mildly teasing in quality—an admixture of affection and controlled aggression in both members of the dyad.

However, if hostile aggression has been intensified during the infant's first year due to either physical or psychological trauma, or if the maternal response to the infant's budding aggression is unduly restrictive (Galenson, 1986), such infants become intensely negative in their behavior toward their mother and other people as well. It is this libidinal–aggressive imbalance which appears to interfere with the developing symbolic function, specifically in regard to the emergence of expressive language. Under these circumstances infants are unable to communicate fantasies and affects through the socially agreed upon vehicle of speech, and may indeed be impeded in the actual development of fantasies as well as in their deliverance to the social world. Certain types of first year experience appear to be particularly traumatic and apt to stimulate hostile aggression. These include prolonged separation from the mother, serious body illness, serious injuries, and surgical procedures.

Normally, the passage through the anal phase during the second year heightens separation anxiety because of the threat of anal loss. This gives rise to the sphincter struggle between retainment and discharge, opposing impulses which color much of the psychological functioning of this period.

When excessive trauma of the type mentioned above occurs during the first year, the mouth becomes invested with excessive oral aggression which cannot be adequately discharged subsequently through the normal anal channels, and the mouth is not available for the verbal expression of ideas and feelings under these circumstances. Another potential source of distortion of symbolic development is the similarity between the sphincteric structure of the mouth and larynx and that of the anus (Greenacre, 1969). Anxiety regarding anal loss, particularly when it has been preceded by an earlier experience of object loss, leads not only to an intense anal sphincteric struggle between retaining and discharging anal contents, but the use of oral and laryngeal sphincters which are needed for the development of speech may be inhibited until the anal struggle is resolved.

Analytically informed observation of the development of a little girl during her second year provides support for the hypotheses described above. Julie, a sturdy 12-month-old girl who was the younger of two sisters, had been developing well during her first year. She was securely attached to her mother as her primary caretaker and had also spent time during each week with a part-time caretaker, Anne, of whom she was very fond. Shortly after Julie's first birthday the family moved to a new city. Julie lost her familiar surroundings as well as her well-loved part-time caretaker. She gradually adapted to her new circumstances and became attached to a new part-time caretaker, but she refused to acknowledge Anne, her former baby-sitter, when Anne visited the family in their new home three months later.

In her attempts to master these separation experiences, Julie developed a large repertoire of hide-and-seek games, as well as other play which involved the theme of organizing inanimate objects of various kinds according to their appearance and function. Shoes were lined up meticulously side by side, blocks were gathered in piles, and puzzles became a favorite pastime. This type of obsessional play helped Julie to organize her new outer world and her inner world as well.

This behavior was readily accepted by Julie's family and by her new caretaker. Soon Julie, now 15 months old, began to object to wearing diapers, insisting she could withhold her urine and soon her stool as well, until she got to a potty or toilet. This self-imposed toilet training was due in part to her desire to be able to do whatever her 2½ year older sister did, but her need for control was undoubtedly an added factor. Despite her parents' clear communication that they did not expect Julie to conform in this way, and indeed were often at their wits end when Julie insisted on finding a proper place to urinate during a family drive, Julie would not, and mostly did not, wet or soil her diaper during the day, although she could not exert this excessive control at night and agreed to wear diapers when she went to sleep.

Julie continued to control her family's activities in this way for the next four or five months, and she often had temper tantrums when her parents could not or did not conform to her toileting needs. In parallel with this struggle, Julie's symbolic development took a remarkable turn; not only did her formerly rich and free semisymbolic play become repetitive and passionately obsessional, but she also remained stationary in her language development. Clearly able to satisfy her needs and wants by communicative gestures, she also understood what was said by others, but she continued to vocalize many idiosyncratic wordlike utterances and only a handfull of identifiable single words. Expressive language was definitely delayed.

As Julie approached her twenty-fourth month, her behavior began to alter in several areas. Her favorite transitional object, a blanket ("Blankie") was used for comforting as before, but Julie added an increasingly large family of "baby dolls," as she now began to call them. She fed, washed, undressed, and comforted them and began to actually *speak* to them in a kind of "baby talk," if one can use that term to describe the speech of a 24-month-old child. This spurt in semisymbolic play, and the equally impressive advance in her language which accompanied it, was truly astonishing. Julie soon began to use quite advanced sentence structure, language which appeared to have been readied silently, only waiting for a critical developmental push before it could appear. This new developmental step had been preceded by a real resolution of the anal and urethral sphincter battles. Now sphincterally competent, she could easily control her urination and defecation during the day, although not yet at night.

Julie continued to show the determined personality of her second year; she soon began to insist on learning how to "read" and to do "arithmetic"—nascent activities which seemed to serve this striving and sturdy child very well. It remains to be seen whether her early separation experience will affect her later on, but this psychologically competent toddler had managed to use a variety of ego capacities as she dealt with the exaggerated aggression of her second year, without coming into serious conflict with her environment. She was certainly aided in great measure by her parents' capacity to abstain from responding to her hostile aggression with an aggressive response of their own. Not all children are reared under such fortunate circumstances. Nor are early traumas recognized for the influence they may exert during this highly vulnerable period of the first 2 years of life.

## CONCLUSION

My research and clinical data from both normal and pathological infants suggest that conflicts over oral aggressive impulses which normally emerge during the last quarter of the first year may be intensified by anal phase conflicts over sphincter control and the accompanying anxiety during the second year. Important precipitating factors include a change in the infant's relationship with his or her primary caretaker, particularly if there is a break in the continuity of this relationship at the highly vulnerable age when object permanence is just beginning to evolve and separation anxiety is peaking.

In addition to its nutritive function, the mouth carries out the important sphincteric function of speech. This function may become involved in conflict when the anal sphincteric function of retention and loss begins to express both positive and negative affects, as well as anxiety. While receptive language may be proceeding normally in its development, an infant who is engaged in serious anal conflict as the result of earlier object loss may be unable to utilize the oral sphincter for the production of speech. Such infants usually acquire a complicated gestural repertoire which temporarily serves communicative purposes in lieu of speech. When the conflict over the issue of object and anal loss is resolved, either through the infant's own capacities or through intervention from the environment, both anal and oral sphincters become available for their appropriate function and the symbolic function proceeds to develop in the form of semisymbolic play and speech.

If my hypothesis concerning the dynamic relationship between oral and anal aggression is correct, it would elucidate many of the puzzling features of distortions in language development, particularly the delay in the emergence of speech. I suspect that it is precisely in those instances where the mother–child relationship has been invaded by an undue degree of hostile aggression that the dynamic relationship between the libidinal aggressive drive balance and language development will be evident. I believe this is the situation in many single parent families where the mother cannot help her toddler to modulate the normal early hostile ambivalence of anal phase development in the absence of paternal support for both mother and child.

## REFERENCES

Galenson, E. (1986), Some thoughts about infant psychopathology and aggressive development. *Internat. Rev. Psychoanal.*, 13:349–354.

Greenacre, P. (1969), Discussion of Dr. Galenson's paper on "The nature of thought in childhood play." In: *Emotional Growth*, Vol. 1. New York: International Universities Press, pp. 353–364.

Stone, L. (1979), Remarks on certain unique conditions of human aggression (the hand, speech and the use of fire). *J. Amer. Psychoanal. Assn.*, 27:27–33.

5.

# Loss, Aggression, and Violence: Two Groups of Traumatized Children

## JO ANN B. FINEMAN, M.D.

For the past five years, I have been acting as child psychiatry consultant and program supervisor for two tribes of Southwest Indians, both of which are located in the southern desert of the United States. These tribes are of Mexican origin, probably descendants of the ancient Toltecs. They migrated from northern Mexico to the southern part of the United States in the late nineteenth century to escape persecution from the religious hierarchy, and to seek better grazing or agricultural land. The migration from northern Mexico was the culmination of nearly three centuries of intermittent warfare between these Indians and the Spanish Mexican dominant population. Theirs was a unique culture which resisted the authority of the Catholic church, attempting to preserve a culture rich in native Indian elements of religion, social organization, and language. In the 1960s, approximately 200 acres in the southwestern United States were set aside by the U.S. Congress for this tribe, but only in the late seventies was it recognized by the U.S. government and granted the same status and benefits as all other American Indian tribes. As of this writing, the total acreage of the reservation has grown to approximately 900 acres, and the tribe to roughly 5000 enrolled members. Despite the increase in land, there are still many tribal members who intermittently move to the regional large cities, in search of better living conditions and employment opportunities. Only about one-third of the adult members of the tribe are regularly employed, and the median income for a family of five stands at approximately $5000 per year (IHS Headquarters Briefing Book, 1987). While this figure is at the poverty level, there are some benefits which partially augment such a low income: medical care provided by the Indian Health Service; subsidized housing (when available, often with a waiting period); educational opportunities for qualified high school graduates; and some tribal employment furnished by enterprises such as gambling casinos, landscaping businesses, and others. Only 3 percent of tribal members have college degrees, and only 8 percent have any formal training past high school, while three-quarters of the adults have not finished high school. Given this grim population profile, it is not surprising that the infant mortality is approximately 66 percent above that of the proximate geographical area, while the mortality rate from all causes is 22 percent higher, quoting mid-1980s statistics. Alcohol and drug abuse have become and remain a significant psychosocial problem for the population both on and off the reservation. In the children, fetal alcohol syndrome and its related fetal alcohol effect is clearly at levels above those of the surrounding population, even though this particular tribe does not have well-documented statistics. The accompanying incidence of violence, related somatic diseases, and death by car accident and suicide are also unusually high. Seven years ago, a child mental health team comprised of a child psychiatrist and child analyst (JBF), a social worker, and a tribal mental health worker of great skill and sensitivity began to evaluate and design psychotherapy strategies for a group of children aged 3 to 5½ years, identified through the preschool unit located on the reservation, and for older children referred by the tribal social service. This program has continued and flourished, the only program of its kind to provide such services on any Southwest Indian reservation. Over the years, we had child psychiatric fellows joining this team in six-month elective rotations, which augmented the opportunity for psychotherapy and follow-up in the later developmental phases when the children go on to grade school. These tribes seem to have been dealt a losing hand, since their reservation land is largely low desert with little or no grazing for livestock, and still less arable land for agriculture. Despite these hardships, the tribes have struggled (as have most North American Indian groups) to maintain a sense of dignity and cohesion, of village and family, in the face of shattering odds and harsh realities which require defenses and ego states often aimed at denial and avoidance. This, in turn, I believe, has contributed to a unique attitude toward their children and their child-rearing practices. The remnants of their traditional ritual and religious practices, intertwined with Catholic ritual and dogma, have also produced a special blend of beliefs, either articulated or covertly held, which, from a psychoanalytic point of view, produce a linkage between death, loss, intrapsychic failure to mourn, and the emergence of a particularly tenacious identification with the aggressor (historical, cultural, and intrafamilial) with its generational consequences. While none of the children reported has been in psychoanalysis, several of them have been in dynamic psychotherapy with the child psychiatry fellows, and we have had the opportunity for informal follow-up of some cases, since the tribe is small, and members of the preschool staff and the mental health technicians, who have been a part of the child psychiatry team for the past seven years, are in touch with families in the village and are apt to know the children as they grow and enter the school system in the outskirts of a nearby large city.

This group of children has, in many instances, experienced extreme trauma in their early years: desertion, violent abuse, and death of major caregivers. Sixty percent of the 3- and 4-year-olds in one of the preschool groups we served had either lost or been abandoned by a biological parent, and there is no reason to believe that this was a unique group since the preschool program is free and open to any tribal family. Thus, cultural and personal loss, often determined by extreme economic and social privation, have become almost a standard feature of the developmental experience in these children. Coupled with these losses, physical punishment of the children may become brutal when the depression and rage in the adult caregiver breaches the boundaries of the ego defenses.

My own focus of interest in this work over the past seven years, in addition to the clinical goal of treating as many of the children as possible with the resources available, has been the relationship between catastrophic early loss, later aggressive and violent manifestations, self-destructive acts and fantasies, and affective object attachments. From a countertransference point of view, this work can become extremely frustrating and discouraging. The chronic and ubiquitous depressive affect which understandably pervades the population, and which often leads to an attitude of despair and therapeutic avoidance, can become deadening for the therapist and discouraging in the extreme. The motivating energy must often come from the impetus to learn and to understand the more global relationships between early loss and later aggression toward the object, in the hope that such knowledge can in some way be transmitted to the therapeutic goals in working with this population. And, one becomes attached to the children, and to the tribe in general, as they struggle in isolation, little noticed by the surrounding culture except as rather romantic and colorful dancers in the public ceremonies attended by tourists.

In psychoanalysis, a theory of aggression seems to have been fraught with more controversy and varying points of view than has libidinal theory. Perhaps, as a child analytic patient in my training years once wisely said to me, "The trouble with being mad is that you have to do something about it right now." In childhood, as in adulthood, loving, with its pleasureful aim and beloved object, produces a sense of contentment, and we all attempt to preserve that affect and sense of love in whatever way. On the contrary, aggression and violent affects and fantasies push to be discharged immediately, so as to rid the self of pain and to literally put outside of the boundaries of the psyche such an alien and disturbing set of affects and fantasies. Several authors have addressed the elusive problem of revisions of psychoanalytic thinking on aggression (Buie, Meissner, Rizzuto, and Sashin, 1983; Fonagy, Moran, and Target, 1993; Rizzuto, Sashin, Buie, and Meissner, 1993). Fonagy et al. (1993) is clear on the point: "Psychoanalytic thinking on aggression lags behind many other aspects of our normal and clinical models of the mind." Anna Freud (1972) emphasized that the problem of normal infantile aggression was still full of uncertainty (A.

Freud, 1972). Parens (1979) described a closely studied consid-eration of the development of aggression. In his first named type of aggression arising in childhood, he indicates that it is "unpleasureful discharge of aggression" which ensues when the infant or child is overwhelmed with pain or frustration. Here, I would add, we see the failure of the environment in the form of the parenting (mothering) figures to provide the minimum necessary climate of comfort, safety, and object related plea-sure. This rather begs the question of innate "drive" or reactive expression of a hostile intent. But leaving aside this theoretical dilemma, these authors have delineated theoretical narratives of the development of aggression in early childhood. Yet, from the observations of these groups of children, there seems to be a special effect from object loss or separation in early life, and later attachment to objects in which tormenting and sadistic attitudes prevail.

The questions posed are in the realm of the earliest inner representations of the hurtful and frustrating objects, the sub-sequent loss of that object, and the preservation of the internal representation by identification and acting out of the tor-menting and/or aggressive object representation. In many of the children whom we have observed or treated, there is a remarkable need to retrieve the lost, pain producing object, even in the face of replacement of that object by a more benign soothing and loving caregiver (Novick and Novick, 1987). In his longitudinal studies of infants, John Benjamin (personal communication, 1958) endorsed the concept of what he then called "non-hostile aggression," very akin to Parens' similar con-cept. Recently, a Boston group (Rizzuto et al., 1993) has brought forth the theoretical proposition that to some of the former theories of aggressive development must be added a statement that the aim of aggression is to overcome an obstacle, that is, aggression is called into play toward gaining a goal, either psychical or physical. Perhaps in reference to the chil-dren in these two groups described, the original "goal" of a basically gratifying object attachment has been thwarted consis-tently, and the resultant aggressive action and accompanying fantasies, when present in the preconscious or unconscious mind, can be thus understood. Again, I would add a salient early determinant, that of early traumatic object loss or separation from the primary object, with the additional psychic attribute of a persistent need to retrieve the lost object, however pain producing that object may have been.

The clinical case study described in this article, that of the Manuel children, portrays a family group caught in internal and external forces which result in the sequence of loss, abuse, and object attachment pathology. Especially in Lorenzo, the 6-year-old boy in the sibling group, the precursors of destructive aggression and violence can be unmistakably identified.

The Manuel children all spent time on the village road, watching for their deserting, drug-abusing mother, who locked them in a closet and almost starved them. They played out sequences in which they called her on the phone to ask her when they could go back to her, and they developed fantasies of her whereabouts, which were unknown. As though to hold onto this image, they were tormenting and brutally sadistic to one another, physically and sexually, with little affect or sense of any level of gratification. As the 6-year-old boy, Lorenzo, said, "We play momma and daddy."

These particular children were a representative example of the developmental traumas faced by many of the children in the tribe. While this family was one of the more pathological, it was by no means novel or singular in our clinical experience in the tribe.

The four children ranged in age from 7 to 1½ years, with the oldest a girl, Maria, and a boy, Lorenzo, 10 months apart. The mother was a heavy heroin and crack abuser, as well as one of the village dealers, and the father was severely alcoholic. The children were found in the house (after neighbors notified the Tribal Social Service unit) in a state of extreme physical neglect with marks of blows from one of the parents. Later the mother left the family; it was believed she traveled to the California border to work out a drug deal. They were placed in a foster home, where it was later revealed that all of them were victims of sexual abuse, probably from an older male cousin. Even before this repetition of their earlier abuse, they played out sadistic sexual scenes, with Lorenzo taking the role of the male in oral and genital sexual acts with the younger sisters. In recounting these, for us, almost depraved and unnatural activities, one might expect fantasies of ugly and monstrous children to be operative; not so with these children. Lorenzo and the younger sisters could be warm, expressing their neediness by climbing on the laps of the observers and sharing toys amongst themselves. The oldest, Maria, 7, could assume a caregiving and organizing role with the others, a remnant of her early identification with what caregiving the parents had been able to provide in their brief episodes of sobriety and attachment. Even in the midst of such relatively calm play, Maria was heard to remark to Lorenzo, quietly and without affect, "Would you like me to suck you?" Their everyday language was replete with such explicit sexual references, as well as sadistic acts and fantasies, biting, beating, and stabbing of toys, dolls, and one another, graphically acted out in play. The function of this overtly sexualized, perverse genital and anal play may not be only an identification with the abusing and sadistic treatment the children have received, or observed; but may also represent an attempt to maintain closeness. The early absence of soothing and comforting kinesthetic body experiences predisposed them to distorted anal and genital play, as active repetition of passively experienced somatic trauma, now also utilized to maintain the object attachments to one another. Only Maria, the 7-year-old, is beginning to display attempts at what appears as appropriate superego formation, with compulsive counting and lettering, as well as beginning disgust directed toward Lorenzo and the younger children in their sadistic and sexually explicit play. She, alone of the siblings, at times repulsed Lorenzo's attempts to play "making babies and sucking" with her, and was turning more and more to the adults in the foster home to aid her.

It can be postulated that brutal sexual play had been a lifelong method of need gratification for them, as well as the mode of attachment between the siblings—they probably shared one bed in the original home, and clung to one another as both sexual and aggressive objects. The polymorphous perverse nature of the libidinal and aggressive fixations was illustrated by Lorenzo's stealing of food from the cupboards at night and hoarding it in his bed, his relentlessly sadistic approaches to his two younger female siblings, and his anal stabbing play in therapeutic sessions. There was, in Lorenzo, an early dysjunction between act and affect. For him, these sadistic and violent actions seemed devoid of real affect, a chilling portent for later violence; and the most affective content was directed toward the longing for the lost mother, either once more to experience masochistically the attachment to her, or (and this is inferential in the extreme) to make the mother the object of his sadistic and violent impulses and fantasies. We had little evidence for this latter speculation other than a remarkable drawing by Lorenzo in one of his last sessions, of himself with a 'knife-penis," so named and drawn, and in which he also depicts himself as a maternal figure, with the youngest sibling on his outstretched arm, going into the house. This is a primitive but graphic illustration of a merged identification with the brutal and lost mother (Figure 1).

In the report of a panel of the Fall Meeting of the American Psychoanalytic Association, December 1988, Robert Gillam commented that "we really do not understand why some patients will identify with sadistic parents or parental figures, and why others will select masochistic solutions. . . " (Panel, 1990, p. 799), a statement which my observation of the children discussed in this paper strongly endorses. I would suggest that the combination of a predominantly depriving, brutal, and sadistic parent, coupled with the *loss* of that parent in the early years of life, brings about a special constellation of later sadism, attachment to the lost object without mourning and relinquishment, and a driven need to repeat the sadism in the service of maintaining the inner representation of the lost object.

Another boy from the tribe illustrated a more organized sadistic character development, one in which the child can displace the impulse and fantasies into drawings, but also act out violently with other children. Ernesto, another child from this tribal group, age 12, turned on playmates in the schoolyard (a Catholic parochial school), knocking them to the ground and brutally kicking them without provocation. He also, on one memorable occasion, stood up during Mass and pummeled an attending nun, shouting, "fucking bitch" at her, behavior which resulted in instantaneous expulsion from the church and from

Figure 1

the school as well. Ernesto was particularly preoccupied with torturing large insects—plentiful in the desert—pulling legs and wings off and closely watching the insects struggle and lurch as they tried to crawl or fly.

Ernesto was adopted by a neighbor woman when he was 3 years old following abandonment by his biological mother, who later died of unknown causes in an adjacent state. He seemed genuinely puzzled about his vicious acts and had a sort of curious affect when observed as if saying, "Is that me doing all these things?" His therapist reported only one observed episode of true affect, occurring when he was told he was being sent to another school. He said, "I'll go," then paused, and added, "If they want me." His wistful sense of longing to be cared for may have echoed his inner search for the lost mother, abandoning and abusing though she was, and thus added another determinant to the hypothesis relating early object loss of an aggressive and sadistic object.

Another group of children and adolescents, non-Indian and largely of Hispanic or Anglo heritage, within the same geographical region, have been seen in psychoanalytically informed interviews over the past two years. These children were referred to an inpatient unit for seriously acting out children and adolescents, including substance abusers. Over this two-year period, about fifty youngsters were evaluated and interviewed. In reviewing these life stories, there was seen to be a preponderance of early parental loss, as well as parental brutality, particularly between father and son.

As I sought to review these data in more detail, another striking characteristic emerged that seemed to corroborate our observations of the younger Indian children.

I refer to the lack of observable affect, and the juxtaposition of the utmost sadism toward some humans and animals, coupled with caring and protective attitudes toward others. This is notably present in the adolescent males' attitude toward girls to whom they are attached. This may also be confirmatory of the notion that early loss of a sadistic parent may lead to internalization (rather than relinquishment through mourning) and identification with the sadistic object later acted out. The emergence of loving and protective attitudes and behaviors toward females during the adolescent period suggests an attempt to preserve an early fantasy of the loving mother, despite abandonment, sadism, or final loss by death. The majority of children and adolescents seen were males, but there were a small number of females, referred after being apprehended for prostitution and drug dealing. We do not have the in-depth material on these young women, since they were rather quickly sent to a girls' residential treatment center, which offered longer term evaluation and residential therapeutic intervention. The boys, on the other hand, because of the limited resources of the region, were necessarily kept in the evaluation center for much longer, thus allowing us to spend more time in interviewing and after-care planning in order to locate suitable therapeutic services. The young women seen, however, paralleled the male population in sadistic actions and affective impoverishment, as well as having experienced early loss and brutality.

I will briefly mention two 18-year-old males, both white Anglos, who were for several years engaged in lives of violence and cruelty. Ken, age 18, had been a drug and alcohol abuser probably since the age of 7 years, when he first began to drink leftovers from his father's weekend binges. The father was a rural farmer and a committed hunter in the mountainous region where the family lived. Ken grew up with violent and destructive assaults on animals, but also frequent fights with his sadistic father. Ken fought back, and on one occasion, when he was about 12 years old, father and son engaged in a wild west knife battle, resulting in slashing of both parties. Such ruckuses are devastating and leave literal and figurative scars for life. Ken proceeded to pot and hard drugs; was able to kick these addictions, but maintained a brutal and destructive relationship with most of his peers. He left home early, at 16, and relying on his innate intelligence, got a job fixing cars in a small northern Texas town, breaking rodeo horses (a harsh and dangerous occupation), and fighting whenever the opportunity presented.

Remarkably, he admitted himself to the inpatient unit, just before his 18th birthday, after his girl friend, with whom he was living, threatened to leave him unless he changed his ways.

When I saw him, he revealed himself as a bright, unusually introspective adolescent, looking much older than 18, and proudly showing me his scars and broken teeth. He was consciously aware of his hatred of his father, and vowed he would kill him some day, after perhaps torturing him. Along with these primitive and disturbing fantasies, he felt tender and loving toward his girl friend of two years, and worked hard to support her through his jobs at the garage and on the rodeo circuit. He cried unashamedly during the interview when he told me that at the age of 2, he had accidentally injured his mother. While alone with his mother on the porch of their ranch house, he had picked up a loaded deer rifle, and as he fingered the trigger, the gun had fired. His mother was struck in the throat. She had survived, but with terrible damage to her throat and larynx, such that she was left mute, and for many years was fed by gastrostomy. Ken's mother had finally left his father, and Ken had remained with his father. He is still ridden with guilt over the accident, and is even more rageful toward his father, for leaving him alone on the porch with the loaded gun. His methodical sadism and violence seem relentless, despite his intelligence and areas of warmth toward women. Gratification of his aggressive impulses is offered by the particular cultural and social sanctions of the area in which he lives, as well as his chosen work of rodeo riding, and altogether the outlook for treatment or modification seems bleak.

Another case is that of Jason, age 17, who was referred when picked up in a large city in southern Texas for street fighting and possession of drugs. Jason was an adolescent hit man for organized crime, recruited because of his age. If caught he would be remanded to the Juvenile Detention Center and sent to a psychiatric unit for diagnosis and treatment, if he so chose, rather than being incarcerated in the state Boys Home. His father had been mysteriously murdered when Jason was 7 years old, probably shot in a drug deal gone awry, but Jason had never been told the actual circumstances and had overheard snatches of (his mother's) conversation which allowed him to piece the story together. His mother and a brutal stepfather had divorced shortly before his arrest, and various 'ings were parceled out in neighboring states, either with relatives or on their own. Jason had astoundingly little affect concerning his former profession of hired killer. He had carried a gun since age 14, and had used it with lethal effect on several occasions, he reported. He was never caught, probably because he had no guilt and looked upon his actions as a job to be done, for which he was employed by the bosses and well paid. His ambition was to get to "a big city" like Los Angeles, and continue his current life-style. He told me that any feelings "simply go away" after an act of violence, at which point he liked to get high on marijuana, watch television, and eat pizza. Diagnostically, he was probably on the way to a schizoid development, dominated by the acts of violence without affect or discernible guilt.

The adolescent cases, particularly, leave one with a sense of hopelessness and frustration as to treatment resources, especially in the current and worsening climate of limited public funding for the supportive and long-term therapy of such children.

What can analysts do about violence? Certainly one approach is to gain further understanding of the relationship between early loss, the internalization of the aggressive and sadistic lost parent, and the resulting latent fixation of the sadistic treatment of objects. The failure to begin or complete mourning in such a constellation of circumstances is central, preventing later identification with more benign objects which could modify the supergo in its archaic and harsh character. It appears from the clinical observations we have been able to make in the two populations of children mentioned, that there is, in the face of early loss of a traumatizing parent, a perverse need to internalize the painful attachment to the lost object, identify with the sadistic nature of the attachment, and repeat such attachments in their own object choices. The role of affect, or the lack of it, seems crucial, in that the sadism is often largely without any discernible conscious gratification, calling into question the designation of "sadism" to describe the violent or tormenting acts. Much remains to be learned regarding violence and its precursors, especially in a world where violence is increasingly sanctioned by political and cultural systems.

Another developmental determinant for these children, since many of the losses tend to cluster within the developmental period of separation individuation, is the relative failure to convert externalized action into internal representation, and symbolization, as well as to merge affective meaning and consequences with outer directed action, especially when such action is aggressive in intent. Thus, one might postulate in such children and adolescents a more firm linkage between aggression and violence; one which may be more fixed and embedded in character formation and affective life. In the theoretical proposition mentioned above (Rizzuto et al., 1993) the psychological obstacle may be thought of as the need to form and preserve an attachment to the primary object, even if that attachment has been torturing, or the object has been lost. Any object, even one united with the child in a painful tie, is preferred by the psychic apparatus than the absence of any object attachment at all.

## REFERENCES

Buie, D. H., Meissner, W. W., Rizzuto, A. M., & Sashin, J. I. (1983), Aggression in the psychoanalytic situation. *Internat. Rev. Psychoanal.,* 10:159–170.

Fonagy, P., Moran, G., & Target, M. (1993), Aggression and the psychological self. *Internat. J. Psycho-Anal.,* 74:471–485.

Freud, A. (1972), Comments on aggression. *Internat. J. Psycho-Anal.,* 53:163–172.

Indian Health Service Briefing Book (1987), Office of Health Program Development, Indian Health Service, Health Program Review, Tucson Area.

Novick, K. K., & Novick, J. (1987), The essence of masochism. *The Psychoanalytic Study of the Child,* 42:353. New Haven, CT: Yale University Press.

Panel (1990), Sadism and masochism in neurosis and symptom formation. F. M. Levin, reporter. *J. Amer. Psychoanal. Assn.,* 40:789–804.

Parens, H. (1979), *The Development of Aggression in Early Childhood.* New York: Jason Aronson.

Rizzuto, A. M., Sashin, J. I., Buie, D. H., & Meissner, W. W. (1993), A revised therapy of aggression. *Psychoanal. Rev.,* 80:29–54.

# 6.

# The Small House Program: Learning to Play

## ERMA BRENNER

At New York-Cornell Medical Center Westchester Division, the author was offered an exceptional opportunity to create and direct a program of her own choice for emotionally disturbed children. The unit assigned to her was the day students' division which could accommodate about twenty-five children between the ages of 4 and 13. The students were enrolled in school at the day hospital because they were too difficult and disruptive to be maintained in the regular public school system. Their daily program was the usual one. Besides regular classroom work it included extracurricular activities such as music, art, recreation, and occasional trips away from the hospital. There were five classrooms within the unit where the children were taught by special education teachers who were assisted by teachers' aides. The classes were small with no more than five children in a room. In addition to the normal school activities every child received psychotherapy twice a week.

The children's records revealed the kind of information familiar to those who work with emotionally disturbed children: histories of sexual abuse, violence, physical abuse, overcrowded housing conditions, parents addicted to alcohol or other drugs, inadequate or psychotic parents, fathers and sometimes mothers away in prison for long periods of time, and not infrequently outright abandonment. Foster home placements were common. For the author the most poignant aspect of such devastating deprivations was the sadness and lack of joy in these children's lives—the normal kind of joy that rightfully belongs to all children.

The author's decision was to offer a program of imaginative play, to be available to each child as part of the curriculum. She hoped that in this way she could provide these deprived children with a measure of some joy in life that they had never known. With rare exceptions they had never had the opportunity to experience the special joy of playing at "make believe" with a caring adult.

Naming the program Small House came about because the only available space was a classroom—small indeed. Nonetheless it was designed not only to incorporate a great variety of toys and art materials, but was set up with appropriately sized furniture to look and feel like a special magical house created just for children.

Children came to this child's world as part of their school schedule to play on a one-to-one basis with their special adult companions. The Small House was open for play five times a week from 8:30 a.m. until the students were dismissed for the day. Each play period lasted for 40 minutes.

To apply her concept of how adults can play effectively and pleasurably with emotionally disturbed children the author decided at first to take only one child at a time into the Small House to play with her. After only a few weeks the Small House program proved to be extremely successful with the children. Now it was time for the author to train a small volunteer staff. With an increased staff the Small House could schedule two children at a time.

The adults chosen to play with the children were from a hospital volunteer pool. Above all else they had to be genuinely interested in children. Over a ten-year period, among the volunteers who applied a number were college trained women and others who had only a high school diploma. One volunteer had a master's degree and had worked with deaf children, another had been a demographer at the United Nations, still another was an Australian special education teacher between jobs who was looking for more training and experience with this group of children. Among another group were two high school graduates who had returned to school and were working toward a college degree. All of those applying to work in the Small House were interested in learning about emotional disturbance in children and how to play with them. Several of the volunteers were African-Americans; one woman was planning to work with children at day care centers and two others were attending college. One extremely gifted woman who had been abused as a child herself was particularly eager to learn the techniques for working in the Small House. Added to the staff were a number of fourth year psychology majors from local colleges who before graduation wanted to acquire some firsthand working knowledge about emotionally disturbed children. Occasionally a retired man who wanted to work with children would be added to the program. A few of the mental health workers who wanted to increase their skills came to the Small House to learn our special techniques for playing with the children. They applied their newfound knowledge with the children during recreational periods.

The adults who were chosen to play with the children in the Small House program were not required to have had any previous knowledge of emotional disturbances or training in psychology. As part of their training they learned about early child development and some of the causes for developmental lag seen in so many of the children in this group. In addition they learned the special techniques for playing with emotionally disturbed children. Of great importance, they were particularly advised not to interpret the children's play to them.

During fantasy play the adults were to let the children take the lead in the play and were not to try to dissuade the children from playing out their fantasies. Instead they were to be willing to accept the many different kinds of roles the children asked them to assume to animate and dramatize the play.

The adults were always to be mindful that in a magic child's world adults don't ask questions of children about their fantasies but follow the children's wishes in all the different kinds of fantasy play or games. For obvious reasons it was advantageous to have each child play with the same adult during each play period.

The reason the program was called Learning to Play was because for nearly all the children imaginative play of this sort was a new experience.

Soon after the Small House had been opened with a trained volunteer staff it was ready to accommodate all of the children in the day school.

## WHO SHOULD PLAY WITH WHOM?

The policy was flexible. If two children wanted to play together rather than separately they were allowed to do so. It often took much juggling of the schedules to accommodate all of the children, particularly if their allegiances to various "best" friends shifted. It wasn't surprising though that once the play started the special friend often was abandoned, but not out of anger or dislike. Rather it was because the child actually craved the undivided attention of her or his adult friend. One could easily understand why a deprived child would not want to share this "special" adult companion with another child, even a good friend.

The youngest children, the 4- and 5-year-olds, were given extra time during the day. Their teacher felt that they needed this extra time to play since they were more of a kindergarten age than first graders. In the Small House these young children were introduced to imaginative play which offered them not only a chance to play, but to have enjoyable, cognitive learning experiences.

The Small House provided all of the children with a great variety of play equipment from which to choose. It had been thoughtfully chosen to stimulate fantasy play for all age levels. It included special equipment for the younger children such as: water table, boats, sea animals, blocks, puppet stage, zoo and domestic animals, early child development toys, a kitchen play unit with dishes, pots and pans, tables and chairs, dolls, blocks, musical instruments, trucks, small metal figures, doll house and furniture, dress-up clothes, dolls and doll clothes. A real automobile steering wheel, simple games, and a host of other new toys were also part of the equipment.

The older children who had not played with younger children's toys at first scorned them: "Baby stuff," they said. But as they became more at home in the program and felt free to express themselves, they began to play "house," or "store," or the "father," who went to work. They used blocks for the first time, played at the water table, and used the puppet stage. They went on imaginary trips, taking their "food" to sustain them on a long voyage. They built airports, tall buildings, towns, and houses.

As some of the teenagers vacillated between fantasy play and more age appropriate activities, we introduced into their play the use of special tools and equipment. We guided and encouraged the older children if they wanted to make something of their own choice. Model airplanes and car models were offered as well as woodworking, art materials, bead making, leather articles, or other materials. Such projects helped to build a bridge over which they could cross from time to time as they grew older. Such activities were a way of introducing and interesting these 13-year-old children to more adult activities. We offered them a typewriter, some simple office equipment, play money, checks, stamp pads, and realistic looking telephones with which to furnish an office or bank. As the children played out more mature fantasy games they chose new roles both for themselves and the adults. Secretaries were employed to help the boss run her or his business or bank. Men and women were bank presidents. They owned restaurants, employed help, made out the menus, or waited on imaginary customers. Others pretended to be homemakers. Several of the boys went into the construction business, ordering blocks for new buildings. They drew up blueprints, and explained them to the construction workers. In all of these imaginative games the adults carried out the play to suit the children by taking on the different roles appointed to them. Such games opened up the world of adult pursuits to these children. It gave them a sense of adult responsibilities and a feeling of personal gratification. For example, an infant busy box, with which the younger children played, became a computer for an older child, or a place in which to insert a credit card. All of these imaginative games gave the older children roles they played out with relish.

Board games and checkers were used as a springboard to a child's imagination. Both older and young children could make up their own rules for playing their favorite game in order to win. And why not? In a magical room a person can make up her or his own rules and win each time—in the everyday real world it is impossible. Naturally, it was explained to the children that the Small House was a very special place where you could win and have fun, but that outside the Small House those magic rules wouldn't work.

There was laughter, excitement, creative play, and fun in the Small House. It was difficult for observers who watched the children playing to believe that they were emotionally disturbed.

However, not all of the children's games were calm, normal, pleasurable or purposeful. There were times when even the young children's play turned to bank robberies, murder, escapes in fast-moving cars, fires burning, bad guys fleeing, cops chasing bad guys, jail doors slamming on both good and bad guys. Sometimes the bad guys won out and the good guys were put in jail.

While the gamut of real and fantasied events was being played out the adults playing with the children did not interfere with the games, but played along acting out their given roles. Although the adults never remarked on the play to the children we often learned much from the play about the turmoil that was part of many of the children's everyday life. Often through enactments we got a clue, or confirmation of something that was going on in a particular child's home life. Sometimes what was acted out was fear of abandonment, of parents separating or divorcing.

Weddings frequently were enacted with dress-up clothes. The new bride, sometimes a small child but more often a teenager, invited her many children, the dolls, to come to the wedding. It was of particular interest to us that the imaginary groom was hardly ever more than a shadowy, undefined male who had no real role in the ceremony. The adults were instructed by the bride how to set the table for a wedding feast. It was a fervent wish of most of the girls to have a wonderful wedding with a spectacular party after the ceremony.

Divorces too were acted out by some of the children.

For example: Sam, a boy of 10 whose mother had left her husband for a man Sam hated and feared, sat quietly drawing a picture for his teacher. Showing neither anger nor keen disappointment over his parents' divorce he began to speak to his adult companion.

"Are you married?"

"Yes."

"Is your husband two-timing you?"

"I don't think so."

"I bet he is. You know somethin'? If my wife ever tried to divorce me I'd kill her. And then after I killed her I'd say I was sorry. See this pitcher I'm drawing? I'm making it for my mom."

We sat at the same table, each drawing a picture. Soon Sam began to speak openly about the new man who took his father's place.

"He's a dirty rat and has a machete. He takes it out all the time and swishes it in the air. My father's a real man. He doesn't have a machete. Only a gun, and he doesn't take it out in the house."

Sam, who obviously was vulnerable and "needy," left that morning with a polaroid picture of himself, extra pipe cleaners, and a gift for his mother. It took months of such play sessions for Sam to be able to find some pleasure in fantasy play. Eventually he began to use the blocks to build airports. He played at being a chef, a policeman, a robber, and a loving, generous father who gave lots of money to his son at Christmas to buy gifts for his friends.

Some young children's play showed that they were being asked to assume adult jobs far beyond their strength or abilities. Armand, who was only 9, played mostly at the kitchen unit. He pretended that he was cooking for his "little brothers," because his mom had to work all the time. That's why, he said, he was always late for the school bus.

The Small House staff kept copious daily notes on each child which were discussed at the end of the day. Much valuable observational information was recorded and shared with the children's individual psychotherapists and psychiatric staff.

The teachers also found our notes helpful in understanding some of the children's problems. Concerning the older children, they very much appreciated the cognitive skills the children brought back to the classroom from their Small House play. Such activities often gave a child an opportunity at "show and tell" time to exhibit and talk about a drawing, a game they played, a string of beads for a friend, or something they built of blocks, and a polaroid picture of their play.

Of course there were some rules for playing:

No throwing things.
No screaming. No fighting.
No swearing or calling other children bad names.

In administering such a program it is important to remember a few simple but basic facts:

Children take time to accept strangers.
Children take time to feel at home in a new environment.
Children take time before they can begin to trust an adult.
Children need to be sure that the adults they come to care for
    and trust will be there for them in their lives as constant
    caring and reliable people.
Children thrive on humor and lightheartedness.

There were many reasons for our assuming the role of reasonable, nonjudgmental, accepting adults with these children. The children needed to be accepted by us regardless of their disturbances, anger, anxieties, depressions, and low self-esteem. Although they did not show it, we were very aware that they wanted desperately to feel that we cared for them—even if they had a bad name or record. It was for these reasons that all the children who crossed the threshold of the Small House were accepted into a safe and secure magical child's world.

In playing with these children it was important to keep in mind that on pain of punishment many of these children were bound in secrecy by their parents or caretakers never to talk about what went on in the home. The child who fears reprisals from home may consciously suppress and conceal what goes on in that home. These children out of fear may withhold valuable information from their therapist thus thwarting and impeding the treatment.

Because of the atmosphere of trust in the Small House a fearful child often found emotional relief in acting out real life experiences. With dolls and puppets they could show what it is like to be beaten; they may play "pretend" in burning another child's hands over the stove; a young girl played out with dolls that a strange man came to her bed and tried to rape her.

Although most of the children came to the Small House eager to play, children did not have to play if they didn't feel like it. Instead a child could choose to sit and relax on the big rocker. It was possible that the child didn't want to play because she or he needed time to sit and think. Or perhaps the reason the child didn't want to play was because she or he was upset, angry, or depressed. Some children, whether on medication or actually very tired, wanted to sleep on a mat for a while. A shy child might just want to watch for the first ten minutes. The adult would always ask if the child wanted to play, but if the child said no, the adult honored the child's need for privacy. She would withdraw to a nearby table, busying herself by playing with some clay or making a simple picture, but ready to play if the child changed her or his mind.

Regardless of the child's affect, the child's adult companion accepted the child's behavior and did not show annoyance or impatience.

The Small House staff kept detailed daily records on every child who came to play. Among the topics covered were the child's affect, the nature of the play activity, the content of any imaginative play, and any other pertinent facts.

We shared our information with the children's therapists, and at staff conferences were included in the discussions concerning individual children.

In addition to being a source of pleasure to the children, the Small House proved at times to be a place of solace and comfort. For example, one of the children, Billy, became acutely upset by the death of his father, who was shot and killed in the street near their home. Billy reacted with extreme agitation and fear.

After an absence from school for a week, on entering the Small House Billy was extremely agitated. Since he didn't want to have anything to do with the adults we said we would wait and play by ourselves but were there for him if he wanted to talk with us. At first he sat in the rocking chair rocking himself violently. Then shouting and screaming he put on a soldier's helmet, found a long block which he used as a gun, and pretended to blow away and kill his father's murderers. He stood looking at himself for a long time in front of the long mirror brandishing the gun and making ugly faces. The play went on for about ten minutes at which point he asked for some cookies and a soda. After a short time he repeated his play and asked us to watch him kill his father's murderers. He left asking us to walk with him back to his class.

"I ain't afraid. I just like company," he said.

This first session was only one of many sessions in which he acted out his bitterness, anger, and blinding grief. His adult companions stayed close by him at all times. They talked if Billy wanted to talk, they played out many roles for him, and withdrew if Billy said he didn't want to talk but wanted to be alone. The agitation and tears were so extreme one day that we took him to the bathroom and helped him to wash up his hands and face. We told him that we and everybody else in the school were very upset and sorry for him because of the terrible thing that had happened.

On that first day when he was so agitated we asked him if he would like to stay a bit longer in the Small House. When he said yes we called his teacher on the intercom who was very appreciative of our offering the child extra time.

"He needs it badly," he told us. "Billy said the only place he wanted to be in was the Small House."

On returning a few days later to the Small House, Billy was calmer but talked only about his dead father and the funeral. It was clear that what Billy was totally unable to cope with was having seen his father's dead body in the coffin. He asked for a cold drink and some cookies and then said he wanted to build something and asked his adult friend to bring him enough blocks to "build something around him." As she started to build he insisted that his sneakers be removed and instructed us how high to build the enclosure and how many flat boards to bring to make a roof. Once he was completely enclosed he began to giggle and make jokes. He knocked on the sides of his building. We knocked back and said we could hear him. When in response to all the jokes and knocking on the building he was asked, "How is it inside there?" He shouted, laughingly, "It's cozy."

We thought that he felt safe because we were nearby, and although he couldn't see us he kept in voice contact through jokes, singing, and knocking on his coffin.

"Take a pitcher of me," Billy shouted from inside his coffin. "Get the camera."

"Now how can I take a picture of you if I can't see you?" his friend asked.

"I'm comin' out," Billy shouted. With a kick he threw down the front of his house, waving frantically at us. As the polaroid camera clicked and the picture popped out it showed a boy smiling and waving at us as he kicked down the coffin.

"Gimmy the pitcher!" he said jumping up, snatching at it. He stood staring at the photo for a long time saying he was going to keep it. Then he kicked the blocks as hard as he could, scattering and destroying the coffin. After another cold drink, the session was over. As he left he clutched the picture saying he was going to show it to his teacher.

It was evident when he asked his friend to "take a pitcher of me," with the polaroid camera that he wanted to see how he looked coming out from inside the coffin, and to be reassured that he wasn't dead. In fact he could easily have escaped from his coffin. In acting out this fantasy play in our reassuring presence we made it possible for Billy to imagine how it might feel to be dead in a coffin and to get free. Obviously what Billy was doing was an attempt to experience death. Not only what was it like to be dead, but what was it like to be inside a dark cold coffin. Was it dark and frightening?

"No!" he shouted to us. "It's cozy."

It was a good place. It was like a good warm house. Billy could now pretend he wasn't frightened at all. Through acting out the fantasy he could deny the terror. Like Billy, his father was in his "cozy" warm home.

Several weeks later after having played the coffin "game" three more times, Billy arrived at the Small House saying he wanted to play something new. He wanted to use the blocks to build a castle. We felt that Billy had worked through some of his initial terror and seemed ready to move away by building a dream castle populated by kings and queens and a cook to bring the king (Billy) all kinds of delicious food. This castle was elaborate and full of riches. The king was kind and generous to his people and the queen was beautiful.

It seemed to us that the building of this fantasy castle was Billy's way of taking a small step to distance himself from the horror of his father's death and the buried coffin. It also seemed that his elaborate fantasy castle was an expression of his great need to create a better world for himself.

Lest one think that by building the castle and playing other normal games it was the end of Billy's terror, we were not surprised when several months later he wanted to build a coffin again. A year later on the anniversary of his father's death Billy built the coffin for the last time.

At the age of 14, after Billy had left the hospital to return to regular school, he made a surprise visit to the Small House. He was warmly greeted by the adults who were delighted to see him. As he looked around the room he remarked how small it was. Turning to his favorite adult friend who had played with him when he was younger, he asked her:

"Do you remember when I was a little kid how scared I was?"

"Of course I remember."

"And how I made that coffin a lot of times?"

"Yes, I remember."

"Well I ain't scared no more. Can you take a pitcher of me? I have to leave soon."

"You're lucky Billy," his friend said, "there are just two more films in the camera."

Billy who was by now taller than his favorite companion took off his shades, made a big grin, and posed with his arm draped over his friend's shoulder. As soon as the films developed he looked carefully at both pictures.

"Can I have one to keep for myself? I'll let you have the other one to put on the bulletin board for the kids to see how I look now."

"That's a good idea Billy. We'd love to have your picture. Here, you put it up where everybody can see it."

"That's cool. Man that's cool! I bet some of the big kids miss me."

"We miss you too Billy, but we're proud of how well you're doing now."

"See you around," he waved as he left the Small House.

Encouraged by experiences like Billy's, one of the teachers called on the intercom one day:

"I was thinking what to do with Anthony," the teacher said. "He's having a very tough time in class. I don't want to have him sent to the quiet room. I think that if Anthony could play in the Small House, even though he's not scheduled to come, it would be helpful to him and us. Maybe if he has a chance to play instead of being in the quiet room he'll be more manageable when he returns. I think it's worth a try."

Although there were two other children playing at the time we gladly accepted Anthony, who came eager to play. The other children weren't pleased to see him but we felt it was important to follow the teacher's intuition and help this child to gain some degree of psychological equilibrium through play in the familiar Small House.

Anthony said he wanted to build something and went immediately to his favorite activity, the blocks.

"I'm going to make a tall, tall tower. You'll see it'll be taller than anybody. And then I'm gonna knock it down."

"Can I be your helper and bring you the blocks you need?" his adult friend asked.

"Yeah. Sure. You bring me lots and lots of long blocks. This tower is gonna be tall. I mean tall, man."

As soon as it was finished he gleefully knocked it down with a deafening crash.

"I'm gonna build it up again. And this time you better watch out it's gonna crash all over the place!"

Tower after tower was built and crashed for a good part of the session. Anthony was excited as each tower crashed, but after a while he got tired of that game. He said he wanted to string some glass beads to make a necklace to give his girl friend. Two other children along with adults were busy playing with boats at the water table. Anthony decided he wanted to play with them, but the other children resented his presence and said he couldn't play with them. Anthony was mad, but decided to make the necklace, and with his adult friend's help brought the beads to another table where he strung a long colorful necklace. Since the necklace was a present, he wrapped it in pink tissue paper, drew a heart on pink construction paper and printed his name under the heart. Anthony was very pleased with his present, chose some stickers which he put in an envelope, and left the Small House with the other children when the session was up. He was still jittery but not as belligerent and aggressive as he had been in the classroom.

"Anthony was still excited when he returned," his teacher reported to us, "and found it hard to settle down, but he wasn't nearly as angry and hostile as when he left. It was a big change from how he usually behaves after returning from the quiet room."

What had the teacher learned about how to help modify the behavior of an upset disturbed child?

What she had learned was that a timely use of the Small House can make crisis intervention unnecessary. By sending a child to the Small House, at the point when he or she was beginning to be very upset, one could prevent the development of a classroom crisis of the sort that had in the past led to the child being sent to isolation in the quiet room. She saw that the Small House could be useful as a means of *crisis prevention* in the classroom. It appeared that the Small House had some temporary therapeutic value as well as being a source of pleasure to the children in the day hospital. In the classroom as in many other situations, crisis prevention proved to be far more desirable than crisis intervention. When crisis prevention as practiced in the Small House was seen as a reasonable way to help modify the behavior of disruptive children most of the teachers sought it. They were convinced that through play with a familiar, understanding adult companion, the disturbed child was given an opportunity to act out in the Small House what might have been so troubling to the teacher that the child couldn't remain in the classroom.

Now the concept of crisis prevention in handling children who were on the edge of going out of control in the classroom was added to the usefulness of play in the Small House.

It was demonstrably obvious to the teachers that crisis prevention through play in the familiar safe child's world made teaching an easier task. Crisis prevention which is child oriented obviated the need for using the more drastic concept of crisis intervention which utilizes the barren, unfriendly quiet room.

This concept of crisis prevention was the beginning of what became a very important function of the Small House. Some of the hospital staff expressed the fear that children would take advantage of the teachers and act up simply to have a chance to come into the Small House, or that we were rewarding a child for poor behavior. In fact these fears proved to be unfounded.

Adding crisis prevention to the program was such a big advantage to teachers and students that it became our practice to have three adults in the Small House at all times rather than two, so that one would always be available for crisis prevention if necessary. Although the room was small it always could be divided to accommodate another child.

The two vignettes that follow are offered as illustrations of how the Small House functioned in crisis prevention.

Death was not an uncommon theme. Two other children made coffins for themselves, and these enactments often were repeated four or five times. Each time we followed the exact instructions given to us by the child on how to build his coffin and bury him. Repeating the acting out in such detail was part of how we accepted the child's need to act out his idea of death.

Brett's foster mother was dying of bone cancer. She was the only person he had ever known who loved him wholeheartedly, and he returned that love. Finally, after a long and painful illness she died. Brett was devastated, particularly since he was not allowed to make a final visit to her before she died. The last he saw of her was at the funeral in her coffin before she was buried.

After her death his behavior in the classroom threatened to be so disruptive that time after time his teacher felt that the only place in which he could cope with his great sorrow was in the Small House. When he came he repeatedly played out a ritual game of death.

First he stood on his head for several minutes. Then he fell down yelling, "I'm bleeding. Take me to the hospital."

As he lay in the hospital he screamed, "Fix my leg. Hurry, I'm dying."

Every kind of life support was offered him: oxygen, bandages, and an operation; all to no avail. Brett expired and pretended to stop breathing. As he lay there he began to give instructions as to how to bury him.

"Get the big blocks and make a coffin." Then he lay back as if dead. When the coffin was finished he sat up ordering the adults as to what to do next.

"Carry me to my grave and put me in my coffin." Again he lay lifeless as he was carried and lowered into his coffin. He lay there, eyes shut tight, arms crossed over his chest. Then he sat up to give more instruction.

"You should bring flowers. Lots of flowers. Put them on my grave." Again he lay back. But he still wasn't satisfied and sitting up again he said, "Cry. Cry harder. Harder." At last he seemed satisfied, sat up, and climbed out of his coffin.

Each time before Brett left the Small House to return to class the adults told Brett that they were glad he could come to the Small House to play. They repeated that his play was a game and they'd play the game as long as he wanted to do it. The adults emphasized that his play was only a game in order to minimize the reality of this game of death and burial.

After each of the sessions in the Small House in which he enacted these vivid scenes he was able to return to the class and participate in the work rather than being on the verge of disrupting it.

After many weeks the ritual did become a game for Brett and he then began to play it more like a game than an enactment of fear of death and dying. At long last he was able to return to his normal schedule and play with another boy. He was no longer a threat to himself or the other students. Now in the Small House he began a new game of being a banker with a lot of money.

Tinna, a child of 6, became so agitated one day that her teacher asked to have her spend some time in the Small House lest she completely disrupt the classroom. This child was from a mixed racial background: her father was in jail and her mother was a prostitute. Tinna came into the Small House in a state of uncontrolled anger about being abused by her grandmother who screamed at Tinna and beat her all the time. Tinna's play was to beat up her grandmother, put the grandmother in jail, lock her up, and scream at her. Then she laughed when she locked the grandmother up and took away the pretend key.

"I'm never, never, never gonna let her out!"

Revenge was sweet to this child when she could pretend to incarcerate this evil witch. She then acted out another role, that of a tough male. She donned the costume of a gangster who outsmarted the cops, rode her motorcycle, and robbed banks. She soon discarded this role and became a pitiful abandoned infant who lay in her crib crying for her bottle and her mommy. One of the adults stayed close to her when she cried, patted her, and sang to her. When it was time for Tinna to leave we were not at all sure that she could remain in class without becoming disruptive again. We assured her teacher that if Tinna could not remain in class she could return during lunchtime.

Several weeks went by when Tinna, who seemed to be back on a more even keel, came in to play in the Small House at her regular sessions. One day, however, a call came from her teacher that Tinna was too distraught to stay in class any longer and asked if we could take her in.

The moment she bounced into the Small House Tinna yelled and said she wanted to make a show.

"I'm gonna make a special show," she yelled. "You! You get out the stage and hurry up."

The adult helped her to set up the puppet stage and gather the puppets. Tinna rummaged around trying to figure out which puppets she needed and chose a blond nurse puppet (her mother was blond) and a black policeman puppet. The adult told Tinna that she'd come to the show but was going home to get her friend. She picked up the steering wheel, jumped into her car and drove home to get her imaginary friend.

The adults, who played with the children often, used an imaginary friend to talk to, which enhanced the play. Children need time to think about what their play will be. A disturbed child needs even more time. We adults often talked to an imaginary friend in order to carry on a realistic conversation. It is particularly useful to carry on a bit of chatter while a child is preparing to create a puppet show. The adults, one real, one imaginary, stretch the time by pretending to buy their tickets and popcorn before the show. When they take their seats they talk to each other about the wonderful show they came to see. This conversation gives the puppeteer plenty of time to prepare before opening the curtain—in preparing for a show most children take lots of time behind the curtain.

Soon the curtain parted, and Tinna held out a blond woman and black man who started talking.

"Hey honey wanna go to bed?" the male puppet asked.

"Sure, come on," the female puppet responded.

The male puppet jumped on top of the female and from then on to the end of the play this child puppeteer showed in detail a variety of sexual acts, including perversions, with all the sounds and language that accompanied the actions. The curtain closed and the child came out to take a bow.

Since our technique is not to comment on the children's revelations, show displeasure, or shock, we, the adult and her imaginary friend, clapped at the end and said we hoped we'd see another show soon. Tinna then said she wanted to make another show, went behind the curtain and soon appeared with a baby puppet she introduced as baby Jesus. The show of about five minutes was about how loving Jesus is, how sweet he is, and how much she loved him. Then Tinna sang some Christmas songs in a soft, loving voice, kissed the baby tenderly, and closed the curtain. We clapped again, thanked the puppeteer, and said we'd come to the next show.

We were reasonably sure that Tinna had been warned not to talk about her mother, her boy friends, or her prostitution. We had suspected for a long time that Tinna was sexually overexcited much of the time. Here was an example of the usefulness of the Smalll House in helping an agitated, sexually excited child express herself to adults whom she trusted. She smiled and looked happy after the first play as if relieved by showing us the sexual acts she had witnessed. The relief and pleasure we felt came from her being able to show us the violence of the perverse sexual acts she had seen. Tinna was much more relaxed when she expressed love and tenderness for another abused baby—baby Jesus. This small, frail looking child understandably was overstimulated all the time by living in an adult world of aberrant sexual excitement. Her teacher now had a better idea of what suddenly set this child off, and was able to send her from time to time to the Small House where she could act out what at the moment was the cause of her sexual overstimulation.

Members of the hospital staff have, at times, questioned whether the Small House might be too stimulating to a very disturbed child. Our experience indicates that this is not the case. Over a ten-year period even the most disturbed children were invited to come to play. One 6-year-old boy who had been severely abused by his mother and a grandparent was so disturbed that he could only play a game of "car." From the age of 3 his grandfather had made him sit on his lap to steer the car. The child's anxiety was expressed on every visit by his constructing a car, which always was defective. He would start to drive his car but it broke down, then it ran out of gas, it crashed into another car, or it had to be repaired. He showed his frustration and despair when once repaired it broke down again. This child felt himself to be like that car, out of control, and utterly impossible to fix. If he bought a new car and took his children for a ride, it broke down, and the children had to go to MacDonald's for supper. Sadly and all alone he stayed behind with the broken down car to wait for the tow truck. But the truck never came and he was stranded in a far away place with his useless car.

This child, Albert, was in therapy and was on medication. He was constantly in a state of fear and deep depression. However, he begged to come to the Small House as often as possible although his depression never lifted. The Small House may have been of some help to Albert but over time there was no change in his depression or fearfulness.

A 10-year-old psychotic boy, Herbie, was confused about his identity. His play was to build toilets in the Small House, questioning the adults whether he should sit down to urinate or stand up. He was told that he was a boy, and that boys usually stand up. Despite his psychosis this boy had an extraordinary artistic talent and used clay to create small animals, toilets, and perfectly formed feet especially the toes. He seemed to find great pleasure in coming into the Small House and screamed if he thought he was being deprived of his session. Only once was his play somewhat normal as he prepared a party for a doll with champagne and fruit. He always undressed the dolls, looking to see if they had a penis or a "hole" instead. We never refused to have Herbie come to play. His teacher said he kept track of the printed schedule in the classroom of the times he was to come to play in the Small House. If Herbie found pleasure in the Small House we were pleased to have him come and to play with him.

Although play in the Small House rarely exacerbated a child's emotional disturbance, in our experience, not every child could make use of the Small House.

Andy was so disturbed, so angry, aggressive, and out of control that it was impossible for us to have him come to play. He wanted to destroy the room, throw everything on the floor, and empty the water table. Despite therapy and medication he couldn't study, learn anything, or have any friends. Andy spent much time in the quiet room.

One last vignette is of Carla, a 12-year-old girl. This child had an IQ of 70. She was sweet and compliant in the Small House, playing house, scolding her children if they were "real bad," and was happy to be playing with her grown-up friend. She was jealous of another girl who was playing in the Small House but always gave in to the other girl's wishes, reluctantly but self-deprecatingly.

Carla's therapist told us that she suspected that the child was being sexually abused, but she could never get enough information during the therapy session to confirm her suspicions. We had no indication either of sexual abuse, although we saw her enact physical abuse when she would beat her baby very hard because she was a "real bad" baby. But we didn't observe sexual abuse in her play.

Just before school was dismissed one afternoon the principal of the school knocked on the Small House door. Carla was with her screaming.

"I brought Carla here because she came running to my office in terrible distress crying and repeating she had to go to the Small House. I don't know what can be the matter but maybe you can find out. I have to go now but call me before you leave."

Carla ran to her adult friend. She clung to her, shivering and crying, but was unable to speak coherently. Suddenly Carla broke away and threw herself on the floor where she writhed and moaned as she rolled around on the floor. She seemed oblivious of our presence as tears ran down her face. Then she pulled up her skirt and put her hand over her vagina. As the moaning got louder she opened her mouth and almost brutally forced her thumb into her mouth shoving it back and forth as she continued to roll around on the floor. The scene played itself out as an exhausted Carla lay quietly on the floor, eyes closed as if in sleep.

Her adult friend went over to Carla, put her arms around her and rocked her in her arms. The child responded by weeping softly.

"I understand what you showed us Carla," the adult said. "I'm glad you could come here today. You're safe with us in the Small House."

There could be no more moving enactment than what we had just witnessed. This child's desperation was overwhelming because she felt trapped. Where could she go to tell what had happened to her? She turned to the Small House. There she felt it was safe for her to show her friends what an awful thing she had lived through.

This dramatic acting out of an overwhelming experience confirmed the usefulness of the Small House as a sanctuary. The child sought it out as a last resort because of the trusting relationship she had with her adult friends. In the Small House with her nonjudgmental, empathic adults Carla felt free to reveal what had been happening to her. With this realistic, dramatic evidence of sexual abuse it was possible for the psychiatric staff to intervene and help this child. She was removed from her present home and sent to a good, suitable foster home.

In summary:

Although the Small House originally was created as a place for pleasurable imaginative play, it soon developed an additional function, that of crisis prevention. Besides the Small House being a place for pleasurable play experiences, the usefulness to the teachers of crisis prevention became in itself a cogent and compelling reason for having a Small House. The several vignettes clearly illustrate the usefulness of crisis prevention.

Moreover, although the Small House was never developed or used as a formal therapeutic program it became a reliable source of additional information which could be shared with the therapeutic staff.

# PART II:

# Child Analysis on the National Mental Health Scene

# 7.

# Wins, Losses, and Challenges: Child Analysis on the National Mental Health Scene

## PETER BLOS, JR., M.D.

In an attempt to provide historical focus on this vast topic, I shall begin with a brief reflection on my own professional career. Obviously this will not be a scholarly review, nor all-inclusive, and many important persons, their contributions, and events will not be mentioned: I trust that this will not be seen as a slight.

In 1952 I began my medical training at the Yale School of Medicine. This was the era of Theodore Lidz and Fritz Redlich in the Department of Psychiatry. They lectured to us, as did Norman Cameron, who in the second year gave a series of lectures on psychoanalytic development. Dr. Milton Senn was Director of the Child Study Center where Marianne and Ernst Kris were regular consultants and observers of the nursery school scene. Sally Provence and Al Solnit had academic appointments at the Child Study Center with concurrent appointments respectively in pediatrics, and psychiatry and pediatrics. Both regularly taught medical students in the pediatric wards and Clinic calling our attention to the practical aspects of bio-psychosocial concepts. I recall Jean Piaget coming to speak at

First presented at the Vulnerable Child Workshop, December 16, 1993 at the American Psychoanalytic Association meetings in New York City.

the Medical School with Kathe Wolff serving as translator and lecturing without notes on his remarks. Not too long before I arrived Edith Jackson had started the rooming-in unit for obstetrics with the radical notion that a neonate and mother should be together. My senior thesis in Medical School was entitled *An Investigation of the Healthy Child's Understanding of the Causes of Disease* (1956) which I completed with the help of Dr. Morris Green in Pediatrics. My first experience as a psychotherapist was as a senior medical student under the supervision of Daniel X. Friedman who was at that time in psychoanalytic training. Excellent neuroanatomy and neurophysiology instruction, especially that offered by Drs. Fulton and Delgado, was provided during this period, and it went side by side with the psychological without apparent contradiction. To be sure, there was not integration either except for Dr. Paul McLean who was working, as I recall, on the psychophysiology of the limbic system.

What I am trying to illustrate is how much psychoanalysis, child development, and the concept of mind and the individual were an important part of medical education in the United States in the late 1950s. As students in that era we were taught to include psychodynamic ideas in our thinking abut patients regardless of age or illness and ideas of psychosomatic illness, and the biopsychosocial model seemed quite logical. Many of my classmates were very stimulated by this exposure and went on to careers in psychiatry, while others admittedly saw it as not particularly relevant to the learning of medicine. I was among those who found these ways of thinking stimulating and challenging.

In July of 1956 I began two years of Pediatric training at the Bronx Municipal Hospital Center associated with the Albert Einstein Medical School. Both institutions were just in their beginning stages. Psychological and developmental ideas also played a role in this work. I recall being assigned to do some nursery school child observation at the Bank Street School. A long observational course on normal child development was given to the pediatric and psychiatric house staff. The instructors included Sybille Escalona and Eleanor Galenson, both of whom are still at work today. In other words, we were encouraged to think about normal development as we worked with sick children and their parents. One patient from these years still stands out in my memory. I worked for some months in my internship with a young adolescent Puerto Rican boy from the Bronx who had a precarious diabetic condition. We met fairly regularly to keep track of his condition and talk about his life. At one point he brought me a page torn out of a book which he had found: it was about the psychiatric problems of the juvenile diabetic. I was amazed and curious and requested he bring in the book. It was an old edition of Kanner's (1935) *Child Psychiatry!* Unfortunately, despite his lively mind, obvious intelligence, and capacity to relate to me, I was unable to successfully prevent his experimentation with and denial of his diabetes, and he died one evening in the emergency room. The mind and the body became for me indelibly and ineluctably indivisible.

I began my adult and child psychiatric training at the same center. Supervision, courses and seminars, and case conferences were often taught by psychoanalysts who came up from Manhattan or down from Westchester. Fenichel's *The Psychoanalytic Therapy of Neurosis* (1945) was considered required reading and everyone had a copy. Dynamic formulations were a part of every case evaluation. Again the biopsychosocial model with its inherent developmental component was at the heart of what we were taught. Note again, this was not in any way to the exclusion of biological diagnosis and treatment. Most of my house staff mates went on into psychoanalytic training as did I.

I should note that this was a time in which psychoanalytic ideas of development, formative relationships, conflict, defense and symptom formation, psychic structure, and a dynamic formulation of mental structures were significant, not only in adult and child psychiatry but also to burgeoning interest in the adolescent patient as well. And it was a heady and hopeful time for the field as a whole.

But in the late 1960s and early 1970s, as we all know, a change began. The dynamic interest in the individual, the family, the group, began to wane; by the 1980s it was thought to be useless, archaic, and even dead. DSM diagnosis became the cutting edge of thinking and classification of the mentally ill. Symptoms were the focus of attention since it was thought that they could be objectively listed as results of biological disorder like fever or cough or limp. The idea of symptom as final common pathway, to use Sherrington's felicitous neurological phrase, and that it could be the expression of both mind and body, came to be considered old fashion and irrelevant.

Perhaps this marked shift in thought and theory was inevitable since psychoanalysis, it might be said, had become quite grandiose. Psychoanalysts were talking about a general psychology based on psychoanalysis. For many in the United States it was the century of psychoanalysis, just as for other hopefuls it was the century of the child. Popularly, it was thought that to have an analysis would let you remove your inhibitions, resolve your conflicts, let ego be where id had been, and you could joyfully become whatever you wanted to be. America, responding to its inevitable disappointment in a characteristic way, lost interest. As the love affair with psychoanalysis ended, America, like a lover in search of new romance, turned to better living through biochemistry where change could be achieved by medication, training, and even potentially gene change and repair.

Perhaps our question today is to ask what has been retained from the thirty- to forty-year period which was sometimes bravely called the age of the child and could in retrospect perhaps be called the golden age of psychoanalysis? In the present as we look at the current national mental health scene for children I think we can see some contributions from psychoanalysis still extant. Let me list a few:

The upsurge of research and intervention in the life of the infant has very rich, powerful, and current connections to child analysis. Some of the prominent contributors such as Selma Fraiberg, Eleanor Galenson, and Robert Emde were all trained as child analysts. Berry Brazelton, the pediatrician, was made an honorary member of the American Psychoanalytic Association in 1993. I believe child analytic training has had a formative influence in their work, but at the same time they have gone beyond it. Currently, one of the areas of considerable psychoanalytic interest and controversy is the importance of infant experience in clinical analysis. This is not talking about Kleinian formulations about the mental life of the infant below the age of one year, but about the infant's mental capacities for memory and the influences of this memory later on in development, and the possibility of reconstructing something of this experience in an analysis.

In a similar vein, in recent years, there has been a growing interest in toddlers and therapeutic nursery schools. One fountainhead for this in the United States has been the Cleveland Center for Research in Child Development and the Hanna Perkins School. There are now similar independent therapeutic nurseries growing in the Chapel Hill area of North Carolina and in Houston, Texas, as well as some nursery consultation situations elsewhere.

I think it can safely be said that developmental psychoanalytic thinking made an important contribution to the thinking and development of the Head Start program and the Early Assessment program. However, I must also note that these programs are chronically and severely underfunded, and the teachers are both inadequately trained and paid.

The field of adolescence in which my father pioneered and contributed is an area where I think psychoanalytic thinking has been a leader. But I am afraid that here too its influence is fading as well.

A more mixed impact can be seen under the heading of popularization. Many analytic terms have become part of our culture as revealed in language usage. Terms such as *identification* (a recent newspaper headline stated "President Clinton Identifies With JFK"), *defensive, regressive, be in touch with your feelings,* and so on. Unfortunately, these words do not seem to foster mutual understanding and respect, but frequently convey a pejorative meaning.

How will all this fare under the new national health care plan currently being formulated in Washington? At this point no one can say. But I fear that mental health care for *children* will not fare well and psychoanalytic contributions to their care will be less than ever. I find the concept of short-term mental health intervention misleading, letting people feel they have truly and lastingly helped children suffering from psychological difficulties when there has been only symptom relief, if that.

It is my impression that training programs in early childhood education and care give short shrift to understanding the mental functioning of toddlers, how they express their feelings and needs in a unique way, and how adults in their lives can foster their biopsychosocial development.

These, of course, are among the losses of my title, but there are others. Psychoanalysis as a way of thinking about individuals has been cast out from the centers of power. Within the child mental health movement, which includes child psychiatry, social work, and psychology, the emphasis is more on management, symptom removal, and economics. I won't belabor this point since it is a familiar one but let me list some of the losses which I think are important:

1. The child guidance clinic, whether run by a hospital, social agency, school, or privately, has largely disappeared. This is not to say that there are not good places with dedicated individuals providing real help to children and their families. Rather I wish to point out that their numbers have been decreasing and their focus has been narrowing. Dynamic psychotherapy for a child or adolescent in a low-cost clinic setting is very difficult to find. A case in point is the condition of Attention Deficit Disorder (ADHD) and associated learning difficulties, which in my view has been much overdiagnosed. One can readily obtain pharmacological treatment in a psychiatric or pediatric clinic, and perhaps some counseling on management techniques. But the comorbidity, to use the current phrase, of neurosis, depression, and anxiety is ignored. Here the final common pathway of behavior, the symptom—hyperactivity associated with social and learning problems and an inability to concentrate—is managed rather than understood as an expression of multifaceted causality which must be treated.[1]

2. Residential treatment for children and adolescents, the dynamic milieu, and work with delinquents has become another relic. Fritz Redl, one of the brilliant and charismatic practitioners and teachers of this area of work, is all but forgotten.

---

[1] This observation, unfortunately, has been repeatedly confirmed in recent years through my participation as an examiner on the Adolescent Section of the oral part of the Board examination for Child Psychiatry.

(It is ironic that this loss was brought home to me in the Detroit area where he worked for so many years but whose name and work are now virtually unknown.) There are many other analytically trained workers in this arena whose work has also been forgotten; names such as Eleanor Pavenstadt and Edward Mason come to mind. In fact the whole concept of residential treatment has been deemed "too expensive" with insufficiently "proven" results.

3. Funding for research of a dynamic and clinical nature has almost vanished. I find the interest is more on management than understanding, and whereas understanding could lead to helping individuals to help themselves, management only leads to more management. Whether it is through conditioning, behavior modification, and/or the use of medication, it seems to me the objective is the same: control rather than learning and self control. I hasten to add, that the individuals who are providing this kind of help are very dedicated and committed to their young patients who often benefit. But nobody wants to investigate or acknowledge the effect of transference in this transaction.

4. Recently published by the American Academy of Child and Adolescent Psychiatry, *Parameters for the Assessment and Treatment of Anxiety Disorders* (1993) gives little credence to the effect and importance of fantasy in the life and behavior of the young. To my mind the reality of events and biological imbalance have been disconnected from the life and influence of the mind. In other ways too the *Guidelines* do not sufficiently underscore the importance of developmental thinking in understanding and treating the young.

So far, I am afraid, I have painted a rather gloomy picture of the fate of child analytic contributions to the mental health care of children. Despite this I think that if we shift our focus to the future we will find that child analysis is not dead and it is therefore important to find and face the challenges. Our influence will be slow, I believe, but significant. And my suspicion is that child analysis will rarely be given due credit for its contributions. But we should not be discouraged.

I am inclined to identify five areas whose challenges are of paramount importance:

1. Services to the birth to 4-year-old. This is an area where child analysis has a great deal to offer. The kind of knowledge we analysts have of this early period of development is without equal in that we know so much about both sides of the child/parent relationship. I believe that the only plausible way to bring our contribution to any large population is by consultation: to nursery schools, to day care centers, and to Head Start programs. This can lead to teacher and parent guidance and, when necessary, to treatment for the child. Consultation is an art in itself and deserves its own discussion. Suffice it to say, that our understanding of children in this age group—their needs, methods of communication, concerns, interests, modes of thinking in an affective–cognitive way, and anxieties—is unique among those who work in these programs. Individual teachers or parents may have intuitive awareness, but are often unsure and unable to express these ideas. We also know something of special value concerning the emotions of caretakers, both parents and teachers, and the feelings aroused by their young charges.

2. Case studies, clinical vignettes, and theory building have been the primary modes of discourse among analytic practitioners, and that will probably continue. But this is effective and respected only by those already committed to the psychoanalytic approach. It has been a long time since the fields of child psychiatry, pediatrics, psychology, social work, and teachers have considered psychoanalytic observations to be of scientific interest and validity; methodologies which are considered sufficiently "scientific" by those other disciplines tend too often to be considered to be reductionistic by psychoanalysts.

I think we need to find ways to present our data that will demonstrate convincingly how our understanding of the mind and emotion of the child contributes to "practical" interventions. With ADHD for instance, it would be useful to be able to demonstrate the contributions which a dynamic understanding can make to the development of a treatment plan which includes psychotherapy as well as practical guidance, remedial education, and support to parents and teachers. The same is true for many other forms of child psychopathology.

3. We need to demonstrate more adequately the efficacy and cost effectiveness of the dynamic psychotherapies including psychoanalysis. In child work this is very difficult to show because of (a) short-term focus of most outcome studies; (b) the impossibility of convincingly mapping the road *not* traveled (i.e., what would have happened without treatment); and (c) the uniqueness of the individual, which prevents making matched groupings for in-depth, psychodynamically oriented study.

4. Because of its cost in time, effort, and commitment child analysis, even setting aside the financial expenditures, will always be a rare undertaking in this world. We need to take a hard look at the relationship between child analysis, psychotherapy, treatment via the mother, and other forms of dynamically oriented treatment. We need to find suitable ways to unify clinical analytic work with children and to do away with the implicit caste system and discrimination.

5. Analysts, as a professional group, need to reconsider their avoidance of political activism. However this particular stance came about in our field—in part I think it reflected a rationalization about the effect of political visibility on our treatment work.[2] For instance Greenacre (1954) states that "[psychoanalytic therapy] demands . . . the sacrifice on the part of the analyst of conspicuous public participation even in very worthy social and political 'causes' to which he may lend his name or his activities" (pp. 682–683).[3] We cannot afford to remain isolated; we need to be much more active. We may not shrug aside responsibility, noting at the same time that Selma Fraiberg's experimental political statement, her *Every Children's Birthright: In Defense of Mothering* published in 1977, had remarkably little impact or discussion at that time or since. Right now the struggle for a national health plan calls for effort, energy, and attention. Such activism will be necessary at the national, state and local level and requires staying power for

---

[2]Dr. E. Galenson suggested that the tradition of little political activism in psychoanalysis also stems from the fact that many of the analytic pioneers were political refugees who felt constrained from publicly expressing their political views in a new country.

[3]I am grateful to my colleague Dr. James W. Kern for bringing this reference to my attention.

the long haul. If we fail to respond, we can hardly complain about the outcome.

Perhaps we can think that child analysis is like parenthood itself, where the contributions are perceived as self-evident and taken for granted, and the shortcomings are the focus of comment. Secure in the knowledge that our field has much to offer we may be better able to tolerate that it will not be given much credit. This is difficult to live with perhaps, but, as they used to say, virtue has its own rewards.

## REFERENCES

American Academy of Child and Adolescent Psychiatry (1993), Practice Parameters for the Assessment and Treatment of Anxiety Disorders. *J. Amer. Acad. Child Adolesc. Psychiatry*, 32:1089–1098.

Blos, Jr., P. (1956), An Investigation of the Healthy Child's Understanding of the Causes of Disease. Unpublished Thesis, Yale University School of Medicine, New Haven, Conn. Incorporated into Blos, Jr., P. (1978), Children think about illness: Their concepts and beliefs. In: *Psychosocial Aspects of Pediatric Care*, ed. E. Gellert. New York: Grune & Stratton, pp. 1–17.

Fenichel, O. (1945), *The Psychoanalytic Theory of Neurosis*. New York: W. W. Norton.

Fraiberg, S. (1977), *Every Child's Birthright: In Defence of Mothering*. New York: Basic Books.

Greenacre, P. (1954), The role of transference: Practical considerations in relation to psychoanalytic therapy. *J. Amer. Psychoanal. Assn.*, 2:671–684.

Kanner, L. (1935), *Child Psychiatry*, 2nd ed. Springfield, IL: Charles C Thomas.

# Discussion

## JULES GLENN, M.D.

Like Dr. Blos, whose excellent paper outlines the problems we face, we all bemoan the possibility that the tremendous amount of knowledge that analysts have acquired about normal and pathological development will be ignored or minimized by those who attempt to build a national mental health plan. We have hopes that Hillary Rodham Clinton, having spent productive time at the Yale Child Study Center, and Tipper Gore, an ardent advocate for children, will not allow this to happen. Since economic factors—and pseudoeconomic rationalizations—play a vast role in determining what is deemed practical and what Congress will enact, data from psychoanalytic sources may well fall by the wayside. The concerted effort to discredit analysis as a treatment and as a science may justify such an outcome. People may decide that child psychoanalysis, dynamically oriented child psychotherapy, and other modifications are not "cost-effective."

The psychoanalytic knowledge I refer to is extensive. It derives from analyses of adults (including memories and reconstructions); analyses of children; to a lesser extent psychotherapy; direct observations of children, such as those made in the nurseries of Margaret Mahler and her associates (Mahler, Pine, and Bergman, 1975), Roiphe and Galenson (1982), Galenson (1993); of the Cleveland group (Furman and Katan, 1969), the Hampstead nurseries (Freud and Burlingham, 1939–1945). It also comes from planned studies, some using experimental procedures by analysts, like Brody and Axelrad (1970), Robert

---

This discussion took place at the Vulnerable Child Discussion Group, Theodore Cohen, Chair. December 16, 1993.

Emde (1988a,b), Daniel Stern (1985), and others inspired by analysis. All of these studies verify, challenge, and expand analytic theory.

The knowledge derived from these sources has been effectively used in treatment of patients. In addition to informing the types of therapy I have mentioned, it has been helpful in guiding parents of infants and older children, altering environments, establishing therapeutic nurseries and framing nurseries for normal children. We can be proud of the data we have amassed and of the innovative and imaginative applications we and our colleagues have inspired and instituted. Many important contributions to sensible child rearing practices have derived from psychoanalysis. At the same time, misapplication, mostly by nonanalysts, has had deleterious effects. Some parents erroneously try to avoid neuroses by exhibiting themselves nude before their children or by avoiding discipline; they thus overstimulate their children or interfere with adaptive superego development. Some overzealous opponents of child molestation have misapplied analysts' observations that children whose neuroses are significantly determined by such traumas may deny or repress the pathogenic experiences, and have falsely accused innocent caretakers of molestation. Such unfortunate calumny of adults can blind us to the many actual cases of child abuse that do exist.

Beyond that, our society has produced conditions of fear, overstimulation, failures of conscience, and deprivation that interfere with sublimation. I will mention but a few. Children and adults in impoverished ghetto neighborhoods and other areas live in terror of injury and death to themselves and their loved ones, a terror that fosters denial and identification with aggressors (Meers, 1970, 1973; Burland, 1984, 1986). Crowded quarters with little privacy and repeated exposure to primal scenes as well as aggressive encounters, facilitate uncontrolled behavior and learning difficulties. Television shows can stir children's sexuality and aggression without offering the mastery and healthy resolution that were supplied by frightening nursery stories. Unemployment, low income, and homelessness have always plagued us, but now the problems seem more malignant and insoluble. Currently, an unprecedented number of patients who have been released from mental hospitals without adequate outpatient care roam the streets. Drug usage is rampant, and guns on the street and in schools are commonplace.

Some people criticize statements that working and absent mothers may be a source of their children's difficulties; such statements have been called "politically incorrect." Economic and social reality may make maternal absence inevitable. A single mother, for instance, may have to work to afford the required food, clothing, and shelter; many families cannot get along unless both parents work. Nevertheless we must face the fact that children will not survive and thrive without supporting and stimulating caretakers. It is unconscionable that many government officials refuse to attempt to solve this urgent problem by supporting decent day care centers and cannot find the funds for headstart programs.

Things are indeed a mess. As a result there are too many children with pathology involving inadequate and maladaptive superego formation; excessive aggressive and libidinal urges; feelings of inadequacy due to insufficient contact with parents and good substitutes; learning disorders based on maladaptive defenses; and failures to cope adequately with treacherous environmental circumstances. Biological disturbances occur also, many a result of dietary deficiencies, poor prenatal and postnatal care. These and other biological conditions, such as perversive developmental disorders, schizophrenia, manic depressive disorders, attention deficit disorders, often or usually result from interaction with psychological environmental circumstances.

Our society has neat solutions that won't work: Be cost effective; give medication; restrict psychotherapy and good nursery and other school facilities because of economic considerations.

What can we do?

Dr. Blos suggests that we become political. We must inform the public and the politicians that the "solutions" I mentioned won't work. We must somehow make it clear that medication without supplemental health care has quite limited benefits, that psychoanalysis (which is optimal for a minority of patients with emotional disorders, but can be potent when indicated), psychotherapy, guidance, and environmental change can effect palpable changes. Indeed they are necessary to help many patients. We must make it clear that social change is necessary to prevent many (but not all) types of maladaptive disturbances. In addition, we must show that knowledge such as that which Dr. Galenson described, and types of nursery help that Dr. Barrett described can help us get out of the morass we and our children are in.

Dr. Galenson demonstrated that direct observation of children as well as therapeutic intervention have helped us understand the vicissitudes of aggression in youngsters and adults. Dr. Barrett described the sensitivity with which the Cleveland Center for Research in Child Development (CCRCD) helped a commercial company, TRW, establish a day care center for the children of their employees and other families in the community. Rather than impose plans on TRW, CCRCD acted as consultants who elicited and shared ideas with the day care center personnel. They set an example for the personnel to work with the children and their parents in an empathic sharing way.

We have a personal interest in the survival of adult and child psychoanalysis, but there are additional objective reasons for our hoping they will continue to prevail and grow. As I mentioned, psychoanalysis is an excellent and helpful treatment. It also provides us with information that can be used to build and correct theory and to apply it to other means of therapeutic and preventative activity.

There are several threats to analysis. A national health plan may deny patients the right to analysis. A national health plan may impose conditions that make analysis impossible, such as prohibiting confidentiality and establishing a limited duration for individuals in analysis. The conditions stated may pose a threat that the treatment will be cut off before completion, thus making it difficult or impossible for patients to feel safe during the analysis. Managed care by insurance companies often incorporates these features.

One possible means of protecting the future of psychoanalysis which many advocate is the exclusion of psychoanalysis from the national health care system while allowing patients to obtain analysis privately. Such an arrangement would be elitist and undemocratic. Only patients with enough money would be able to engage in the treatment. People who need it but cannot afford it would be excluded. It would be a pity if the government did not find a place for analysis within the system while allowing others to obtain the treatment on their own. The erection of a national health plan can provide the public with much needed mental health care or it can destroy much that has been achieved.

## REFERENCES

Brody, S., & Axelrad, S. (1970), *Anxiety and Ego Formation*. New York: International Universities Press.

Burland, J. A. (1984), Dysfunctional parenthood in deprived population. In: *Parenthood. A Psychodynamic Perspective*, ed. B. J. Cohler, R. S. Cohen, & S. H. Weissman. New York: Guilford Press, pp. 148–163.

———— (1986), The vicissitudes of maternal deprivation. In: *Self and Object Constancy*, ed. R. F. Lax, S. Bach, & J. A. Burland. New York: Guilford Press, pp. 324–347.

Emde, R. N. (1988a), Development terminable and interminable. I. Innate and motivational factors from infancy. *Internat. J. Psycho-Anal.*, 69:23–42.

———— (1988b), Development terminable and interminable. II. Recent psychoanalytic theory and therapeutic considerations. *Internat. J. Psycho-Anal.*, 69:283–296.

Freud, A., & Burlingham, D. (1939–1945), *Infants Without Families*. New York: International Universities Press, 1944.

Furman, R. A., & Katan, A., Eds. (1969), *The Therapeutic Nursery School*. New York: International Universities Press.

Galenson, E. (1993), Infant psychiatry with high income and low income multi-risk families, 1980–1990. In: *Prevention in Mental Health*, ed. H. Parens & S. Kramer. Northvale, NJ: Jason Aronson, pp. 61–84.

Mahler, M. S., Pine, F., & Bergman, A. (1975), *The Psychological Birth of the Human Infant*. New York: Basic Books.

Meers, D. R. (1970), Contributions of a ghetto culture to symptom formation: Psychoanalytic studies of ego anomalies in childhood. *The Psychoanalytic Study of the Child*, 25:209–230. New York: International Universities Press.

———— (1973), Psychoanalytic research and intellectual functioning of ghetto-reared, black children. *The Psychoanalytic Study of the Child*, 28:395–418. New Haven, CT: Yale University Press.

Roiphe, H., & Galenson, E. (1982), *Infantile Origins of Sexual Identity*. New York: International Universities Press.

Stern, D. N. (1985), *The Interpersonal World of the Infant*. New York: Basic Books.

# 8.

# Applied Child Analysis: The TRW/ CCRCD Early Intervention Alliance

## THOMAS F. BARRETT, Ph.D.

Child analysis has historically been a profession that has not limited its focus to the consultation room. Pediatrics, education, the juvenile justice system, and all areas of child care and development have provided opportunities for intervention and consultation. Anna Freud began her professional career with work in a day care center, and the findings of the Hampstead War Nurseries provided a foundation for understanding the developmental lines of childhood.

At the Cleveland Center for Research in Child Development (CCRCD) our course in child psychoanalysis has included extensive training and experience in a variety of applied child analysis settings. Beginning in the fifties, child analysts from the Center consulted with the nursery schools and day care centers of the Cleveland Day Nursery Association. Many such consultation relationships have continued over the ensuing forty-plus years and new ones have been formed. There is now a series of Extension Division courses for preschool teachers and day caregivers. Our experience has convinced us of the importance of two factors present in any consultation effort. First, we are not there to teach or inform but to learn and understand so that we can think and work together with a staff that knows our respect for them as professionals. Second, it must be clear that our commitment is a long-term one that will enable our relationships with a center or school director and staff to develop and deepen over time, leading to a sense of mutual trust and respect.

These two concepts were central when we began discussions in the fall of 1992 with representatives from the TRW Foundation, headquartered in Cleveland. Mr. Joseph Gorman, the CEO of TRW, is unique among his peers in that he has long been an advocate of business and industry being concerned about early childhood development and education. Specifically, he has stressed the view that every child deserves an advocate. Our belief, that an attitude of advocacy can only develop in the context of a relationship, was one that resonated with Mr. Gorman. As he became aware of our long-standing investment in the growth and development of preschool children and of our consultation experiences, he shared our concerns regarding the increasing number of children in day care and the ways in which those settings interfered with the development of a child's capacity for relationships. During the years following World War II it was typical for only one parent to be employed. With most mothers at home, businesses knew who was raising the next generation of employees. Now, the vast majority of those future employees are being raised in substitute or multiple mothering settings. There is good reason to question and be concerned about how such settings prepare children to be empathic, conscientious, and able to achieve a sense of pleasure in work and productivity. An enduring, consistent relationship with a primary caregiver is a crucial component in the child's progression on the developmental line from play to work.

It was Mr. Gorman's wish that CCRCD work with the TRW Foundation to develop an early intervention program. TRW employs more than 60,000 persons world-wide and it was important to their Foundation that they provide support for programs in various communities where TRW facilities are located. At first, they asked if we could provide training to day care workers and early childhood educators that they might transport to Cleveland from various other cities. We pointed out that such an approach would be disrespectful in that it would be presumptuous and would not allow for the development of a relationship over time.

The Foundation representatives concurred and committed themselves to working with us to develop a long-term program that would effectively unite the business sector with specialists in child development in efforts to promote healthy development and readiness to learn in young children. Individual divisions of the corporation would adopt a day care center in each of their respective communities. The four selected include Detroit, Dallas, Huntsville, Alabama, and San Bernadino, California. A major component of the "adoption" commitment would be to support the consultation services of a child analyst or specialist in child development. Other ways of involving business representatives with the day care center would be explored and might include participating on the center's board of directors, or providing financial support for special projects such as playground improvements, etc. Not only did the Foundation representatives agree with our contention that a program could only be successful if it could confidently anticipate enduring support, they backed up this contention with a ten-year commitment. It is our mutual hope that, if the first four sites prove this to be a successful format for developing such consultation programs, we will later expand to other sites in our cities. Furthermore, TRW has expressed interest in helping us find ways of approaching other businesses to enlist similar forms of support.

When the project was inaugurated in January of this year a number of preliminary stages were anticipated. Four child analysts from Cleveland, of whom the author was one, were selected and paired with each of the four respective TRW sites. From each site a business representative was identified and a joint meeting was held in Cleveland where the concepts of the program were explained in conjunction with an orientation to the work of the Center and its sister organization, the Hanna Perkins School. The TRW representatives and the Cleveland analysts then began efforts to identify potential day care centers and child analysts or child development specialists in each of the respective communities. It was with these efforts that the project began to take on the individual community distinctions we had expected as the differing child care centers and child mental health resources were researched and studied in each city.

The TRW facility chosen in Detroit, where the author was assigned to work, is actually in a distant and even somewhat rural suburb. The business representative there felt it was important that TRW involve themselves in that community rather than in Detroit proper, and she identified a large day care program sponsored by the community education department. It provides services to more than 3000 preschool children in a number of sites throughout the district. As a beginning point of intervention for the consultant, she identified a program for approximately seventy 3- and 4-year-olds, housed in an old elementary school building and serving a culturally and economically diverse population.

I was initially delighted, and over time am even more so, with the willingness of Dr. Kay Campbell to serve as the local consultant to the program. Dr. Campbell is not only a child analyst, she has had extensive experience providing consultation services to a large inner-city program working with teenage mothers. In addition to her knowledge of child development she recognized from the start the importance of understanding the roles, the relationships between and the sometimes differing priorities of the various administrators, directors, and staff who work in the program.

The project design involves my serving as a consultant to Dr. Campbell as she develops her consultation relationship with the Detroit area day care center. Her recording of her experiences and observations in a journal-type format provides documentation that will assist us in evaluating the program and in planning for the development of additional sites in the future.

From the outset the administrators of the center were intrigued but also made a bit anxious by the interest of TRW and CCRCD in their program. A first step was to explain our reasons for wanting to provide support. To accomplish this, after Dr. Campbell had formed a beginning relationship with the program administrator and the program director, they scheduled a joint meeting that also included the overall director from the community education department, myself, and the TRW business representative. A result of this meeting was that the overall goals and rationale for the program took on a clearer perspective, and the day care director and her supervisors came to have an understanding of their participation in a project designed to support their efforts to provide quality care to preschool children.

I think it is fair to say that an important consequence of this support is that the day care director in particular has felt an increased valuing of herself and her staff as professionals working on behalf of children. Some of the issues for discussion that have surfaced early on have involved points of potential conflict between financial considerations and quality care. For example, the administrator wanted to make short-term care available for children whose parents were hospitalized or unable for some other reason to be at home with their children for a brief time. With the support of the consultant, the program director expressed concern regarding the confusing impact of these comings and goings on the children who were in regular attendance.

In recent correspondence, Dr. Campbell reported on the outcome of this and other administrative issues. She wrote:

> [The administrator] was eager to tell me that my "seeds" had "sprouted" and they were now planning to have two groups in the . . . program: one consisting of children who are there all day every day and the other of children who tend to come and go, are there part-time, are there as emergency placements. Furthermore, each child will be assigned one of two caregivers as their primary person. Each teacher, in other words, will be responsible for the same nine (9) children every day inasmuch as those children are present.

Another change provides for the same two caregivers to work consistent shifts. That is, two caregivers in the morning and two in the afternoon will no longer rotate mornings for afternoons. "That way each child will come to know that 'Susie' cares for him or her in the morning and 'Jane' will do so in the afternoon." Dr. Campbell enthusiastically supported these changes and added the observation that "the morning person would then be able to speak with the parent each day and the afternoon person each evening, providing a continuity of care that has not been provided previously."

Dr. Campbell and the director and her staff have also been able to address individual problems and concerns as they have surfaced involving various children. One example involved a girl who was transferred from the toddler program into the 3-year-old group. Following the move, she had become quite aggressive with episodes of hitting and biting the other children. The troubles had persisted over three weeks and nap time had been especially difficult as the child had refused to nap and had instead used this time to run about and disrupt the other children. When staff tried to contain her, she cried loudly. Dr. Campbell helped the staff think through what they knew about the little girl's home life and her relationships with her parents. They reported that her father had confided that he hated to make his daughter cry so he seldom made any demands of her. Bedtime patterns at home were also unclear and changing. The staff acknowledged further that all of the children who had transferred from the toddler to the 3-year-old program were having a hard go, though this girl had seemed the most troubled.

Dr. Campbell then learned that the little girl had made the transition without her parents' direct involvement in the move. "She was simply dropped off as usual after having one brief visit in the program a few weeks earlier." Dr. Campbell could then talk with the director about what the staff and center could do to make such a transition more manageable. "[A] system of 'getting familiar' would probably help parents and child (as well as staff)." Dr. Campbell suggested that: "[T]he transferring children be invited to spend an hour with their mother present, and then a full morning and lunch, and then a full morning, lunch and nap before making the final change." She reported that the director, "was enthusiastic about establishing a protocol to assist the staff in becoming familiar with the child as well . . . it was clear that the staff needed to be oriented to the child just as much as the child needed orientation. There was no one around who really knew (this child) and could help the staff cope with her behavior."

Essential in this intervention by Dr. Campbell was her simultaneous support of the staff in terms of acknowledging their frustration and concern, even as she helped them think of the little girl's "misbehavior" as a communication, a cry for help. An offshoot of this intervention was that the director of the infant and toddler program became interested in learning of the availability of consultation and she has made plans for future participation, especially with regard to the transitioning of the children from the toddler to the 3-year-old group.

Another example serves to illustrate how knowledge of child development and awareness of community resources can also prove helpful. Dr. Campbell was told of another child, C, who had, "a history of having been abused. He is an unattractive child, who plays with his feces and has a speech problem." During the summer his behavior became increasingly aggressive, especially during a few weeks when the program was moved to a different building so that the primary facility could undergo painting and repairs. Dr. Campbell wrote:

> I learned that C was not comfortable making the change from the old school to the summer school building and it had been difficult for him to get used to the new building and playground. He looked forward to returning to "his school." I also learned that his grandmother had died, his friend had moved away, and coupled with the loss of familiar surroundings, I concluded that his fecal play and aggression had a lot to do with the various losses he had endured. I encouraged (the director) to help the staff talk with C about these things and help him plan for those things that were within his control. I was concerned about his speech problem and recommended the parents request an educational assessment through the Child Find Program for Early Intervention and explained to (the director) how they could do that (e.g., contact the county school system office of Special Education and request services). The director was not aware the county schools were participating in programs to identify preschoolers with difficulties and offer services prior to their entering school. I also discussed the importance of understanding what was unattractive about this child and what its effect was upon the caretaking staff. I urged that he be paired with a childcare worker who found him appealing. . . .

It perhaps goes without saying but should also be stressed, that another kind of "community resource" that a consultant can help a day care staff think about are mental health services available for children and parents as deemed appropriate. In Cleveland, some of our consultation efforts have gradually expanded into what we now refer to as "outreach sites." These are day care centers or nursery schools where our therapists spend as much as four to six hours per week, on site. By virtue of their extended involvement, in addition to conferring with staff, they might be asked to observe a particular child and then, should it be deemed appropriate, they are able to provide direct, developmental guidance services to the child's parents, employing the kind of "treatment via the parent" model that we have typically used at Hanna Perkins School.

As we approach the culmination of our first year of involvement in this Early Intervention Alliance project with TRW we are more convinced than ever in the efficacy of such efforts at applied child analysis. Child analysts are not surprised to note the findings published over the past several years by the Research and Policy Committee of the Committee for Economic Development. They have stressed that efforts to educate children need to focus on the first five years of life, the period that provides the foundation for all future learning. Studies of Head Start Programs have been cited as proof that early childhood education can improve children's ability to learn in school and to perform in the work force, and will decrease their chances of turning to drugs, delinquency, and criminal behavior. These and other studies have shown that $1 invested in young children can save anywhere from $4 to $6 in later expenses. As stated in the 1985 CED (Committee for Economic Development) report, "it would be hard to imagine that society could find a higher yield for a dollar investment than that found in preschool programs for at risk children."

A basic tenet of our understanding of child development is that it is only in the context of a stable and enduring, "good enough" relationship that a child can grow in a healthy way. With the majority of mothers now working, the personalities of most children now develop in situations of substitute or multiple mothering. This means that the development of the ability to form and maintain relationships, to care for oneself and others, and to develop a feeling of pleasure in learning and working, is jeopardized and at the very least, stressed for these children. I think we might all agree that, under these circumstances, it would be hard to imagine a better application or investment of our child analysis resources and expertise than in this area of day care consultation.

## REFERENCE

Committee for Economic Development (1985), *Summary Report*. Washington, DC: United States Government Printing Office.

# Discussion

## JULES GLENN, M.D.

Dr. Barrett's description of the actual work of the Cleveland Center for Research in Child Development (CCRCD) as a consultant to and ally with TRW in their attempts to provide good day care for their employees' children is inspiring.

Dr. Barrett assesses the motivations of TRW and CCRCD. TRW, a commercial and profit-seeking organization, is both altruistic and self-serving. The CEO, Mr. Joseph Gorman of TRW, wants to further children's development and their capacity for relationships by improved day care center activity. He also wants to create a future work force that would be capable of furthering the company's productivity. TRW hopes it can, through proper child care now, create good workers they can employ one day. The plan is more altruistic than that; not only do their workers' children attend the day care centers; so do other children. Perhaps as a byproduct of its good works it is attempting to create healthier adults per se and a better work force for other companies as well as its own. Indeed, if the venture succeeds TRW hopes to encourage other companies to start and support similar enterprises.

Although we do not know Mr. Gorman's full motivation for propelling TRW into this excellent and far-reaching undertaking, it seems likely that personal, perhaps childhood, experiences have stimulated rescue fantasies which have adaptive functions. Probably other entrepreneurs who undertake similar idealistic and practical projects would have similar motives.

Dr. Barrett and his many colleagues also hope to improve day care throughout the country starting with four cities and then expanding. They follow a proud psychoanalytic tradition of community service long established through the work of pioneers like Anna Freud (1930–1980), Dorothy Burlingham (1972), Anny Katan and the Furmans (R. Furman and Katan, 1969; E. Furman, 1974). They know that psychoanalytic knowledge can inform and inspire useful child rearing practices.

CCRCD's method includes keeping careful records which will have research value beyond the evaluation of their results. They do not want to impose preconceived notions on TRW or the personnel of the day care centers. Rather they seek discussion and mutuality at every level: between CCRCD and TRW; between the local consultant and the Cleveland consultant; between the administrators and directors of the Detroit center and the local consultant; between directors and teachers; between teachers and parents. In that way new ideas will be generated, making for practical gain and research advances. Probably there are contacts between the CCRCD and teachers at times, but that is not clear.

I want to reemphasize Dr. Barrett's emphasis on careful attempts at empathy with all involved, the desire to allow individuals their autonomy. Not that the consultants do not give advice; they do, but they don't impose it. This modus operandi is based on analysts' principles and analysts' respect for their patients. It is also based on practical considerations; respect for individuals works! In addition, eventually the teachers, through identification, increase their empathy with and their respect for the children and their parents. When we hear the design of the project and compare it with the original suggestion that the personnel of the day care centers come to Cleveland for a course, we can shout hosannahs at the wisdom of the current plan.

I want to ask a question about the specifics of discussions between teachers and children or their parents as well as between the consultants and child care center personnel. I presume that emotions are labeled and situations clarified. I assume that the consultant may use information that the teachers tell them about the children and the families to help them understand the children's and families' dynamics, and how one may deal with situations. I imagine that the consultant does not interpret the workings of the child's mind to the child, or of the parent's mind to the parent. But perhaps there are times that such interpretation would be helpful.

We all have reservations about sending children of 3—or even 2—to day care centers away from their parents for many hours a day. Dr. Barrett mentions 11 hours, surely a challenge to the adaptive capacities of the children and the capabilities of the substitute caretakers to help the children. He describes attempts to diminish the adverse impact of multiple parenting and multiple separations. They divided the total group into two subgroups. One contained children who would be away a great deal. The other was comprised of those who were present at the day care center with regularity. In addition to constancy of peers they also established consistency of caring persons. Further, they encouraged caretakers to be intimate with the children, to understand them. In a beautiful example,[1] one caretaker asked a child who thought she was ill why she thought so—with clarifying and gratifying results. The little girl realized someone was interested in her as a thinking and feeling person.

They aimed to create an atmosphere in which the feeling of being deserted was minimized. Hence the aggression associated with being left would be minimized and masterable. The child could proceed through separation-individuation more successfully. He would have a better chance of achieving object constancy, self-constancy, and a sense of autonomy.

It would be erroneous to think that day care centers necessarily advance development when parents work and when children have no primary parenting for long hours. Nevertheless, many nursery schools which look after children for a reasonable length of time help children tolerate separation and provide healthy nontraumatic outside-the-primary-family experiences akin to those available in the extended family of old. Even nursery schools which aren't classified as "therapeutic" can help a child cope with a potentially pathogenic home situation. The mother of Mary, a sweet 3-year-old little girl I see in psychotherapy, is dismayed that she cannot help her daughter whom she loves tenderly as much as she wishes. Mrs. A's underlying depression is complicated by her feeling weak and needy, a

---

[1]This example appeared in a longer version of Dr. Barrett's paper.

result of periarteritis nodosum. Mrs. A has difficulty tolerating her daughter's desires for contact with her. She feels that Mary clings to her too much, and indeed Mary has become too clingy in reaction to what feels like her mother's rejection of her. She in turn rejects the housekeeper's trying to play with her, dress, and feed her. At the therapeutic sessions with me and at nursery school away from her mother, she can engage in helpful expression in play and can enjoy consistent caring and joyful relations with other children. The nursery dilutes her mother's potentially pathogenic influence.

The Cleveland program that Dr. Barrett described has great significance for national child mental health care. Obviously it carries enormous preventative potential, and should be attempted not just in four nurseries in four cities, but throughout the country. It should receive funding not only from private industry and private sources, but governmental support as well.

The TRW/CCRCD early intervention alliance as described for Detroit does not include an inner city population, which would involve families with serious economic problems living in dangerous areas plagued with overcrowding, traumatization, and illness, and infested with drugs, guns, and murder. As I write this the New York City schools chancellor reports that there is even more crime in the schools than had previously been reported. How much preventative and curative work can be done in such an area is problematical. Psychoanalysts, including Eleanor Galenson (Roiphe and Galenson, 1982), Dale Meers (1970, 1973), and Alex Burland (1984, 1986), have described the overwhelming conditions that challenge children and those who want to save them.

Dr. Barrett mentions that some of the children in the Detroit preschool come from families in which separations and inconstancy are so rampant that the group had to be separated from those children in less disturbed families. I would appreciate his telling us whether he thinks we are prepared to help those children find the road to adaptive development.

I thank Dr. Barrett and his coworkers for treating us to a wonderful description of exciting work and congratulate them for continuing their pioneer work.

# REFERENCES

Burland, J. A. (1984), Dysfunctional parenthood in a deprived population. In: *Parenthood: A Psychodynamic Perspective*, ed. B. J. Cohler, R. S. Cohen, & S. H. Weissman. New York: Guilford Press, pp. 148–163.

—— (1986), Vicissitudes of maternal deprivation. In: *Self and Object Constancy*, ed. R. F. Lax, S. Bach, & J. A. Burland. New York: Guilford Press, pp. 324–347.

Burlingham, D. (1972), *Psychoanalytic Studies of the Sighted and the Blind*. New York: International Universities Press.

Freud, A. (1930–1980), *The Writings of Anna Freud*, Vols. 1–8. New York: International Universities Press.

Furman, E. (1974), *A Child's Parent Dies*. New Haven, CT: Yale University Press.

Furman, R., & Katan, A. (1969), *The Therapeutic Nursery*. New York: International Universities Press.

Meers, D. (1970), Contributions of a ghetto culture to symptom formation: Psychoanalytic studies of ego anomalies in childhood. *The Psychoanalytic Study of the Child*, 25:209–230. New York: International Universities Press.

—— (1973), Psychoanalytic research and intellectual functioning of ghetto-reared, black children. *The Psychoanalytic Study of the Child*, 28:395–418. New Haven, CT: Yale University Press.

Roiphe, H., & Galenson, E. (1982), *Infantile Origins of Sexual Identity*. New York: International Universities Press.

# PART III:

## Adolescent Mothers and Children with Constitutional Deficits

# 9.

# Developmental Psychiatry for Infants, Young Children, and Their Families: An Inner City Setting

## MARGARET MORGAN LAWRENCE, M.D.

A DREAM

I was walking along cradling a brown, black baby in my arms. The feeling was a joyful, serene one. Suddenly, I looked down. I had dropped the baby. Horrified, I replaced the baby in my arms and continued my happy way. The scene repeated itself [Lawrence, 1963].

"Yes," I responded to Elizabeth Davis, then chief of psychiatry at Harlem Hospital Center, New York City, "I will come back to Harlem." It had been twenty-one years since I had completed an internship and residency in pediatrics at Harlem Hospital. Some background notes for my return to work with infants, young children, and their families in the Harlem community in 1963, as child psychiatrist and psychoanalyst, may be helpful. Hartmann (1964) speaks of the analyst as, "not only an observer of the field, but also an actor in it, [and] that analysis introduces new factors, factors neglected by other methods of observation, not only into the analytic situation but also into the direct observation of children. . . . By acting in the field and studying action and reaction, data are made accessible that had not been accessible to other methods. . . (p. 101).

In 1942 and 1943, I studied for a year at the Columbia School of Public Health, including a course in Child Public

Health with Benjamin Spock. After four years of teaching Pediatrics and Public Health at Meharry Medical College in Nashville, Tennessee, my experience with medical students in well child clinics and pediatric wards led me to seek further knowledge of the psychological processes of the children and families whom I served. My children's nursery school director lived across the street from my home. I noted that each time her professor husband left the family for a working trip, my neighbor called with the complaint that her 2-year-old girl was having respiratory symptoms.

By 1946, psychoanalyst Viola Bernard and a coterie of supporters from various walks of life, had made public their concern for the lack of first-rate psychiatric residences for qualified minority persons. In 1948 I became a resident in psychiatry at the New York State Psychiatric Institute and Hospital and a trainee at the Columbia Psychoanalytic Center. Sandor Rádo, Abram Kardiner, John A. P. Millet, and David Levy were my teachers. The Child Development Center, headed by Nathan Ackerman, provided a fellowship in child psychiatry, in a psychoanalytic setting, for the study of early childhood problems. It included a therapeutic nursery in which I was pediatric consultant. At the Center, Peter Neubauer organized and led interdisciplinary consultation teams to serve community day-care centers, their directors, teachers, and family counselors. Consultation to day-care centers was accomplished by a clinical-educational team through individual child observation and study with all day-care staff.

This apprenticeship was followed in the 1950s and 1960s by work in other child development centers and a City University educational clinic. In 1954, Dr. John A. P. Millet, psychoanalyst and veteran founder of community mental health programs, and I, with the help of numerous persons from the mental health disciplines, organized community mental health services in Rockland County, New York. The programs under my direction were, in turn, children's therapy, a school consultation service, and a child development center.

In 1963, Virginia Wilking, Chief of Child Psychiatry at Harlem Hospital, and Elizabeth Davis welcomed my concern for the Harlem community's infants, young children, and their families. A composite picture of nature, nurture, and trauma had become integrated into my understanding of the developmental dynamics of children of impoverished families. Knoblock and Pasamanick (1953), who did their own internships and residences at Harlem Hospital, had documented with their extensive epidemiological studies, the relationship among socioeconomic status, maternal and fetal factors, and neuropsychiatric disorder. My own work in Harlem's schools and day-care centers, presumed to be populated by normal children, had brought recognition of the ubiquity of minimal brain dysfunction (the classification attention deficit disorder does not assist us in the understanding of the contribution of constitutional deficit to the problems of development). At Harlem, our therapeutic nursery established, we found that more than two-thirds of these preschool children showed constitutional deficits: their mothers had had inadequate prenatal care; some babies were born prematurely or even if not, were "small babies" at birth; nutrition, health care, and housing were faulty. The vicissitudes of poverty often did not support good "nurturing" on the part of parents, especially single mothers, and traumas for both children and families were everyday occurrences.

Deficit, delay, and dysfunction confronted us as we began working with Harlem's young inner city families. These signs and symptoms had been taught throughout my medical education as a given of this population's social reality. However, in my psychiatric training I had seen few black poor; and confronted with their delay and dysfunction, we had rejected dynamic psychotherapy in favor of supportive therapies. Rather than explore the possibilities of models of dynamic psychotherapy demanded by the dysfunctional symptoms presented, we had denied that a dynamic approach could serve the needs of a poor black family.

With the help of Dr. Wilking and Dr. Davis we began the organization, in 1963, of a developmental clinic, later called the Developmental Psychiatry Service for Infants and Young Children and their Families. Regular consultation to child health stations, renamed pediatric care centers, and day care centers, was the source of the first referrals to the Developmental Clinic.

[T]o deny, in effect, that unconscious conflicts, *as well as* external stresses, contribute to symptoms, dysfunctions, and distress on the part of those who are underprivileged is to inflict still another subtle form of discrimination upon them; it is as though one were saying that, in their case, the fundamentals of psychiatry, as to psychic structure and function (including malfunction) do not apply [Bernard, 1971, p. 76].

Children are nurtured in Harlem, in spite of stressful circumstances. They are subject to the same developmental and neurotic conflicts as are more affluent children in our city. Intervention by mental health workers in the nurturing processes of Harlem children requires something more than general sympathy or even empathy, more than willingness to share our largesse. The Harlem community requires our best understanding of familial and developmental dynamics, unconscious conflicts and dated emotions, the creation of self-images and the roles and limitations of drives, ideals and goals. This knowledge is needed in the infant day care center as well as the carpeted nursery. I agree with Sandor Rádo . . . that psychoanalysis should begin in the nursery; that is, the best we know of emotional education should begin where nurturing begins [Lawrence, 1975, pp. 55–56].

These statements represented the aims of an infancy and early childhood service in the Division of Child Psychiatry at Harlem Hospital. Our beginnings coincided with the formation of a national Joint Commission on the Mental Health of Children which culminated in a report, *Crisis in Child Mental Health, Challenge for the 1970's.* More than twenty years later we may still write about the social scene that confronts those who serve young children and their families in an inner city setting: "Poverty, in this the richest of world powers, is still our heritage. Racism, in a country dedicated to its people's inalienable rights, speaks as clearly of 'man's inhumanity to man' as did slavery" [p. 1].

"The story," of the families which the Developmental Clinic team saw, this author wrote:

[D]id not begin in Harlem. It is an urban, exaggerated variant of lives lived by parents, grandparents, and great-grandparents of these families, chiefly in rural Southern areas. Because of injuries in ancestral social scenes, young families are a ready prey to the more concentrated traumata of the city. These are young persons fleeing families and communities, scenes of conflicts unbearable to them, in which they had seen no hope of productive lives. The story is not a tale of unrelieved despair. Strength abounds in these families and it, too, is a reflection, to some extent, of the survival of an inherited strength by all the avenues open to inheritance: nature, nurture, and culture [1975, pp. 130–131].

It was with this assumption of ego strength both visible and latent, in the lives of these young families, together with our full awareness of their personal and familial conflicts, that our clinical-educational team sought to join them toward the identification and demonstration of their ego strengths, as well as their psychopathology. We were cognizant of the racism, poverty, and oppression that are for these families a social inheritance. But we did not agree with "the culture of poverty perspective [which] has tended to see the poor as an almost separate culture, often ignoring the large body of common cultural assumptions which they share with the rest of the population and generally oblivious to the presence of ego strength among even the very poor (Lawrence, 1977, p. 78).

Many children studied in Harlem day care centers, pediatric care centers, and in the Developmental Psychiatry Service and its therapeutic nursery, satisfied our criteria for the diagnosis minimal brain dysfunction. In our consultation to these preschool agencies the presenting problem was often "delayed development," poor, or no speech, withdrawn or hyperactive behavior. Histories revealed possible genetic problems, deprivations, physical and/or emotional traumata, pregnancies complicated by illness or drugs, birth injuries, low Apgar scores, and "quiet" babies. These children seemed to be poorly "put together," had various congenital anomalies, showed neurological "soft signs," inadequate speech, and visuomotor and perceptual problems.

Our first concern, therefore, was with ego development, Hartmann's "conflict-free" ego sphere. Fine and gross motor development were often impaired, and opportunities for learning diminished. More significant perhaps was the reduced opportunity for object relations. The "quiet baby" does not reach out to or make the usual demands on the caregiver. He does not provoke the caregiver's responsiveness. The infant's constitutional defects, therefore, are significant for impaired object relationships. The neurologically impaired infant may make fewer demands for food; he may not suck as aggressively. Because of his "quietness" all stimuli from the environment are diminished. The impaired child himself is partially responsible for the caregiver's lack of responsiveness. Interferences with emotional and physical growth, learning, and socialization follow. Nagera writes (1966):

> Because the central nervous system of the human infant is quite immature at birth, some of the basic organic structures necessary for the performance of many complex functions are not yet developed. These functions cannot properly be performed until the physical maturation required has been completed. Thus at this early stage there exists the closest relationship between actual physical maturational development (especially of the central nervous system) and psychological development. . . . It seems that with the achievement of the basic physical maturation a given potential for psychological development has been laid down. How far the latter will reach is now largely dependent on phenomena of a psychological nature—taking in part at least the form of specific stimuli from the environment and the interaction with the objects [p. 14].

The caregiver's responsiveness is even more crucial to the constitutionally impaired child than to the normal child. We have seen in Harlem preschool centers great awareness on the part of mothers regarding the "difference" and needs of impaired children. One mother said of her 2-year-old, "Somehow he is different from the others; so I pick him up and cuddle him more." We were encouraged to teach mothers, fathers, and grandmothers ways of assuring communication with these children. "Treatment" of a 9-month-old with delayed development, odd and assymetric facies, and nystagmus consisted of a bimonthly appointment with child and mother, where repeated evaluations and instructions were given. This child, at 3 years, was admitted to our Therapeutic Nursery. In Erikson's words, "basic trust" was established through the mother's effective contact with her child. In the meantime treatment of the mother toward a better self-image, "trust in herself," was simultaneously accomplished. Separation of child from parents may put an added severe burden on the child with constitutional deficits. The family and community, however, may provide substitute "objects" in Harlem or "down South." These are often grandparents, including the paternal grandmothers of infants of unmarried fathers, stepfathers, and boyfriends.

Not every "separated child" is so fortunate, and separation from the caring person is a frequent "developmental interference" experienced by the Harlem child in his early years. Even in families where good object relationships have been established during the first year, stable identities may not be achieved when confused messages are given the child concerning the identities of the chief figures in his life. A 15-year-old cousin who brought a 3-year-old to the Service said in the latter's presence, "He thinks my mother, his aunt, is his mother, and that I am his brother. I'm not. I'm his cousin." Since constitutional deficit was a part of this child's picture, developmental interference was further compounded. This 3-year-old, chiefly because of his constitutional deficit, had little ability to communicate verbally. He, therefore, was restricted in the opportunity to ask for clarification of his role in the family. He had developed symptoms of withdrawal. Traumata, physical and emotional, derive from the daily lives of the children of poor young families, and may constitute severe developmental interference.

Drug abuse and AIDS have markedly increased the suffering of African-American and Latin infants, young children, and their families who present themselves to Harlem's Division of Child Psychiatry in the 1990s. Cocaine and "crack" babies regularly show serious constitutional deficits. Families are having greater difficulty in caring and providing for their children, or even surviving, than they did five years ago. Mental health workers, supporting staff, and teachers are almost overwhelmed by the extent and severity of the needs of families. They court despair.

The Developmental Clinic at its beginning was made up of a team that included a clinical psychologist, a psychiatric social worker, a psychiatric nurse, two child psychiatry residents, for a period of six months, and a child psychiatrist-psychoanalyst. Team aides joined us for varying lengths of time;

some came from community training programs and others were parents who had gone through our evaluation process with their families. They became "transportation aides," shared family visits with other team members, and became our connecting link with hard to reach families. In this regard, a team nurse was more acceptable to some families than a representative from any other mental health discipline. To these families she was a "caring" person, rather than an investigative one; the opposite of a doctor, who finds out "what is wrong with you." One group of Therapeutic Nursery mothers regularly cuddled "boarder" babies on the newborn pediatric ward.

Initially a pediatric consultant joined the team's child and family evaluations. Later, a Screening Clinic was established in which a pediatrician, a child neurologist, a pediatric nurse, and members of the Developmental Clinic came together for brief evaluations of children and families applying to the Clinic. A Screening Conference was immediately held following the screening process, and decisions made as to which of the available hospital services for children, including the Developmental Clinic, could best serve the child and his family, and in what order. A plan was made and the family informed. Unfortunately, although this scheme clarified greatly the presenting problem and what could be done about it, the Screening Clinic was lost after several years, when staff were no longer available. Subsequently applicants to the Developmental Clinic, now the Developmental Psychiatry Service, and staff suffered considerable loss of time and energy in their attempts to refer to other departments in the hospital.

The Therapeutic Nursery, which had been organized by Dr. Paoli, a child psychiatrist, Ms. Balliett, an educator, and Ms. Heffner a social worker, joined the Developmental Psychiatry Service. Through that Service's consultation to day-care centers, specifically the Sheltering Arms Day Care Center, Harlem's Therapeutic Nursery became the Harlem-Sheltering Arms-Therapeutic Nursery for therapeutic education and psychotherapy of young children. The twenty children of the Therapeutic Nursery were a part of a large City day-care center partially supported by a private agency, Sheltering Arms. The original Developmental Psychiatry Service team, the Nursery teachers, a coordinator and directors, a speech therapist, and an additional clinical psychologist and social worker, became a clinical-educational team. It may not have been accidental that almost all mental health workers had been or were in analysis or psychoanalytic psychotherapy. These were remarkably concerned persons, black and white, each of whom, through various combinations of group meetings, formal and informal, knew the stories and progress of each child and family in evaluation or in the Therapeutic Nursery. When an urgent need was presented by a family, the team member who was on the spot at that time, could respond to the crisis. Another team member, perhaps a family member's therapist, could relieve the first clinician or Nursery staff. This was indeed "mutual identification" and "mutual responsibility" by persons well grounded in their own disciplines.

Child Health Stations were an early source of the Service's referrals. They were also extensions of our clinical-educational team; a training ground in which together we studied infants and their families. Our monthly conferences were planned well ahead by the Service's psychiatric nurse, and the Child Health Station or Pediatric Care Center pediatrician and nurse-in-charge. Young children showing serious or urgent problems could be referred directly to the Developmental Psychiatry Service for evaluation. We proposed child and family study at the Pediatric Care Center's monthly conference, of a child about whom typically it could be said: "You may be able to help this child within your own Center structure. Should you need us after our Child Study, we will respond. Since you will have many children like this one, the study of one child will teach us much that will be helpful in serving others like him. . . . "

Holt, a 3½-year-old African-American boy, was chosen for study by the Center's pediatrician and its chief nurse, in consultation with the Service's psychiatric nurse. The Team's psychiatrist and clinical psychologist responded to the Center's invitation to make the regular consultation with the Center's staff. By the time of our arrival at the Pediatric Center on the ground floor of a public housing project, most of the babies, small children, their brothers and sisters, mothers and grandmothers who had had preventive care and treatment that day, had left early. The Center was ready for the Harlem Consultation. The pediatrician, chief nurse, two other nurses, clinic aides, and the regional Bureau of Child Health social worker were slowly gathering in the "baby weighing" room. The pediatrician, a slender young Asian woman, presented to the consulting team and the Center staff, Holt's medical history, the results of pediatric examinations, supporting tests, and his progress since entering the Center. Holt was the product of a normal pregnancy. The membranes had ruptured prematurely. Holt weighed 7 pounds, 4 ounces at birth. At one week he had had difficulty in breathing that required intubation. Subsequently he had normal developmental milestones.

Mrs. Tanner sat in the waiting room with Holt and his 7-year-old sister, waiting to be called. We had caught sight of Holt as he ran wildly about the Center. Twice he came into the room where the conference was being held. Holt was apparently of average height and build for his age, a handsome boy. A nurse's aide called Mrs. Tanner and her children. Although appearing to run aimlessly, Holt began and ended his forays at his mother's side. His sister, a mild-mannered girl, remained close to her mother. After the introductions, Mrs. Tanner explained quietly that Holt had "speech problems." He didn't seem to understand and was withdrawn from the rest of the family. He sucked his thumb. She said that he didn't seem to be different from his 7- and his 13-year-old sisters in his physical development. While his mother talked, I engaged Holt in balloon play. He hit the balloon accurately and vigorously. He was well coordinated and showed no unusual associative movements. I could discern no signs of constitutional deficit.

I sat on the floor and gently pulled Holt near me. I gave him family dolls, mother, father, baby and two sisters. Holt ignored all but the parent figures. He made them fight. Holt did not speak; however, his play was well focused and occasionally he looked at me. From his behavior he gave the impression of having good intelligence. Mrs. Tanner and the psychologist talked briefly. I resumed my seat on Mrs. Tanner's other side. A handsome woman, she looked sad and old for her 36 years. "I've stayed home since Holt was born," Mrs. Tanner related. "Then too my mother was sick and I had to take care of her.

My husband is a taxi driver and he wants me to stay home and take care of the children; but I spend more time in my mother's house than I do at home." Mrs. Tanner became quiet.

I asked about other members of Mrs. Tanner's family of origin. Almost inaudibly she responded, "I had a younger brother, but he was killed on the street when I was pregnant with Holt. My mother went blind when my brother died; he was the favorite. It was as if the shock blinded her. Her diabetes got worse and her mind 'isn't the same'." Mrs. Tanner told us that she was a high-school graduate and had wanted to be a dental assistant. Although her husband was against it, she had planned to return to school when her second daughter went to nursery. Her pregnancy with Holt, her brother's death, and her mother's illness had ended that.

The two consultants exchanged glances. Both began the conference with the expectation that Holt's history of "difficulty in breathing" during the first week of life and absence of speech at 3½ might lead us to a diagnosis of "constitutional deficit." Holt's facile balloon play, and the mother's family tragedy refocused our attention on Holt's prenatal and newborn environment—"the arms that cradled" him. Mrs. Tanner was well aware of the changes in her mother following her brother's death. She was less able to see her own sense of loss of both brother and mother, and her anger toward her mother for always having "favored" her brother. For Holt there had been little of a caring environment from before his birth until the time of our conference. Physical care had been more than adequate. Nagera concludes (1981), "Since the first two years of life seem to be the critical period for . . . [developing structure in the central nervous system] it follows that if the right kind of stimulation is not provided during this phase, the result may be a structure that, though not necessarily "damaged" (in the sense of brain damage), has certainly not developed to its full potential" (p. 73). We had seen symptoms many times, similar to Holt's, associated with evidence of "brain damage," and without the picture of family trauma; however, the mother's trauma, related to the family trauma, could not, in this instance, be ignored. This mother's depressed state, before and after Holt's birth, did not permit an adequate affective response to

Holt's beginning affective thrust. Kohut (1977), referring to the "infantile sexual drive," states, "The primary psychological configuration (of which the drive is only a constituent) is the experience of the relation between the self and the empathic self-object" (p. 122). Stern (1983) also writes of the primary nature of this pair: "[T]he self-experience involves an affective, sensorimotor, and cognitive part of the self that cannot be experienced without a concomitant complementary experience of the other; it cannot be experienced alone" (p. 73).

Here we observe not only the psychodynamics of the mother–child pair, but a kaleidoscopic view of mirrored dynamics involving at least three generations. Holt's symptoms and behavior represented this generational dynamics which had become for him a "developmental interference." It "constitute(s) an 'interference' with the conditions under which development ought to have proceeded" (Nagera, 1966, p. 17). "[U]nderstimulation of the brain during the first few months of life, . . . may well lead to an inferior quality of brain structure (less dendritization, connections, and functional pathways)" (Nagera, 1981, p. 73).

Holt and his mother came to the Developmental Psychiatry Service for further evaluation. Properly titled introductions were made, and handshakes were exchanged. Psychologist and psychiatrist were again present. The psychiatric resident, Dr. Ghia, had been assigned to work with both Holt and his mother. We anticipated that the Therapeutic Nursery would best serve Holt's needs. The attending psychiatrist would be Mr. Tanner's therapist. This evaluation was the beginning of a two-year interdisciplinary effort. Here, too, was an opportunity to begin to demonstrate the Team's awareness of our common humanity, and our intent to assist the Tanners in identifying their ego strength. They would be members of the therapeutic team. We had learned with Greenspan and his colleagues, in their six-year in-depth study of infants in multirisk families (1987), that in addition to the "intensive work . . . teasing out the hidden needs, the often difficult to observe psychopathology . . . most important [are] the special abilities and strengths of each family" (p. 9).

The evaluation begun, Dr. Eisold, the psychologist, and Holt, sat in one corner of the large "developmental" room. This was a brief encounter in which she offered Holt a few test items chosen on the basis of her observation of him at the Pediatric Care Center. A full battery of psychological tests was not indicated at Holt's apparent level of maturity; however, during his two-year stay in the Therapeutic Nursery his psychological functioning would be compared repeatedly to his earlier functioning; he would be compared with "himself." Dr. Ghia had her first brief interview with Mrs. Tanner and a plan was made for regular meetings with her, while Holt was in the Nursery. Mr. Tanner was not present at the evaluation, although we had clues to his important role in the family. Holt, in his "Family Play" at the Pediatric Care Center, had pictured his father and mother battling. Mrs. Tanner had twice related that her husband wanted her to stay at home to take care of the children. Mrs. Holt expressed both guilt for Holt's "condition," and anger toward him for interfering with her plans to return to school after her younger daughter started school. When he was 2½ Mrs. Tanner had thrown Holt's bottle away before his eyes.

In the conference that followed the evaluation, the Team, not including the family, compared and integrated observations, test behavior, history, and psychiatric examinations. Dr. Ghia listed Holt's "assets" as well as signs and symptoms of psychopathology. She described him as a healthy-looking, handsome boy. He related to people easily, played, and laughed. Fine and gross motor behavior were normal for his age. He completed puzzles and played with cars, blocks, and mechanical toys at his age level. He fed and dressed himself. His greatest deficits were in the area of language; he used sentences of five or six words, interspersed with jargon. He rarely answered simple questions appropriately.

We had learned through our valuable association with Katrina de Hirsch that language is only learned in relationship, and that, "In practically every case [of severe language deficit], one has to search for the complex interactions among variables. . . . The child's constitutional endowment, his inherent strengths and weaknesses—genetic, physiological, emotional, and linguistic—interact with environmental forces: the affective climate of the home, the quality of mothering he receives, and his social and cultural milieu" (1975, p. 118). De Hirsch, in her study with us of a 5-year-old whose "linguistic deficits . . . interfered with ego development," called attention to Anna Freud's (1936) description of the essential nature of language in ego development:

> The attempt to take hold of the drive processes by linking them with verbal signs which can be dealt with in consciousness is one of the most general, earliest and most necessary accomplishments of the human ego. We regard it as an indispensable component of the ego, not as one among its activities [p. 178].

Holt's father, Mr. Tanner, was not present when Dr. Ghia reported the Team's evaluation findings to Mrs. Tanner. Our attention was often called to the fact that the only man on the clinical-educational team was the director of the Therapeutic Nursery's Day-Care Center. This was a reminder that the search for fathers would require more than usual effort on our part. Mrs. Tanner also seemed reluctant to invite her husband to join us. Inquiring about Mr. Tanner's tour of duty, driving his taxi, we asked to visit the family at home at a time when we could be sure that Mr. Tanner would be present. Dr. Ghia and I would visit. We asked Mrs. Tanner if she would have some coffee or tea for us. We had learned that "asking to be fed" gave us assurance of our acceptance in homes; and that such a request gives the least impression of an impending "investigation." A father is more apt to be present at home if the proffered occasion has some element of being "social." From Holt and his mother we had begun to hear that Mr. Tanner was playing ball with Holt and that they had gone out together for hamburgers. The family visit would be my first "appointment" with Mr. Tanner.

It was four in the afternoon. On the third floor landing the aroma was unmistakable—fried chicken. Mrs. Tanner greeted us warmly and ushered us into the small, neat, and comfortable living room. Mr. Tanner, a sturdy, shy-looking man, came in slowly when his wife called him. Holt was leaning on his arm. Soon Mr. Tanner sent his son off to play. With Dr. Ghia's help I related for Mr. Tanner's benefit the evaluation findings concerning Holt, beginning with the positive ones. Mr. Tanner responded that at times he thought that Holt was as smart as any child he had. He recognized that he was slow in talking; although, and he smiled, "he seems to say 'bad words' pretty good." The father added, "Holt keeps asking me to let him ride with me in my taxi."

Dianne Elise (1991), in her study of gender-related differences in separation–individuation, concludes:

> In his identification with the father, a boy has another chance at autonomy no matter how unsatisfactory his own particular relationship with his mother might have been. . . . However, the fact that it is the father, a male, who represents the real world beyond the symbiotic orbit cannot be divorced from the power differential in sex roles in patriarchal cultures. Furthermore, that powerful adult is the model of the boy's future position in the scheme of things [1991, p. 59].

Mr. Tanner had grown up in the middle of a family of seven boys, in a small town in South Carolina. His father had died when Mr. Tanner was 15. Following his graduation from high school at 18, he came to live with a maternal uncle in New York City. He had wanted to be an engineer, but an early marriage and children had made his job driving a taxi essential for the care of the family. Sometimes he worked at a second job. Nevertheless he was firm in his demand that his wife remain at home.

Mr. Tanner talked openly about his wife's response to the death of her brother. Not only was Mrs. Tanner's brother's murder a terrible shock to all of them, but the diabetic grandmother had slowly become blind and mentally unbalanced. Mrs. Tanner, five months pregnant, spent all of her time at her mother's apartment in the same building. Although Mrs. Tanner's father was able to take care of his wife, her daughter insisted on doing everything herself. Mrs. Tanner was markedly depressed; her behavior did not change when Holt was born. Mr. Tanner felt that in the midst of the family's hard times, the two girls, 7 and 13, were neglected; however, they had no particular problems and continued to do well in school. A 15-year-old male cousin had recently started coming to the house every weekend. He was a great help with Holt. Our knowledge of the significance of the father's role in Holt's life was enhanced; it was important for us to engage him in our work with the family.

Holt's constitutional deficits were disclosed in further psychological and speech studies; however, gross and fine motor functioning were intact. Holt even made use of physical activity in compensation for his language deficits. Graphomotor skills were a major strength. Holt's second developmental interference doubtless was of emotional origin. At birth and in early infancy he was denied interaction with his mother by reason of her grief, depression, and long-time neurotic conflicts. He was at the same time denied access to other family members because of their participation in the trauma that engulfed three generations. His father became preoccupied with trying to make a better living for the family. Holt's constitutional deficits and the lack of positive emotionally charged relationships combined to interrupt linguistic growth. Linguistic deficits interfered with ego development, particularly in the cognitive area. Mirroring of himself as a person of value, "worthy of being loved" had all but failed; however, by the time of our family visit, play with father and the 15-year-old male cousin began to offer opportunities for growth in relationship. These opportunities expanded many fold with his admission to the Nursery.

Holt was a member of a group of eight in the therapeutic nursery; he had individual speech therapy. Mrs. Tanner was seen for psychotherapy weekly by Dr. Ghia, who saw Holt twice weekly. Mr. Tanner met with his therapist once a month. Mrs. Tanner, in therapy, revealed a passive-aggressive personality with ambivalent feelings toward Holt, fraught with anger and guilt. In the Nursery, Holt at first cried much of time. Soon, however, he began to play with other children. Spontaneous speech was better than elicited speech. The teacher noted that when Holt directed himself in an activity, he could function better and was most alive. He used fantasy to defend himself against anxiety, to withdraw when tasks were difficult, and also to engage his teachers, therapist, or peers.

Significant delays in comprehension and expressive language initially hampered Holt's work with Dr. Ghia. Play with cars and trucks tended to be stereotyped. Later he accepted the family figures, displaying his fantasy life, and some of the realities of home life: "The little girl crying. Daddy hits her. He sits her on chair. We got to eat said Mommy. She say 'wake up' to boy. Boy says, 'I want a hamburger for breakfast. Shit!' Father says, 'Come here. You come here. You said a curse.' Little boy made a poo-poo. Father says, 'Go to the bathroom. Now finish eating.'"

A few months later: "Daddy hits the little girl and Mommy. Mommy steps on the little girl and girl falls and get hurt." Holt chokes and smashes the girl doll . . . As Holt leaves his therapist, he says, "I want to be a girl."

Dr. Ghia believed that Holt was responding mainly to parental anger and aggressiveness. Was Holt feeling the anger of both parents, to the extent that he punished himself and chose to identify with the female side of the family? "It is difficult to *restore* something to the child that was missed in his early development," conclude Kennedy and Moran (1991), writing of their aims in child analysis.

> At best the therapist can help him to make adaptations to such deficits and the consequent distortion of development. This work is based on psychoanalytic knowledge of developmental needs and involves *an admixture of interpretation and ego-supportive elements within the context of a one-to-one relationship* . . . the provision of a consistently containing and protective environment [becomes] an important feature of treatment [p. 185].

Cohen (1990) speaks of the treatment of a vulnerable child: "The analyst for such a child becomes an important person—a dependable, caring adult who listens and tries to understand" (p. 161). Holt had several opportunities for supportive one-to-one relationships in the Therapeutic Nursery setting. Ego support also meant for the clinical-educational team being alert to Holt's ability to compensate for his deficits. Teachers, therapist, and psychologist observed that Holt used his intact motoric activity to compensate for his impaired speech. Dr. Greene, the psychologist, noted: "At times he is able to make use of his body to demonstrate words and thereby express his thoughts. Holt's excellent fine and gross motor coordination allow him

to utilize this self-referential method of coping with his dys-
nomia and the resulting anxiety." Teachers discovered that
Holt's physical prowess permitted him to make himself felt in
a group, even to the point of "leading" in play. Since most of
our children in the Therapeutic Nursery had constitutional
deficits, the team learned to recognize their compensatory
modes as significant ego strengths that could be assisted to the
level of consciousness.

      In the Developmental Psychiatry Service setting, the clini-
cal-educational team, teachers and therapists, through their
core of developmental psychoanalytic understanding, and alle-
giance to "mutual identification" and "mutual responsibility,"
served the function of "ego support" and even "interpretation"
for child and family. From a background of "self-humaniza-
tion," a humanizing approach was sought that would assist family members in identifying their own "caring" possibilities, as
well as other ego strengths.

      The tool most useful in Holt's therapy was the "Family
Play." This tool had given us clues to his ego strength when we
met Holt in the Pediatric Care Center. With some help from
the therapist, using blocks, he would outline the rooms of a
house. He chose his own "family people." The first time he
followed Dr. Ghia's suggestion, "Show me what they are doing;
tell me what they say." The following time his play was spontaneous and even eager. Dr. Ghia took verbatim notes of action
and dialogue. Within several weeks, interpretations followed
insight and a sense of security on the part of both child and
therapist. The Family Play took a more specific form when
traumatic events were suspected or anticipated. Patterned after
David Levy's (1965) "sibling rivalry" play or play about an "Unanticipated Event," the Family Play found frequent use by all
members of the clinical-educational team; inasmuch as some
children and families in the Therapeutic Nursery would experience trauma every few days. David Levy (1965) wrote: "Sometimes an unanticipated event in life seems overwhelming to the
ego and yet can be modified in the course of time, by going
over the ground on which the event took place or in some way
repeating or reconstructing the event itself" (p. 238). As was
the case in most of Holt's therapy, a child may be encouraged to

give a spontaneous rendition of his Family Play; but in instances when traumatic events are known or anticipated, a "controlled" play is offered. The therapist herself then chooses characters and scene, presenting the traumatic event in action, until such time as the therapist offers the child his self representative, saying, "What does the little boy say? What does he feel?" The child then completes the play, continuing as long as he wishes. Opportunities are given for repetition of the controlled play, usually a total of three times. David Levy completed the third round of the "sibling rivalry" play, when the sibling was a new baby, by saying with fervor, "that bad, bad baby." The child's negative feelings usually escalate on repetition, and his denial is diminished. If the therapist providing "catharsis" of feeling is a stranger, a supportive parent or teacher must be present. In addition, the child can contribute to his own support, if the therapist is able to provide some specific and true evidence that the child has demonstrated his ego strength in the course of the traumatic event. A reminder that there were persons present, at the time of the trauma or soon after, who came to his aid, is also of value. Confirmation that one was not completely over-whelmed, enhances freedom to express the feelings that origi-nally had to be repressed.

Feelings expressed in preparation for a fearful event in the future detoxify negative emotions on the occasion of the event. In this manner the child achieves access to his ego strengths for the potentially traumatic event. Arlow (1987), re-ferring to Waelder's (1933) summarizing of the psychoanalytic contributions to the theory of play, points to "the function of mastery, wish fulfillment, and assimilation of overpowering ex-periences, taking leave from reality and from the pressures of the superego" (p. 32). And yet "mastery," an ego function, is the opposite of "taking leave from reality," in that, with regard to a traumatic event in the past, it confirms that the ego was not overwhelmed; it was able to withstand both trauma and the fearful or angry feelings related to the event. The child's knowledge of his own ego strength is brought onto "the level of awareness." One is often led to say, once the fearful feelings are conscious, "Look, how you helped to save yourself." It goes without saying that one's observation must be true. The same mechanism can be brought into play regarding anticipated traumatic events such as hospitalization. By providing a preview of the fearful feelings through play, one can assist in bringing to awareness the ego strength necessary to face the reality. It is of value also to list the "caring persons" who will be on hand to help. Moran (1987) says, "play with inanimate objects enlarges the scope of, and enriches the child's relation with, the animate world" (p. 12). The Family Play as here discussed is similar to a dream that uses the traumatic event as manifest content. Related feelings, which constitute the "dream work," are initially on an unconscious level. The child may have as much difficulty as an adult in revealing these feelings. In fact he may refuse to make a Family Play. His trust in the therapist is of the essence. Feelings of anger, fear, or guilt disclosed in play about a traumatic event may antedate the trauma in the developmental process; the "dated emotions" may be added to those sparked by the trauma, or negative feelings may be cumulative, with respect to a series of traumata.

Holt continued in our care until he was five and three-quarter years old. His overall functioning remained variable. As we sought to refer him to an elementary school that would continue to provide a therapeutic education and speech therapy, along with psychotherapy for both Holt and his parents, we considered Holt's and the family's assets. Holt's greatest strength in the performance sphere was his graphomotor skill. Tasks making use of this skill gave him great enjoyment. His performance in copying geometric designs was in the above average range. Holt, in his years with us, had achieved mastery in areas where he had important deficits, by learning to substitute acquired skills. In these instances he was relieved of anxiety in relation to the deficit. He had less need to retreat into fantasy. Both parents found opportunities in therapy for catharsis of feelings about the family's major traumata. Mrs. Tanner's parents became more self-sufficient and able to use community resources. Holt's mother and father were more responsive to him and his needs. They engaged in plans for Holt's education and their own continuing education.

Holt still showed dysfunction in both expressive and receptive areas of language. He had difficulty in comprehension and concept formation. His spontaneous speech was better than elicited speech, and he could speak in seven-word sentences with correct syntax. Holt had difficulty processing new material through the auditory channel; but, again, he was continuously active in his attempts at compensation. Withal, by the time we sent Holt into the larger world, his self-esteem had improved. Yet he had little tolerance for frustration in dealing with his cognitive deficits. When his numerous attempts at compensation failed, Holt's anxiety level escalated, and he retreated into fantasy. His major themes involved aggression and needs for nurturance. "Superhero" play was frequent. This play seemed to be an attempt at repairing his self-esteem through mastery and self-nurturance. Angry, destructive feelings were sublimated. They were subsumed into still powerful but positive and benign uses. Holt, when feeling secure, made good use of fantasy to communicate his concern.

Our choice for Holt's and his family's continued care was the Northside Child Development Center, and its private school. Fortunately the Tanner parents initiated much of the action necessary to this important step. Access to City and State funds were required to support Holt's attendance at the private school. The Committee on the Handicapped of the New York State Department of Education evaluated families' needs and granted or denied funds. Mr. and Mrs. Tanner, social worker, and psychiatrist met the day before the interview with the Committee for the Handicapped (COH), for "role play." On the interview date the Tanners arrived at the Therapeutic Nursery well ahead of time, in a taxi driven by a friend. The Tanners were beautifully dressed for the occasion, and so were the members of the team. We again rehearsed our role play on our long ride to the COH office, stopping occasionally to voice our nervousness. The meeting itself was something of an anticlimax. Within a week we learned that Holt would be able to attend Northside.

The Developmental Psychiatry Service for infants, children, and their families of the Division of Child Psychiatry of Harlem

Hospital Center would want to be included in Shapiro and Esman's (1992) recent survey of "Psychoanalysis and Child and Adolescent Psychiatry." They state:

> The past 25 years have produced new models that enhance our view of and the armamentarium for dynamic therapy. Infant–parent observation, theory of attachment and object relations theory, and self-psychological ideas about self-esteem have been absorbed into ego psychological views of human interaction as it influences psychic structure. . . . The new dynamic therapists are freer to be themselves with children and adolescents. They are likely to be more flexible in their integration of work with parents and other family members in the therapeutic process. They will be cognizant of the levels of cognitive and language development of their child patients and their impact on communicative processes in the treatment work. They will be alert to the nuances of transference and their varied meanings. They will probably be less ambitious in their goals . . . [p. 11].

## CONCLUSION

The psychoanalyst's history relative to training and experience is presented in order that the reader may see something of what and who has contributed to the one who plays with the child, his family, and the older generations not seen. An inner city hospital in a Harlem, New York City community is the setting in which a mental health clinical-educational team provides consultation, evaluation, psychoanalytic psychotherapy, therapeutic education, and remediation for a population principally of young African-American families, living on a poverty level. The children are plagued with constitutional deficits, poor nurturing, and traumata, all related to their poverty. A major task for the team was the identification of ego strengths in the team, and in the children and families with whom they worked. This humanizing approach pervaded consultation, evaluation, dynamic psychotherapy, and therapeutic education. One child and his family were followed over a two-year period. Psychoanalytic principles pervade the action in the Pediatric Care Center, the therapy playroom, and the Nursery. Essential to the action was the mutual identification and mutual responsibility of the dynamically oriented, racially integrated team. Absent in the team's achievement of "wholeness" were men.

"Vulnerable" is defined as, "susceptible to being wounded or hurt . . . difficult to defend." In our concern for vulnerable or "high-risk" young children, I agree with Kennedy and Moran's discussion of Anna Freud's (1965) point of view: "that analysts should make a clear distinction between *aim* and *method*" (p. 183). These authors (1991) state the aim of child analysis: "From a developmental point of view the outcome aimed at is the building up of suitable structural organizations which optimize the potential for development, within the limitations set by the child's constitutional, maturational, and environmental givens" (p. 197). The Developmental Psychiatry Service's Team had this *aim* for the "vulnerable" children and families with whom they worked. Our methods, however, stretch the "limitations" of the "constitutional, maturational, and environmental givens." Our expectation is that the tools of analysis can apply to the children and families of poverty. Our methods are enhanced by the help of other disciplines. Ours is a developmental psychoanalytic psychology which recognizes a "common humanity" with Harlem's young children and families, such that they and we may share our "inner worlds" in play. "Psychotherapy has to do with two people playing together" (Winnicott, 1971, p. 38).

## REFERENCES

Arlow, J. A. (1987), Trauma, play, and perversion. *The Psychoanalytic Study of the Child*, 42:31–44. New Haven, CT: Yale University Press.

Bernard, V. W. (1971), Composite remedies for psychosocial problems. In: *Psychiatric Care of the Underprivileged, Internat. Psychiatry Clinics*, ed. G. Belasso. Boston: Little, Brown, 8:61–85.

Cohen, D. J. (1990), Enduring sadness: Early loss, vulnerability, and the shaping of character. *The Psychoanalytic Study of the Child*, 45:157–178. New Haven, CT: Yale University Press.

de Hirsch, K. (1975), Pedro: A language appraisal. In: *Young Inner City Families: Development of Ego Strength Under Stress*. New York: Behavioral Publications, pp. 118–125.

Elise, D. (1991), An analysis of gender differences in separation-individuation. *The Psychoanalytic Study of the Child*, 46:51–67. New Haven, CT: Yale University Press.

Erikson, E. H. (1959), Growth and crises of the healthy personality. In: Identity and the Life Cycle, *Psychological Issues*, Monogr. 1, Vol. 1, No. 1. New York: International Universities Press, pp. 50–100.

Freud, A. (1936), *The Ego and the Mechanisms of Defense*. New York: International Universities Press, 1966.

——— (1965), *Normality and Pathology in Childhood*. New York: International Universities Press.

Greenspan, S. I. (1987), *Infants in Multirisk Families: Case Studies in Preventive Intervention*. Madison, CT: International Universities Press.

Hartmann, H. (1964), *Essays on Ego Psychology*. New York: International Universities Press.

Joint Commission on Mental Health of Children (1969), *Crisis in Child Mental Health: Challenge for the 1970's*. New York: Harper & Row.

Kennedy, H., & Moran, G. (1991), Reflections on the aim of child analysis. In: *The Psychoanalytic Study of the Child*, 46:181–198. New Haven, CT: Yale University Press.

Knoblock, H., & Pasamanick, B. (1953), Further observations on the behavioral development of Negro children. *J. Genet. Psychol.*, 83:137–157.

Kohut, H. (1977), *The Restoration of the Self*. New York: International Universities Press.

Lawrence, M. M. (1963), Supervision of child psychiatry residents in an inner city setting. Meeting of the American Academy of Psychoanalysis, Houston, Texas, 1981, unpublished.

——— (1975), *Young Inner City Families: Development of Ego Strength Under Stress*. New York: Behavioral Publications.

——— (1977), Infant-caretaker interaction research in an inner city community. In: *Child Psychiatry: Treatment and Research*, ed. M. F. McMillan & S. Henao. New York: Brunner/Mazel, pp. 71–81.

Levy, D. (1965), The act as a unit. In: *New Perspectives in Psychoanalysis*, ed. G. Daniels. New York: Grune and Stratton, pp. 218–252.

Moran, G. S. (1987), Some functions of play and playfulness. *The Psychoanalytic Study of the Child*, 42:11–29. New Haven, CT: Yale University Press.

Nagera, H. (1966), *Early Childhood Disturbances, The Infantile Neuroses, and The Adulthood Disturbances*. New York: International Universities Press.

——— (1981), *The Developmental Approach to Childhood Psychopathology*. New York: Jason Aronson.

Shapiro, T., & Esman, A. (1992), Psychoanalysis and child and adolescent psychiatry. *J. Amer. Acad. Child & Adol. Psychiatry*, 31:6–13.

Stern, D. (1983), The early development of schemas of self, other, and "self with other." In: *Reflections on Self Psychology*. Hillsdale, NJ: Analytic Press, pp. 49–84.

Waelder, R. (1933), The psychoanalytic theory of play. *Psychoanal. Quart.*, 2:208–224.

Winnicott, D. W. (1971), *Playing and Reality*. New York: Tavistock Publications/Methuen, 1982.

# 10.

# Vulnerabilities in Preschool Children of Adolescent Mothers: A Narrative Approach

## JOY D. OSOFSKY, LAURA HUBBS-TAIT, ALICE EBERHART-WRIGHT, ANNE M. CULP, and LUCILE M. WARE

Infants and children can be defined as vulnerable for many reasons. Constitutional factors may contribute to vulnerability; children with physical handicaps and medical problems are often vulnerable. Children may have vulnerabilities related to temperamental factors such as increased irritability and fearfulness. There is also a body of literature defining infants as more vulnerable because of heightened sensitivity to stimulation, loud sounds, light, or even touch (Brazelton, 1961; Carey, 1972). Anthony (1987) has emphasized the importance of considering individual liabilities in the context of the environment in which the individual is embedded. Families at risk due to crises such as disability, disease, and desertion may be at even greater risk if they live under impoverished economic and social

This research was supported by the Center for Prevention Research, Division of Prevention and Special Mental Health Programs, National Institute for Mental Health, Grant No. 36895, the Kenworthy-Swift Foundation, and the John D. and Catherine T. MacArthur Foundation.

Portions of the case presented in this chapter have been reported previously in Osofsky, J. D., Eberhart-Wright, E., Ware, L. M., & Hann, D. M. (1992), Children of adolescent mothers: A group at risk for psychopathology. *Infant Mental Health Journal,* 13:119–131.

conditions. Children may be more vulnerable due to malfunctioning and disorganization within the family, poor communication and emotional contact, a lack of routine and organization, and absence of a plan for the future.

Children of adolescent mothers are frequently vulnerable due to the environmental circumstances into which they are born and in which they are raised. For a less constitutionally vulnerable child, a nonfacilitating environment may not be as problematic depending on a variety of other circumstances.

For children of adolescent mothers many different factors can contribute to vulnerability and problematic development. Most adolescent mothers grow up in poverty which can lead to instability and unpredictability in their lives. Adolescent pregnancy in and of itself adds to the instability. Young mothers often have to move from one home to another due to economic or relationship difficulties. Because their relationships change frequently, both mother and child are less likely to be able to depend upon continuity and consistent support. Adolescent mothers often report being unhappy about being pregnant and having a baby, do not feel ready to be a parent, and lack the maturity to take on the considerable responsibilities of raising a child.

In 1981, we initiated a longitudinal study of 180 adolescent mothers and their infants in Topeka, Kansas, 69 of whom were followed for the first 4½ years of life (Osofsky, Culp, and Ware, 1988; Osofsky and Eberhart-Wright, 1988). The purpose of the research component of the project was to learn about the social and emotional development of adolescent mothers and their children. In cooperation with the city/county health department, we developed strategies for intervening with the young mothers and their children. The strategies were designed to facilitate the adolescents' moving forward with their lives despite the pregnancy and becoming a parent at a young age. In addition, we developed intervention strategies to facilitate the infant and child's development.

The adolescent mothers and their infants were observed and evaluated in a homelike laboratory situation when their children were 6, 13, 20, 30, 44, and 54 months of age and periodically in their homes by a lay home visitor. All observations in the laboratory were videotaped. The assessments included observations of mother and infant/child during feeding and play and the administration of self-report self-esteem and depression scales at each of the time periods. At 13 months, the strange situation paradigm was done to evaluate the attachment relationship between the mother and her infant and the Bayley Scales of Infant Development were administered. At 30, 44, and 54 months, observations were carried out during symbolic play. In addition, at 44 months standardized play narratives were administered and mothers were asked to complete the Child Behavior Checklist (Achenbach, 1979) on their children.

An issue of particular interest for this chapter was whether it would be possible to identify vulnerabilities in children of adolescent mothers related to their internal representations of their early experience and world when they developed the cognitive capacity to use narrative skills. Specifically, was there a relationship between the child's external experience of conflict in his or her early life and later internalizations and representations in stories told through standardized play narratives.

Emde (1991b) has emphasized that our understanding of early emotional development and conflict has been strongly influenced by more current knowledge about variations in family experience and child development. Specifically, narratives allow us to learn how the child comes to understand his or her world and the differences between child and parent. Using narratives of the "oedipal" child that combine perspectives from developmental psychology and psychoanalysis, we can learn about how the child represents through language the conflicts and significant emotional themes of family life. An additional research question concerns the extent to which child narrative themes represent constructions from reality or are fantasy based.

These questions were evaluated in our study when the children were 44 months old. They were presented with different conflict situations in the form of standardized play narratives to which they were asked to respond; that is, the beginning of the story was told using dolls to illustrate the action and the child was asked to narrate the end of the story. The story stems were constructed in two areas. One group of stems probed for narrative themes concerning moral development (Buchsbaum and Emde, 1990) and the other group focused on family relationship themes (Bretherton, Ridgeway, and Cassidy, 1990). The story stems in the moral development area pulled for empathic or prosocial responses. Several story stems probed for the child's representations of ways to adhere to a rule in the face of a temptation to behave otherwise. Another story stem focused on the challenge of restraining aggression in the face of conflict. Yet, another story stem presented a complex "moral dilemma" because the stem pushed the child to resolve a conflict in which a prosocial inclination was prohibited by what the child was told not to do by his or her mother.

The family relationship stems were chosen to sample a variety of narrative themes. Two story stems presented situations that called for reparative responses. The reparative stories did not necessarily involve making amends for intentional wrongdoing. The family relationship stems, while overlapping in some ways with the themes addressed by the moral dilemma stems, involved more interdependence among family members. For example, one story in this group addressed children's narrative responses to parental conflict. A final set of family relationship stems tapped into themes of separation and reunion with parents. These stems can be used to study the attachment relationships between the parent and child.

In order to evaluate vulnerability and potential psychopathology in high-risk children of adolescent mothers, we focused on two areas in the responses to the standardized play narratives that are particularly important for socialization: the development of the attachment relationship with mother and manifestations of aggression, both coherent and incoherent. Difficulties in forming early relationships and manifestations of significant amounts of aggressive behaviors may be earlier indicators of problematic development. The responses to the narratives provide systematic data about representations resulting from the internalization of early relationship experience that may not be evident from other observational data.

A coding scheme to evaluate the security of the attachment relationship in the narratives has been developed by Bretherton, Ridgeway, and Cassidy (1990). Clyman, Buchsbaum,

Emde, Cicchetti, and Toth (1991), in a study of narratives with both normative and high-risk abused children, have developed an additional coding scheme to evaluate both coherent and incoherent aggression in preschooler narratives. Both of these systems were used to rate the narratives of 44-month-old children of adolescent mothers in the current study. Two raters established reliability on the scales while observing the video-tapes and then rated the tapes.

The case description below has been selected to illustrate how observations made as part of a research study using standard play narratives helped to identify vulnerability in a child over the first 44 months of life.

*Darcy and Tabatha*

Darcy was 17 when she discovered that she was pregnant with Tabatha following a turbulent early life. Her mother had died when Darcy was a year old and she never knew her father, who was reportedly alcoholic. Although accounts of her early life varied, Darcy reportedly experienced deprivation and little joy while growing up with her aunt, two cousins, and an older sister, thus being raised without a father figure. She considered her aunt's discipline harsh and inconsistent. School provided little relief since she struggled academically. Darcy began having sex at 15, and became pregnant at 17, which prompted her to enroll in our program. She was at high risk for having problems in adjustment and parenting. She faced the birth of her child with no emotional support, no financial resources or job training, no high school diploma, and a boyfriend who could be abusive and who had alcohol problems. In addition, she was obese and had gestational diabetes.

Prior to delivery, Darcy had mixed feelings about motherhood. These feelings were exacerbated by a complicated labor resulting in a Caesarian section delivery. In the hospital after delivery, Darcy was angry about the difficulties this baby was already causing her. She perceived Tabatha as being more difficult than average. Tabatha was a hefty baby weighing over nine pounds. Darcy's response to Tabatha appeared ambivalent. Despite apprehensions about her baby, Darcy decided to breast-feed. The observation during feeding reflected Darcy's ambivalence, in that she divided her time between the baby and the television. At times, she was sensitive; at other times, she showed inappropriate behavior, such as laughing loudly when the baby appeared to be smiling. After release from the hospital, mother and baby were assigned a home visitor. Darcy's mothering continued to be inconsistent and she showed a minimum of affection.

At the six-month evaluation, Darcy showed signs of improvement. She had a part-time job, attended a weekly program provided for the mothers and babies, and had a new boyfriend. She was feeling good about life. However, the early ambivalence in the mother–child relationship was reflected again at this time. Darcy offered Tabatha a bottle of milk but commented that she thought it might be spoiled. She asked, "Are you sure you want it?" During mother–child play, Darcy appeared supportive of Tabatha as a zestful, healthy child. But, at other times during this evaluation, Darcy expressed her difficulty with Tabatha's demands and dependency.

After the 6-month evaluation, numerous problems surfaced. At her aunt's request, Darcy and Tabatha moved out and found a roommate to share an apartment. The apartment atmosphere was stormy, with Darcy and her roommate fighting, men coming and going, and a lack of money. Darcy's problems continued. She became engaged to a man who did not like Tabatha, contracted venereal disease from another man, and took amphetamines which resulted in her being hospitalized. Amidst this problematic environment, Tabatha exhibited temper tantrums for which the home visitor suggested child management strategies.

At the 13-month evaluation, Darcy was more negative with Tabatha than she had been earlier. She complained that Tabatha was hot tempered and difficult to comfort. Darcy's affect appeared blunted. Self-report scales of self-esteem and depression indicated that she had poor self-esteem and high levels of depressed mood. Tabatha's behavior appeared problematic. Her moods changed abruptly and she received a disorganized and disoriented rating on attachment (Main and Solomon, 1990) showing a mixture of insecurity including avoidance and resistance. She showed many of the behaviors associated with a disorganized attachment rating including stereotypies such as putting her hands over her head, cupping her hands over her ears, and scratching the back of her head. She also showed direct indices of apprehension such as putting her hand over her mouth as her mother approached her and sudden stilling with a blank stare.

It is important to recognize that these early observations of disruptions in the relationship and out-of-control behaviors in the child also characterized the child's environment. Thus, Tabatha's internalized experience of her world would include her early chaotic environment. It could be expected that her later representations as depicted through narrative stories would reflect this early experience.

After the 13-month evaluation, as Tabatha approached the age of rapprochement (Mahler, Pine, and Bergman, 1975), Darcy began talking about giving up Tabatha. Interestingly, Darcy was a year old herself when her mother died. Thus, in this mother–child pair, early signs of a repetition compulsion may have been playing an important role in the relationship (Emde, 1991a). The "ghosts" from Darcy's early life were too difficult to put aside but actuated as she attempted to master warded-off memories from a painful past in raising her own child (Fraiberg, Adelson, and Shapiro, 1975). Darcy met with a social worker to discuss relinquishment and was reported to Protective Services because of her negative relationship with Tabatha. Protective Services insisted that Darcy and Tabatha enroll in a center for abused and neglected children. During this period, Darcy and Tabatha moved several times until they finally were able to obtain an apartment in public housing.

During the 20-month evaluation, Darcy tried to make a good impression despite her many problems. She provided positive guidance to Tabatha and was patient with her despite her negative behavior. Tabatha, on the other hand, appeared hostile and destructive. Her aggressive outbursts had by now become more incoherent, a pattern we will see reflected in the later narratives. She smashed small cups used in the evaluation, threw a ball in the examiner's face, and yelled at her mother. At times, however, Tabatha was able to show more compliant behaviors such as focusing on tasks and behaving appropriately with her mother.

After the 20-month assessment, Protective Services intervened again because Darcy continued to neglect Tabatha, leaving her unsupervised in the middle of the street. It is likely that Tabatha was exposed to fighting and violent behaviors that, combined with sexuality, might have led to overstimulation and difficulties with affect regulation. Foster care was considered. Instead, Tabatha and Darcy enrolled in a special therapeutic preschool program. Tabatha was seen in consultation at the Menninger Clinic and began a three-year intervention in the Preschool Day Treatment Center that focused on both mother and child. Tabatha's initial diagnosis, according to the staff at the Preschool Day Treatment Center, was Conduct Disorder, undersocialized, aggressive (DSM-III-R, APA, 1987). Although a full clinical evaluation was not done on Darcy, descriptively, she appeared to be Dysthymic with a Borderline Personality Disorder. Tabatha and Darcy's relationship problems were classified as underregulated, severely disordered (Anders, 1989; Diagnostic Classification of Mental Health and Developmental Disorders of Early Childhood, in press). The classification of underregulated referred to Tabatha's minimal emotional control including explosive affects and behaviors. Severely disordered referred to inappropriate and insensitive affect regulation with mother being unavailable to the child emotionally and the mother and child rarely showing positive interactions and frequently interacting in a negative fashion.

At the 30-month evaluation, many problems continued to be observed in the mother–child relationship. Darcy showed no delight, little or no affect, and a great deal of negativity toward Tabatha. Tabatha's behavior continued to be hostile and destructive as was noted earlier. When Darcy showed less sensitivity, Tabatha's temper flared. Several times during the course of the evaluation, Tabatha hit her mother hard. During free play, Darcy's behavior improved and she was observed to be supportive and patient. Tabatha's behavior also improved and she was able to play out positive interactions between the mother and child during script play.

At the time of the 44-month assessment, the structured play narratives were administered to Tabatha. At that time, Darcy was pregnant, had not finished high school, and was not working. She reported symptoms of depression, a need for financial and emotional support, and desire for a career. Darcy rated Tabatha on the Child Behavior Checklist (Achenbach, 1979) as having significant sleep problems and she received an overall score above the clinical cut-off for psychopathology. Tabatha was difficult to test due to her difficult behavior and poor impulse control. She scored considerably below average on a receptive vocabulary measure. This score conflicted with earlier test performance on which she scored at or above average. Tabatha's behavior during the structured play stories presented a complex picture of cooperation, aggression, and loving relationships. Overall, she was active, oppositional, and manipulative.

Several of the stories told by Tabatha in response to the structured story stems will be described. The following questions will be addressed: In what ways do early prelanguage relationship experiences that are internalized reflect themselves in narratives when the child is 3½ years old? Do we see indications of early moral development? How much aggression do children depict in their stories? Is the aggression coherent or incoherent? To what extent are the stories as a whole coherent or incoherent?

*Lost Keys Story*

In this story, mother and father are arguing in front of two children, of the same sex as the subject being interviewed, about father having lost mother's keys. Father angrily denies losing the keys. The child is asked to show what happens next. Tabatha walks the girl doll Mary in a circle and knocks down all the other people with her arms. She says that Mary is killing Dad and Mom. Then Mom says "thank you" for killing her. When asked why they wanted Mary to kill them, Tabatha says "It is because they have tights on."

Tabatha's response in this story was coded for aggression shown verbally or physically. In addition, the scale takes into account whether the aggression is coherent or incoherent. Tabatha showed much aggression in telling the rest of this story using the child as the aggresssor and the parents as those who were aggressed against. In addition to the child showing coherent aggression, she also displayed incoherent aggression with Mary knocking people down with her arms. This aggressive behavior seemed to "spill out" in response to the stimulation from the argument in the story.

Further, Tabatha's aggressive response was extreme—killing the parents for no apparent reason. As Glenn (1991) said in his discussion of this material, "aggression is rampant and restraint minimal." Tabatha's ego is insufficient to meet the task of following and enforcing her weak moral demands. Not only do we see lack of moral development in the usual sense, but in this child exposed to a chaotic, unprotected environment, we see serious "shock trauma." For her, aggressive behavior may have been experienced as the ideal (Glenn, 1991). As we will see in later stories, there was inconsistency in her responses. While aggression and violation of rules were permitted, the child was also punished.

*Ice Cream Story*

In this story, Mommy and Daddy, Mary and Jane are going to the ice cream store. Jane is riding on a toy horse and falls off. Jane says, "Ow, I hurt my knee. I fell off my horse." The child is then asked to show what happens next. Tabatha has put Mommy on the horse and says through Jane, "Get off my horse." Tabatha says, "It's my turn." She drives the horse around and flies over Mary. The examiner repeats that Jane got hurt. Tabatha repeats, "Jane got hurt." The examiner says, "Does anyone care?" Tabatha runs the horse into Jane and says, "Take her to the doctor." The examiner says, "Who is going to take her to the doctor?" Tabatha says, "Momma. Me." "Hello, Doctor."

This story was coded for both aggression and security of attachment. The aggression that Tabatha showed in this story is done by Mom against Jane. Again the aggression is incoherent with Mom running the horse into Jane. Jane has been hurt falling off the horse and there was no reason for Mom to attack her.

In terms of security of attachment, the relationship was considered secure if one of the parents or the older sister responded to the hurt child's pain by hugging or administering a Band-Aid. In order for the story to have a positive ending, the hurt child's pain needed to be acknowledged. The criteria for insecurity included avoidance of the story issue and incoherent or odd responses. Based on Jane's interactions with her mother as depicted by Tabatha in the story (it was Jane who had hurt herself), we neither saw acknowledgment of Jane being hurt or of the parents or older child taking care of her. Finally at the end, Jane is taken to the doctor. But during the story, the mother attacks Jane who is hurt. We saw some labeling of what happened rather than completion of the story, and Jane's mother's response was incoherent when she attacked Jane, who was hurt, for no reason. All coders agreed that this story reflected a disorganized attachment relationship with a lack of security. Glenn's (1991) comments regarding "shock trauma" in the earlier story would also apply to this one. In addition, since Tabatha's early relationship with her mother was inconsistent and her other relationships were primarily unstable and chaotic, it is not surprising that she shows primarily disorganized attachment relationships with a depiction of adults as not only unreliable but also potentially threatening. Again, based on the experiences she has internalized, aggressive behaviors may be required as a primary way to organize her environment.

*Moral Dilemma Story*

Jane and Mary are in this story. Jane says, "Ow! I hurt my leg! My owie is bleeding! Get me a Band-Aid! It hurts!" Mary says, "Okay. Oh, but Mommy says we can't touch stuff on the bathroom shelf." Mary walks over to an older child and says, "I need a Band-Aid for Jane. (Her leg is bleeding.)" The older child says: "Mom says you can't take things off the bathroom shelf and I need to go now!" Examiner says, "What does Jane do and say now?"

Tabatha says, "Go take that thing out." Examiner says, "What is Mary going to do?" Tabatha: "Get that Band-Aid out." Examiner: "Why did she get a Band-Aid?" Tabatha: "Because she do." Examiner: "But Mommy said you can't touch things on the bathroom shelf. Where did she get it? Did she do it anyway?" Tabatha: "Yeah. Mom's gonna whoop her."

Although most of the children in our sample did not deal with the moral dilemma, Tabatha not only dealt with the dilemma but was aware of the consequences of disobeying her mother. Tabatha had Mary violate the rules, but understood that she would be punished for it in an aggressive way. What does this mean for the child's internalization of parental standards and moral development? According to Glenn (1991) in discussing this case, "Tabatha's ego was insufficient to the tasks of following and enforcing her rather weak moral demands." She had a frail sense of morality that was corrupt. Such responses are not surprising in relation to the chaotic and inconsistent environment in which she was raised.

## DISCUSSION

Standardized play narratives allow us to gain an understanding of how the child has come to internalize early prelanguage experiences that are then represented through language and play. They provide a different level of data than is available from direct observations. Further, eliciting this information from the children in a standardized way can contribute to knowledge in general.

For some children of young mothers, a group at risk for problematic development, vulnerabilities emerging from their chaotic early environment become apparent through both their emotional reactions to conflict situations in the play narratives and their cognitive representations. Their representations depict a world of conflict and chaos that has been internalized. The narrative allows us to enter into the world of meaning (Emde, 1991b).

For many of these youngsters brought up in high-risk environments like Tabatha, it is difficult to differentiate fantasy from reality as the harsh reality of their young lives becomes so overwhelming and takes precedence in their narratives. Thus, even their view of what is right or wrong as reflecting in their developing sense of morality is colored by the fact that whatever they do, they are likely to be "whooped." Aggression and sexuality become everyday occurrences as a way to deal with life and cope with the environment.

Not only is this work compelling in understanding vulnerable children, but also it points to the need for early preventive intervention to help these youngsters cope with their chaotic environments and build a more stable and integrated internal world. Difficulties in early relationship experiences as well as lack of control of aggressive impulses are reflected vividly in the narratives. Further, there is often a lack of coherence which reflects the child's inability to organize and integrate the many diverse and inconsistent early life experiences. Based on our data, it appears that children need "good enough" caretaking environments in order to develop "stable enough narratives" (Wolf, 1992).

## REFERENCES

Achenbach, T. M. (1979), The Child Behavior Profile: An empirically based system for assessing children's behavioral problems and competencies. *Internat. J. Mental Health*, 7:24–42.

American Psychiatric Association (1987), *Diagnostic and Statistical Manual of Mental Disorders*, 3rd ed. rev. (DSM-III-R). Washington, DC: American Psychiatric Press.

Anders, T. F. (1989), Clinical syndromes, relationship disturbances and their assessment. In: *Relationship Disturbances in Early Childhood*, ed. A. J. Sameroff & R. N. Emde. New York: Basic Books, pp. 125–144.

Anthony, E. J. (1987), Risk, vulnerability, and resilience: An overview. In: *The Invulnerable Child*, ed. E. J. Anthony & B. J. Cohler. New York: Guilford Press, pp. 3–48.

Brazelton, T. B. (1961), Physiological reactions of the neonate. I. The value of observation of the neonate. *J. Pediatrics*, 58:508–512.

Bretherton, I., Ridgeway, D., & Cassidy, J. (1990), Assessing internal working models of the attachment relationship. In: *Attachment in the Preschool Years*, ed. M. T. Greenberg, D. Cicchetti, & E. M. Cummings. Chicago: University of Chicago Press, pp. 273–310.

Buchsbaum, H., & Emde, R. N. (1990), Play narratives in 36-month-old children. *The Psychoanalytic Study of the Child*, 40:129–155. New Haven, CT: Yale University Press.

Carey, W. (1972), Clinical applications of infant temperament. *J. Pediatrics*, 81:823–828.

Clyman, R., Buchsbaum, H., Emde, R. N., Cicchetti, D., & Toth, S. (1991), Aggression Coding Scales for maltreatment study. Unpublished scale, University of Colorado Heath Sciences Center, Denver.

Diagnostic Classification of Mental Health and Developmental Disorders of Early Childhood (in press), Arlington, VA: Zero to Three/National Center for Clinical Infant Programs.

Emde, R. N. (1991a), Discussion at symposium on "Precursors of Psychopathology," International Psychoanalytic Association Meeting, Buenos Aires, Argentina, July.

———— (1991b), Emotion narratives in preschool children. Presentation at Symposium on the Vulnerable Child, American Psychoanalytic Association Meeting, New York, December.

Fraiberg, S., Adelson, E., & Shapiro, V. (1975), Ghosts in the nursery: A psychoanalytic approach to the problems of impaired infant-mother relationships. *J. Amer. Acad. Child Psychiatry*, 14:387–421.

Glenn, J. (1991), Summary of vulnerable child discussion group: Moral development in early childhood. Meeting of the American Psychoanalytic Association, New York, December.

Mahler, M. S., Pine, F., & Bergman, A. (1975), *The Psychological Birth of the Human Infant*. New York: Basic Books.

Main, M., & Solomon, J. (1990), Procedures for identifying infants as disorganized-disoriented during the Ainsworth Strange Situation. In: *Attachment in the Preschool Years*, ed. M. T. Greenberg, D. Cicchetti, & E. M. Cummings. Chicago: University of Chicago Press, pp. 121–161.

Osofsky, J. D., Culp, A., & Ware, L. M. (1988), Intervention challenges with adolescent mothers and their infants. *Psychiatry*, 51:236–241.

———— Eberhart-Wright, E. (1988), Affective exchanges between high risk mothers and their infants. *Internat. J. Psycho-Anal.*, 69:221–232.

Wolf, D. (1992), Narrative attunement. Paper presented at meeting on "Narratives: Creating Meaning from Birth Through Adulthood." University of California, Los Angeles, March.

# 11.

# Some Effects of Lost Adolescence: The Child Mothers and Their Babies

## JO ANN B. FINEMAN, M.D., MARGUERITE A. SMITH, Ph.D.

Lady Capulet:
Here in Verona, ladies of esteem are made already mothers. By my count I was your mother much upon these years that you are now a maid.
—William Shakespeare, *Romeo and Juliet*, Act I, Scene 3

This paper presents a curiously timely yet retrospective look at the attempt to understand the psychodynamics of adolescent motherhood and, incidentally, fatherhood, from a twenty year span. Clearly, our population had not yet been assaulted by autoimmune deficiency syndrome (AIDS) or the epidemic of drug use which now complicates the staggering task of understanding and treating adolescent parents and their babies, but, "the more things change . . . ," a close look at today's inner city adolescent mothers and fathers demonstrates the self-same dynamics between mother, infant, and grandmother, but complicated by neurological compromises at birth, "crack babies," and AIDS-infected infants.

This was one of the earlier comprehensive studies to be undertaken by a team of professionals trained in dynamic aspects of child development (i.e., analytically), and to engage in a treatment design which offered individual, mother–child focused intervention via both clinic and home visit contacts.

167

Such studies largely lost funding or were severely compromised in support services by the end of the 1970s, as was the case with the study reported. Nonetheless, the attempt to apply the developmental and psychodynamic understanding to similar populations should be a guiding theory, since the failures of early object attachment and aggressive modification noted here replicate themselves today, as they did twenty years ago.

## I

The familiar wrangle between Lady Capulet and the Nurse, one exhorting Juliet to marry and bear children, the other remembering her infancy and nursling days, brings to a sharp focus the dilemma of the adolescent child mothers we have seen in our clinical services over the past several years. The graceful language of Shakespeare is often duplicated in the pained and bitter conflicts between the adolescent mother and her own mother, as each struggles to contend with the merging and antagonistic developmental phases which are forced upon them with the coming of the child-mother's baby.

We have become aware of the enormous complexity of this problem over the past six years in which we have been engaged in services to infants, children, and their families in the Solomon Carter Fuller Mental Health Center and the Dorchester Children's Services, both inner city areas of Boston, Massachusetts.

In the six years that we were involved in a program for high risk babies and their mothers, we followed a total of 167 families. We would like to discuss here some of the findings from a statistical analysis of this population. We want to highlight only those concerning teenage mothers, but we will need to describe the total population in order to place these findings in context.

To begin with, our Unit was located in the inner city of Boston and served a population that was virtually 100 percent at risk. Figures from the Boston City Hospital's Neonatology Department showed that from 75 to 80 percent of babies born there had some "less than favorable" characteristic at birth, and that between 30 and 35 percent of babies had some obvious, diagnosable birth defect or anomaly of a permanent nature. (This is in contrast to figures of well below 1 percent per year in a nearby suburban hospital.)

Mothers in our sample ranged in age from 14 to 43 and the babies' problems at birth ranged from "none" to severe, multiple handicaps, of a permanent nature.

Since mothers and babies were referred to us as at risk dyads across a spectrum that ranged from the baby having a problem at birth to the mother's situation being the high risk factor, we approached our analysis from several angles: age of mother at birth of baby; condition of baby at birth; severity of baby's problems; reason for referral; age of baby at referral; stability of mother's home situation. Finally, each family was rated on a scale from 1 to 5 on the basis of participation in the program; that is, not in terms of the quality of mothering or state of the infant, but solely on such concrete items as, keeps appointments, is home for scheduled home visits, keeps scheduled clinic appointments, stays with program for duration of need, or until referral to further appropriate program. This caused some difficulty for the staff, because it did not correlate with the subjective judgment of the *quality* of mothering, so that some of our most troublesome families would receive the highest rating of one. The converse was not true, however; mothers rated four or five did not include any whose mothering was otherwise seen as "good" or "adequate" by staff. What the rating did reflect, therefore, was the availability of the family to the treatment team, without a judgment of successfulness of response to treatment.

We were particularly interested in exploring the group of teenage mothers and babies. There were a total of fifty-two mothers ranging in age from 14 through 19 at the time of the baby's birth, but further examination of this group led us almost immediately to a further age breakdown. Since "very young mother" was established with our referring sources as an adequate reason for an at risk referral, this introduced a bias in our younger age samples that began to become evident as we explored the reason for referral; that is, "very young mother" as the sole reason for referral occurred in the 14- to

17-year-old group, while beginning with the 18- to 19-year-old girls, there was a shift to a combination of age of mother plus an additional at risk factor. As we looked into this more, it became evident that in general the 14- to 17-year-old mother was psychologically in a very different position from the 18- to 20-year-old mother. First (at least in our group), the 14- to 17-year-olds were still part of their primary family, living at home, with little or no contact or continuing affiliation with the father of the baby. None had finished high school at the time of pregnancy and birth of the baby. Some specifically used the pregnancy as a reason for leaving school even when other arrangements were offered them.

In contrast, most of the 18- to 19-year-old girls had moved away from the family home, or used the pregnancy as a reason for making this move. They had once or continued to have an affiliation with the father of the baby, had either finished high school, or been involved in some self-supporting work that took them out of the home, even if they continued technically to live there. That is to say, either from their own volition, or because of pressures from the family of origin, these girls were already breaking away from their parents.

One should note, too, the reflection of the societal evaluation of the 18- to 20-year-old versus the 14- to 17-year-old in the fact that age alone was not seen as a sufficient reason for referral as a high risk mother.

Among our 52 teenage mothers, there were twenty-eight in the 14- to 17-year-old group and 24 in the 18- to 20-year-old group. Among the factors that characterized the "very young mother" group were: most of the babies were healthier than those in the other referral groups, even though nine babies were premature. Only three babies had birth defects that would have occasioned a referral to us regardless of the mother's age. And, oddly enough, these were three unusual, and unusually serious, problems: one was a triple amputee, second, a hemophiliac baby, and third, a baby described as a "prune belly" baby. This was the second baby referred to us with this diagnosis and the mother of the second baby was 30 years old. One needs to remember the built-in skew to this group when we state that these babies were the healthiest of the age groups in our sample (i.e., as noted above, the fact that age alone could be the reason for referral). It should be noted, too, that we surely did not have every pregnant below 17-year-old girl in the area referred to us, and figures for "problem pregnancies" among the total number of below 17-year-old mothers in the greater Boston area may be very different from those of our small sample.

Something that our figures do suggest, however, is that perhaps one should explore more carefully the population in this inner-city area with the question in mind, "Do women living in this deprived socioeconomic group tend to have less healthy babies as they grow older?" Or, conversely, does the very young mother in this socioeconomic group have the best chance of having a healthy baby while *she is still very young*? in spite of the fact that *national* figures show this age group (14–17) to be a high-risk group for birth defects.

Of particular importance for the focus of the discussion today is the fact that in this group of 28 very young mothers, there were 25 babies that started out as healthy babies with no real reason not to develop normally and so deserve our best efforts as a preventive intervention program. What was most discouraging about our analysis was that of all our high risk groups, this was the one group with which we had the most difficulty and where the ratings for "availability of the family to the treatment team" was the poorest. In terms of further age splits, or in terms of moderate to severe problems of the baby, all other groupings showed about a 50/50 split in highly rated versus poorly rated families, but in this group of young mothers with healthy babies the distribution was four to one against "accessibility to the family." Specifically, of the twenty-five mother–infant dyads in this group, only three remained in good contact with the program, five stayed in moderate or sporadic contact with the program, and sixteen were essentially lost to follow-up. Unfortunately, we know more than we would like to know about what happens to that group of mothers and babies with whom we lose contact altogether. Many of them are the parallels of the mothers who make up our next line of referrals according to age (the 18- to 20-year-old) now with her second or third baby. Those for whom the additional risk factor on the referral form frequently is "previous baby removed from her care; mother wishes to keep this baby; needs help." The sample of toddlers and preschoolers from Dorchester Children's Services can show us more of what has happened to these first babies as they become 2, 3 and 4 years old.

Dorchester Children's Services preschool unit accepted referrals from preschool children identified either by their day care or prekindergarden facilities, or by outreach consultative services to the neighborhood facilities. Over a two-year period, from approximately thirty children whom we were able to engage in some form of evaluative procedure, we found one-third had been born when their mothers were 17 years old or younger—some approaching Juliet's age of almost 14. As we surveyed these referrals, it became very clear that their psychopathology centered around the capacity to attach and remain attached to caregiving figures, and that modification of primitive aggression had been poor or incomplete. Phrases such as "persistent maladaptive ego disturbances—either withdrawal or uncontrolled aggressive outbursts" crop up with discouraging frequency in the case summaries of these children of adolescent mothers. We found that most often we settled on the diagnosis of developmental deviation to describe the failure of consistent loving object attachment and the wildly aggressive attacks directed toward adults or peers who had to frustrate or limit them, or who were approaching them with nurturing and loving behavior. All of these children of adolescent mothers referred to our service when they were 3 to 5 years of age had failed to achieve age-appropriate internal controls over their destructive impulses and were fragile in their capacities to love consistently and to accept loving approaches from their caregivers (Benedek, 1938, 1959; Berliner, 1947). The fact that we have used the term *caregivers* is significant—our observations from the clinical data we gathered were that more often than not, the biological mother (the adolescent) loses in her struggle to be both mother and developing girl and through some external intervention of societal mechanisms, the baby is placed in foster care usually before the age of 2 years or thereabouts.

Terry, a prototypical child in the preschool unit of the Dorchester Children's Services, had been in two foster homes already at the age of 5. In an intensive summer program, where he was in a full day group of four children, any situation in which he had to share food or toys elicited a rage reaction. He attacked and scratched his caregivers or ran away into the surrounding vacant lot areas, and once broke a glass and tried to stab himself in a self-directed destructive rage. When finally he could be held and contained, he sobbed, but could not cling to the adult comforter. Terry lived in a foster home but from time to time, his biological mother, who was 16 when he was born, came to see him with the welfare worker. His mother approached him with clear ambivalence, and could only relate to him when one of the other adults took them both to a restaurant or to the nearby zoo or amusement park. Within the triad of the older woman social worker, his mother could play and talk to Terry, and he had been able to hold her hand or run to her, only to pull away when any attempt to reach out to him was made. He repeated the same behavioral evidence of failure to achieve sustained object attachment toward his foster mother, and with the therapists in our unit in his group milieu. He, in common with most of the children of adolescent mothers we saw, resorted to aggressive, destructive, and impulsive behavior when involved in close contact with adults, as though the unconscious need was to ward off attachments or to protect himself against closeness which was experienced as pain producing rather than pleasure giving (Freud, 1923; Greenacre, 1944; A. Freud, 1965).

Since we saw a number of adolescent mothers over a period of six years, the best exposition of the problems faced by these families can be given by the story of two contrasting girls and their families. We attempted to study this problem by means of data regarding the individual dynamics of each case, and by an attempt to derive from the conscious and unconscious verbal and observational material some insights into the conflicts which occurred.

From our theoretical formulations and from the clinical case studies of adolescents in treatment we were able to make some pretty accurate predictive statements about why this age group (the 14- to 17-year-olds) might be expected to be a high risk group in terms of capacity to mother, and in the capacity to relate appropriately to an infant (Olden, 1953; Josselyn, 1956; Spitz, 1958). The two case vignettes to be presented will we hope illustrate a point that we would like very much to emphasize: in spite of the fact that these cases are drawn from a low socioeconomic class, from an inner-city population, from a group of people who seem to have every strike against them *anyway*, that the intercurrent problems of mothering and of the infant's developmental progress in these cases are not primarily socioeconomic (Olden, 1953).

II

*Case 1*

We first came to know the Franklin family when Diane—at 14 the mother of an 11-month-old daughter—was taken to court by her mother after a fracas in which Diane had drawn a knife on her mother and tried to stab her. Her mother had warded off the blow and Diane had turned on her boyfriend—her baby Sally's father—in a wild and violent gesture of desperation and stabbed him. His wound was not severe, but he and the grandmother were so angered that they had taken Diane to court and asked that she be placed outside the home. The court wisely sensed the need for psychiatric intervention, so in addition to the placement, Diane was sent to us for evaluation.

The Franklin family proved to be a complex, fragmented one. The grandmother was a large, tired looking but domineering woman, who fiercely held onto her role as the principal caregiver of her daughters' three babies, ages 2 years, 11 months, and 7 months. Diane's older sister, now 16, had given birth to the 2-year-old and the 7-month-old, and had completely abdicated her role as mother. She had gone back to high school for the second time, and relinquished the babies to Grandmother Franklin. Diane, who was just past her 14th birthday when Sally was born, was caught in the struggle for possession of her baby, but could in fact do no caregiving without her mother at her side to instruct her. Diane laughed and giggled when the therapist called her "mother" and turned to grandmother for answers to enquiries regarding developmental information. As we saw the family in the interview, grandmother sat in a presiding position, holding the 7-month-old against her breast, while Sally toddled aimlessly about the room, looking detached and fretful.

They were a poor family, and lived in a crowded housing project apartment. One daughter, the oldest of the five children, had been able to leave the family and was in college. She visited and clearly cared for her mother, but had removed herself from the struggles of her two younger sisters—her emancipation had been successful and she guarded her freedom carefully. At home were the two daughters, a younger brother who was withdrawn and obese, and an 8-year-old daughter, the youngest. The grandfather was disabled from a stroke, and spent his time on the living room sofa, sometimes lunging at one of the girls when the arguments became fierce. Grandmother clearly ruled the home, but she had been unable to accept advice to put her husband in a nursing home. He seemed to be another fractious and dependent child in her home where feeding and fighting anchored grandmother to each person there, and only the oldest had escaped.

The point at which we began the evaluation seemed to be the beginning of disintegration—had not the court intervention taken place, we probably would never have seen this family. The disintegration and the loss of the daughter represented both a fulfillment of the wish to separate, but mobilized guilt and regressive longings on Diane's part, and reactivated the grandmother's need to again have the children dependent and under her control. Frank, the obese and isolated 12-year-old son, had capitulated to the infantile role, but Diane fought against it overtly, while she more and more allowed her mother to take over Sally's care.

Sally, the 11-month-old, had walked early, by 9 or 10 months, but seemed to be unresponsive and did not focus on either her mother or grandmother for special comforting or interacting. She handled toys awkwardly and without pleasure, in fact her most consistent behavior was a kind of wandering, briefly touching or reaching for her grandmother or another adult, then just as briefly manipulating a toy, circling her environment without settling to any one person or thing. She could be held, and with effort would fix her gaze onto a caregiving adult, but seemed anxious and tense when she was put in this close contact, preferring the distance and movement. We theorized that she represented motorically the incomplete bonding between family members, and that in the household everyone moved together then apart, never settling nor separating.

### Case 2

Sarena had just turned 14 when Sammy was born. She was the oldest of six children; her youngest sibling was 3 at the time. Sarena was a shy, pudgy child and at 14 seemed more like a 10-year-old than a beginning teenager. Perhaps this accounted for the fact that no one in the family realized she was pregnant until she was nearly into her sixth month. Sarena herself seemed to have been quite unaware and uncertain about what was happening to her. She had no understanding or knowledge about sex or reproduction and had had one menstrual period before becoming pregnant.

In spite of the fact that she seemed to have been a victim of a seduction by a young man known to the family, they reacted with rage against her when the pregnancy was confirmed. Her father reportedly became furious at her, hit her, and pushed her out of the house. When he was persuaded to let her return, he refused to speak to her for weeks on end, although he laid down very stern rules for her, kept her out of school, and required that she take over almost all of the household responsibility, while the mother worked.

This was not a completely new position for Sarena, since she had always been very much dominated by him, more so than by her mother, and never did anything without his consent. She had often been required to stay home from school in order to care for the younger children while the mother worked, and for a long time had been the one who did the cooking for this family of eight. Now she was not only removed from school altogether but was not allowed to leave the house except for her clinic appointments.

This was still the situation when the mother and baby were referred to us shortly after the baby's birth in December.

Although Sarena could reasonably have returned to school for the second semester, her parents refused to let her go. Much pressure was put on the grandparents by a social worker from a neighborhood health clinic, to have the grandmother stop working and take care of her children herself. But grandmother continued to work and Sarena continued to have total care of the household, now adding to this already heavy burden the care of her own baby. Thus from the beginning, this baby was placed in a position of being like one more younger brother to be taken care of. As if to emphasize this, the baby's crib was kept in the grandparents' bedroom, while Sarena continued to share a bedroom with her sister and 3-year-old brother.

During this period, also, the father was almost always in the house, since his main occupation at that time was remodeling the house for both living and renting purposes.

This meant that Sarena was constantly under his surveillance and there were constant battles between them. Meanwhile, there began to be a good deal of open competition over the "ownership" of the baby. In spite of his continuing anger and refusal to soften his feelings toward Sarena, the grandfather spent much time with the baby, took over a good deal of his care, and when grandmother returned from work she also spent her time with this baby while Sarena was left to care for the others.

Our mother–child counselors were virtually helpless in this case, but could not drop it because they were seen, both by themselves and by the social worker at the health center as being Sarena's only source of support.

Visits with Sarena at home and support of her caretaking of the baby were often very hard to manage, since the grandfather or grandmother usually joined in these visits so that only the briefest of conversations could be held with Sarena alone. Even so, she managed to convey how miserable she was, how she wished so much to be allowed to go to school, and how much she resented her parents usurpation of the baby.

In conference with the social worker at the health clinic, we learned that the reason grandmother had been allowed to return to work by welfare was that she had been depressed following a miscarriage that occurred after the birth of her youngest child (then 3).

In the fall, when Sammy was about 8 months old, grandmother stopped working and Sarena was allowed to go to school. Now there began to be more friction between Sarena and her mother as Sarena felt her mother was taking over the baby and closing Sarena out. Father continued to be at odds with her and insisted that she go nowhere but to school and right back, in case she would get into more trouble.

Twice a foster home was found for Sarena and Sammy, but each time the family refused to let her go. In her conferences with her own worker, Sarena expressed her great ambivalence and confusion about what to do. On the one hand, she wanted very much to get away from her father, and also expressed a lot of bitterness toward her mother and the fact that her mother would not protect her or stand up for her at all. But then she would shift to how lonely she would be without her mother and without her brothers and sister. She also was uncertain about how Sammy would feel about leaving the home, because she saw that he was very attached to them, too, and wondered if he would miss them. She was adamant, however, that she would never let them keep him while she left home on her own.

This was pretty much the state of affairs for the next year, with a constant fluctuation about whether Sarena was to stay or leave. When summer came, Sarena, still not quite 16, was sent out to find a job. Now she worked from 7 a.m to 4 p.m. Over these months, Sammy's care had gradually moved almost completely to the grandparents, and the problem of rivalry between mother and daughter increased. Meantime, during this year and a half Sarena was changing from being quietly depressed and unable to take any stand for herself or ever talk back to her parents, to being more assertive, especially with mother, and finally getting into some open fights with her. Some of the characteristic provocativeness of the rebellious adolescent began to be more evident. Now when school time arrived, she was reluctant to leave her job and return to school.

Sarena now challenged parental rules more often. She insisted on having some of her pay for herself instead of giving it all to the parents; she found ways of spending some time with girl friends even though in quite limited ways. In an act that seemed a show of "mothering" her younger sister and opposing her "depriving" mother, she cashed her paycheck before coming home and bought her sister a jacket she badly wanted and that the mother had refused to buy.

She began to openly use Sammy as a threat in her fights with her mother. She would say that soon she would be old enough to leave home and then she would take Sammy with her, and they would lose him. She would provoke her mother by saying, "No, you take care of him. You might as well, he even thinks you're his mother. Go to mama, Sammy." Both statements caused mother to become angry and upset.

## CHARACTERISTICS OF ATTACHMENT BEHAVIORS WITHIN THE BABY-MOTHER-GRANDMOTHER TRIAD

We have focused on the specific triad of the infant–mother–grandmother and feel that, contrary to another point of view in which the adolescent mother is attempting to act out the need for the oedipal child (Spitz, 1958), our understanding of the adolescent mothers we studied indicates that her primary conflict is the struggle for separation between herself and her own mother. The pregnancy is seen as not so much an expression of oedipal sexual wishes, but as an expression of the revived preoedipal need to separate and individuate from the mothering figure. In most of the girls we were able to study, the pregnancy itself (i.e., the baby as an entity) seemed to be incidental, and an attachment to the infant which would lead to the bond between mother and child seemed to be so clouded by the persistent struggle of the girl-mother to separate herself from her own mother that a continuous cathexis of the infant could not be established and maintained. We saw, in a majority of the observations of the infants of the adolescent mothers, that focused eye contact on the part of the baby toward the mother was intermittent and unstable. The babies tended to gaze indiscriminately at other human faces or at inanimate objects in the environment. It was consistently difficult to get the babies to focus and to maintain a fixed gaze. Their visual behavior seemed remarkably similar to the babies diagnosed as failure to thrive, even though they were not malnourished or starved looking. The element of ego and defense formation failure with which we have been most concerned in our clinical assessments of these babies has been the defective modification of aggressive derivatives—the grandmother who cared for her daughter's 11-month-old baby girl came to us describing Sally as a combination of "hellion and good girl," by which she meant that the alternation between Sally's uncontrollable rage and quiet receptive loving periods was unpredictable and unmanageable.

Most of the adolescent mothers, during the pregnancy and after the birth of the baby, regressed to a more intensely ambivalent tie to the grandmother.

The baby, when the adolescent mother and her infant returned to the grandparental home, became the center of controversy, and the focus of rivalrous confrontation. The mother alternated between her wish to be nurtured as she saw her mother nurturing the baby, and her need to possess her infant; it is at this stage that we saw most regression and revival of the hostility erupt toward the grandmother on the part of the mother. Not always in the direct and concrete form it reached in the Franklin family when Diane drew a knife on her mother, but in forms slightly less violent but unmistakable. One mother described to us literal tugs of war between herself and her mother—the baby was grabbed and held or snatched away by the other in these battles. The mother forgot about the source of the fight—which was usually a disagreement over when to feed or where to take the baby—and became consciously enraged and filled with longing to have her mother cuddle *her*, or to leave her alone and stop insisting on the rules of the household. Gradually, such primitive ambivalence pushed the mother and daughter farther apart, and the solution became a separation; the baby was likely to be placed in foster care, and each member of the triad lost a crucial love object.

# REFERENCES

Benedek, T. (1959), Parenthood as a developmental phase. *J. Amer. Psychoanal. Assn.*, 7:384–417.

——— (1938), Adaptation to reality in early infancy. *Psychoanal. Quart.*, 7:200–215.

Berliner, B. (1947), On some psychodynamics of masochism. *Psychoanal. Quart.*, 16:459–471.

Freud, A. (1965), *Normality and Pathology in Childhood.* New York: International Universities Press.

Freud, S. (1923), The Ego and the Id. *Standard Edition*, 19:3–66. London: Hogarth Press, 1961.

Greenacre, P. (1944), Infant reactions to restraint. *Amer. J. Orthopsychiat.*, 14:204–218.

Josselyn, I. (1956), Cultural forces, motherliness and fatherliness. *Amer. J. Orthopsychiat.*, 26:264–271.

Kempe, C. H. (1962), The battered child syndrome. *J. Amer. Med. Assn.*, 181:17–24.

Olden, C. (1953), On adult empathy with children. *The Psychoanalytic Study of the Child*, 8:111–126. New York: International Universities Press.

——— (1958), Notes on the development of empathy. *The Psychoanalytic Study of the Child*, 13:375–403. New York: International Universities Press.

Spitz, R. (1958), On the genesis of superego components. *The Psychoanalytic Study of the Child*, 13:375–404. New York: International Universities Press.

# PART IV:

# Child Abuse

# 12.

# Resistances in the Treatment of a Sexually Molested 6-Year-Old Girl

## KATO VAN LEEUWEN, M.D.

Analysis of a patient when sexual seduction has taken place is often fraught with difficulties of a profound nature (Williams, 1984; Furman, 1984; Burland, 1985; Toff, 1986).

Most analysts have limited personal experience in this area as few sexually seduced children are referred for analysis or even for therapy because of this particular reason. To remedy the dearth of information, we invited those in the community working intensively with sexually abused children to meet with us so that we might broaden our knowledge.

My interest in the effects of sexual seduction was stimulated by the following:

1. Consultations with parents whose children had been molested.
2. A touching letter in the *Los Angeles Times* (1984) from an "Unidentified Resident of Southern California." In it, the

This paper was previously published in the *Internat. Rev. Psycho-Analysis* (1988), 15:149–156.

A shortened version was presented at the Discussion Group Meeting "Psychoanalytic Observations among Vulnerable and High Risk Children: Sexual Abuse of Children," Theodore B. Cohen, Chairman, American Psychoanalytic Association, May 1986, Washington, DC; Part of Panel "Sexual Abuse of Children: Effects in Childhood and in Adults," American Psychoanalytic Association, 1986, New York; International Psychoanalytic Association, 1987, Montreal, Canada.

mother lamented missing early clues that should have aroused suspicion that her 2-year-old daughter was being molested by the baby-sitter. She accepted the advice of psychologists who declared that nothing could be done to help the child.

3. The McMartin preschool investigation in Manhattan Beach, California.

4. Jeffrey Masson's (1984) accusation that Freud changed his theory of sexual seduction as the cause of neurosis to that of fantasied seduction to protect his friends and colleagues.

There is a dearth of published analytic material on sexually abused children. Kramer (1974) describes the tormenting doubts of two youngsters whose mothers excessively stimulated them for the mothers' own gratification. In "Ego Disturbance in a Young Child" (Furman, 1956), sexual seduction surfaced accidentally late in the analysis and sexual abuse was not part of the heading of the article. Neither were sexual events part of the title of Selma Fraiberg's (1952) "A Critical Neurosis of a Two-Year-Old Girl," about a child who showed marked disturbances after observing intercourse at a visit to her grandparents. Most other articles about the effects of child sexual abuse are retrospective about adults who had been abused as children (Freud, 1918; Katan, 1973; Shengold, 1979) revealing the far-reaching effects of the "guilty secrets" and the feeling that they contributed somehow to the seduction.

One of the foremost investigators, Summit (1983, 1985) talks of the "accommodation syndrome"; children's ability to adapt themselves to living with dreadful secrets to maintain an equilibrium and protect family life, "disclosure" and "windows," temporary openings which allow one access to what happened. Children are too afraid of the consequences to tell or stick to the truth and are inclined to alter their stories. They pretend everything is fine. Often threats of reprisals have been made to the child or his family, should the truth be revealed. There is guilt about participation and the compulsion to repeat. It is important that the child be given emotional support. Frequently, especially with father–daughter incest, the mother prefers not to acknowledge the facts because they threaten the fabric of the family or she is too overcome by the idea of sexual molestation to face it. The paternal role ends, and generational boundaries so essential to family life are violated (Adams, 1986). The molesters in many instances see to it that the child repeats the act with someone else to make them coconspirators. Identification with the aggressor leads the sexually abused child to do the same to other children, and often the perpetrators lead the child into these acts. Sex play with younger children often follows, and an intergenerational pattern may be initiated. Not all abusers are sadistic and violent. Many (Kaz, 1986) are colorless, needy individuals, afraid of their sexual impulses toward adults.

Whether sexual abuse of children is a current epidemic or has always existed is being hotly debated. DeMause (1974) stated that the history of childhood is a nightmare from which we have only recently begun to awaken. We are far from being civilized. Child murder and child abuse are still rampant.

For the sake of clarity I will use the term *abuse* in the sense of sexual seduction by an adult and not include exposure to nudity or playing doctor games with friends.

## CASE REPORT

Shortly after learning that her 6-year-old daughter Lois might have been molested, Mrs. B consulted me at the suggestion of a friend. The alleged offender's niece, Martha, and Lois were playmates. He was suspected of inserting his finger in the little girls' vaginas while they were in the bathtub.

As Mrs. B talked she suddenly grasped the significance of Lois' reluctance to attend school, her fatigue and refusal to continue skating lessons for the past six weeks. It was Martha's uncle who transported the two girls. Furthermore, Lois had developed sleeping difficulties along with a facial tic. No longer did she wish to bathe with her brother, although they had previously enjoyed joking about his penis and her vagina. While excessively affectionate and clinging with her mother, she distanced herself from her father. Mrs. B, a pharmacist, worked away from home from early morning until late afternoon, and she'd welcomed the "thoughtfulness" of Martha's uncle who volunteered to drive the girls to their lessons and frequently invited Lois to his home. Knowing what she did now, Mrs. B reproached herself and felt guilty of gross neglect. She panicked and wept profusely while telling me about this and requested advice about how to deal with the situation and what to tell her daughter.

Lois was her first born, a "good baby," an accommodating child who presented few problems except for extreme jealousy of her younger brother Max, a troublemaker and still a bedwetter. Lois was intent on making sure that he did not get more than she did, and they often fought frantically. Developmentally, the little girl's milestones appeared normal. She had been bottle-fed and colicky at first, but feeding problems ceased when goat milk was substituted for formula. Lois toilet trained herself. Mrs. B had found caring for Lois boring and returned to work when Lois was a year old, leaving her with a housekeeper.

Mrs. B suffered from chronic depression and, though obviously competent, early rivalry with her brother and two sisters had left her feeling unappreciated and inadequate. She felt further burdened by her poor relationship with her husband, Dr. B, who was away from home a great deal and extremely critical of her. Dr. B was also often depressed. He had lost his father when quite young and was resentful of his brother and particularly of a younger sister. Mrs. B had considered divorce because she found her husband's behavior unbearable. However, whenever Dr. B felt better their marriage improved.

Lois was a perky 6-year-old who readily entered my office, visually explored the room, and involved herself with the doll furniture. Setting up a happy family scene including a bathroom, a girl in bed with her mother, and a baby in a high chair, she played that the family got up for breakfast. Soon everyone was watching television. When asked why mother had brought her to see me, she denied knowing the reason; but when I wondered if mother were worried about what happened with Martha's uncle, she nodded in assent. Many references to dirt and orderliness followed, and she put aside damaged toys. My comment that she did not seem to like dirty things prompted a trip to the bathroom leaving the door ajar and assuring me upon her return that she had flushed the toilet. When it was time to put the toys away, I commented on her neatness, asking if she were always this tidy. She answered that her room was often a mess. In the waiting room she excitedly told her mother about playing with the toys.

At the second visit *she related a scary dream about a fire hydrant and being afraid that the fireman would not find the snake which was lost in the bushes and that the policeman on a couch might take her to jail.* Lois quickly assured me of her good behavior at school and earning stars. Her main worry was that her parents no longer allowed her to come over and play with Martha. Any inquiries regarding her friend's uncle came to naught other than that Lois and Martha were bathed together. A drawing of a girl showed only the head; the body was cut off.

The first month of treatment dealt primarily with rivalry with her brother. There were many bathtub scenes and frequent play disruptions. Boy toys were smelly and were heaped on my lap. Fears of being attacked were voiced, something might jump out. To establish that everything was fine, she drew happy pictures of rainbows and talked in a silly fashion. An arrangement of a prayer corner with little roses established further protection.

At times, upon entering my office, Lois would bring her face suddenly very close to mine or threaten to smear my mouth with crayon. Once I was so startled that I instinctively put my hand on her shoulder, and she withdrew in fright. However, immediately after, I was asked to scratch her back just like her mother used to do to put her to sleep. "Boo" games were initiated, and Lois had me roar like a monster while she was the mouse. My suggestion that she seemed afraid of the monster who might do things to her was followed by a wish for candy and thumbsucking; but the following day she acted more spontaneously and joyfully and banged dolls together, something she had not previously allowed herself to do. Open references to my toys as being dirty followed, and talk of peepee diapers. A wedding scene with people dancing was succeeded by fright and play disruption.

Although Lois did not mention it, a visit by Martha and her uncle to convince the parents that nothing untoward had happened to their daughter retraumatized her. Lois regressed, and I would find her sitting on mother's lap in the waiting room. To reassure me and herself of her worthiness, she excitedly chattered about the many presents she expected to receive for her birthday—furniture for her room and, most important of all, a cheerleader costume. This equation of candy and gifts with love and self-esteem remained prominent throughout the treatment.

The expression of defensive anxiety in play led me to remark that Martha's uncle had done what grown men should not do to little girls and that it made them feel scared and dirty. Lois angrily told me to stop talking about such things and volunteered that she and Martha enjoyed taking showers together. Now a king and queen were banged together as well as all the other chess pieces. When I raised questions about what she had seen grown-ups do together, she disrupted her play, throwing the chess pieces in every direction. The extent of her despair came through in her drawing of a child with long dirty black hair in a cheerleader's costume.

Regression continued, as did resistance to exploration of her feelings. Lois talked baby talk, put candy in heaps, and complained of boredom. I finally pointed out how difficult it was for her to have fun in my office and that she often stopped playing when she became excited. She responded by messing up her drawings and littering the floor. However, greater freedom of play followed and the wish for a wedding gown for the "Barbie" doll emerged. Lois wanted to be grown up and married. Barbie was fed lots of food, and then again there was play disruption. Not too long after this, Lois' tic returned. In connection with this, she told a story about a man in shorts and a T-shirt pacing the floor like a lion in the zoo, driving her crazy. I noticed that she touched her genitals after returning from the bathroom and that her behavior became increasingly agitated.

Baby games became the order of the day, with me being baby while she played the mother. I wondered if the baby were scared of all these angry, wild feelings and afraid that mother would not love her any more. She then enlarged the nipple hole of a baby bottle and talked of the devil. Tickling and grooming games with mother in the waiting room were initiated with decidedly sadistic overtones. In my office, the baby, during play, was fed but then thrown wildly in the air or pushed under the water or poisoned while mother busily prepared dinner. Mother did not like a chatterbox, Lois explained.

During a subsequent session, Lois spanked the mother doll, then became bored and retreated under a blanket on my couch. I interpreted both her anger with mother and her wish to be a baby like her brother, and I also remarked as to how hard it must have been for her to have a baby brother while she herself was still little and needed her mommy too. Lois agreed smilingly and began to take pleasure at playing games, beating me at checkers.

She began to mention the boys in her class, then played a game of hiding a pencil which I had to find. In the waiting room, she teasingly lifted mother's skirt.

An artificial cheerfulness on her part prompted my asking if Lois acted happy even when she worried. She told me she wanted to make mother laugh and to be like mother. It would be far better to be either a grown-up or a 4-year-old than to feel like a little baby. Being her own age was bad. Adding an explanation for her craving for chocolates, Lois said: "They make you feel yummy when you do not feel yummy." The dress-up games with Barbie began to replace the baby games; gradually a wedding outfit was added and finally a boyfriend. There were many prohibitions, and she used her rosary as protection against sinful feelings.

Around this time her mother informed me that she overheard her son Max telling Lois that Martha had shown him her vagina and asked him to put his penis into it. This again precipitated a return of her tic and a preoccupation with holes, being hurt, and bleeding. I ventured to Lois that she was too afraid to tell me what happened. She said it is not that she is too afraid but that she is too shy to talk about those gross disgusting matters. The pent-up feelings burst through when she surprised me by suddenly climbing on my lap and bouncing up and down.

Another time Lois unexpectedly embraced me, followed by more baby and mommy play, but this time she was the baby. She drew a big red needy and greedy mouth which never has enough of mommy. Sadistic fantasies emerged about wanting to smash my head, let it roll in the streets; she joked about a rat going up her butt and she called me "butt head."

Lois' preoccupation with badness as a source of her parents' unhappiness played a role too. In one of my conversations with the father, he revealed his hatred toward his younger sister, whom he tended to make feel stupid, and we were able to connect this to his annoyance with Lois' doll play and girlish pursuits. His anxiety about himself extended to his children. He was very goal-oriented and he insisted on reading science magazines with them rather than doing something they enjoyed. It was upsetting to him that his children were so distant, and he wondered what to do about it.

Participating in church activities also had its effects, and Lois' first confession loomed large and was very important to her. She felt good about it being her secret, her own business. With this boost to her self-esteem, she began to talk of things happening within the family: father is slamming the door, locking mother out of the bedroom. She followed this by mumbling a "JMJ" (Jesus, Mary, Joseph). I interpreted her fear of bad thoughts, and Lois volunteered that she let "uncle" tickle her vagina. Several sessions later she talked of playing hot pillow with father, then whispering softly, "I hate men." When I suggested that her anger with men had to do with uncle's playing with her vagina and showing his penis, she quickly denied it all and assured me they were only bathing together.

Subsequently, Lois told me how Max unzipped her father's pants and poured water inside.

Preoccupation with hospitals and injuries followed, with me in the role of nurse putting on ever fancier bandages. She then connected hurts with deprivation and said, "Can you imagine, mother let me cry for six months before she thought of giving me goat's milk?" Frightening kidnap fantasies occurred in conjunction with her wish for me to be her mother.

Concern and curiosity about menses and blood surfaced and were partially satisfied by using Judy Blume's books as a secret source of information. Her embarrassment was disguised by talking Pig Latin, making jokes about pulling down panties, fat ladies and babies, and a snake in the bathroom.

Lois revealed her enjoyment of "our secret language" (Ferenczi, 1933) hiding "gross" things, and told me how mother rats kill their babies, which made her feel like a "NOTHING." It is her ambition to be a girl priest and go to heaven.

During play with Barbie, Barbie's boyfriend suddenly turned into a monster; and Lois reported a *dream of a blue-eyed coyote, a bobtail cat.* However, there was too much anxiety to discuss this further or to associate to the dream.

Although Lois was not ready to quit, a termination date had been set as the family planned to move away. She had been in treatment for over two years, and it was suggested that she resume later. She had begun to make new friends, enjoyed school, and felt more comfortable with herself, although some anxiety and obsessive religious rituals persisted. Concern about leaving me was expressed in worry about whether I would still be there for her birthday and in taking home flowers and fruit from my office for her mother. She wanted to make sure that I would wait until she returned even if it would take a hundred years. Her parting words were, "You are my mother. I have two moms."

## DISCUSSION

This case illustrates the pronounced effect of sexual abuse on the development and character structure of a 6-year-old girl who functioned relatively well before these traumatic events took place. The already present intense jealousy of her younger brother and a sense of insecurity about parental love were greatly magnified by the sexual seduction. Her somewhat shaky self-esteem was further damaged resulting in her feeling defiled, spoiled, rotten, a "nothing." Phobic symptoms pronounced at the onset of treatment were partially replaced by obsessive–compulsive behavior. Prematurely precipitated sexual arousal forced her to deal with issues inappropriate to her stage of development. Excitement and helplessness were contained through denial, repression, and religious rituals. Torn between the wish to be a grown-up and desirable like her mother and an infantile regressive need for maternal care and gratification, she could no longer fully enjoy being a child with playmates. Reaffirmation of her goodness and value was constantly sought by performing well in school, pleasing mother and teacher, and getting gifts.

The question of whether seduction took place was affirmed only after a considerable period of therapy, with great hesitation, unexpectedly and suddenly; then it was quickly retracted and denied.

Suggestions of sexual abuse were abundant in her anxiety about being attacked and the content and manner of her play. More typical was her drawing of a girl with a huge red mouth. The attempt to stuff crayon in my face was reminiscent of Furman's patient (1956) who tried to force lipstick in her therapist's mouth while at a high pitch of excitement saying, "I must not tell." It further appears that these children seem to have knowledge of matters which they only could have acquired by being exposed to sex with an adult. Some of the features seem bizarre and sometimes a strange secret language is used (Ferenczi, 1933). The tic Lois displayed recurred whenever the sexual trauma was rekindled, representing a compromise formation, a reflection of conflict between the impulse to act out aggressive, voyeuristic, and sexual impulses and a warding-off of this wish. The fact that sexual abuse occurred during latency was reflected in a phase specific struggle between impulses and superego, accentuated by Lois' religious beliefs. Her sadistic behavior betrayed identification with the aggressor and the compulsion to repeat what was done to her.

Play disruptions occurred frequently commensurate with the severity of the trauma. She wanted to let me know but was afraid, too shy and ashamed, and did not have the words for the unmentionable "bad" things done to her by someone she trusted. It was particularly difficult to deal with ego dystonic sadistic impulses experienced toward her penis-endowed sibling for displacing her. Though curious and interested, she feared and hated men, feelings she coped with by distancing herself from and discarding them. This was partially too in identification with her mother, who often threatened to leave her husband.

In the transference, I was first experienced as a policeman, superego, then as a seductress, and finally as the longed-for good mother who had the patience to listen, the wish to understand, and who would protect her from harm. Most remarkable and not mentioned in the literature on child sexual abuse were extraordinary suddenness of the nonverbal revelations, the spasmodic reenactments of highly charged feelings closely tied to the anxiety and guilt connected with the traumatic forbidden experiences. In connection with the way these intense feelings may surface, Conner (1986) reported how a 6-year-old girl molested in nursery school between the ages of $2\frac{1}{2}$ and $3\frac{1}{2}$ years, in the fifth month of treatment, suddenly had the impulse to "tell" and did so in little spurts spread over a long time period.

The resistances to revelation were major, difficult to overcome, and often frustrating. Others in the community working with sexually abused children have found the experience wearing and report burnout (Summit, 1986; Powell, 1986).

As has been pointed out (Summit, 1983; MacFarlane and Jones, 1986; Steele, 1986) emotional deprivation makes the child more vulnerable to seduction. This may have played a role with Lois, whose mother, though devoted and providing physical care, was depressed and had difficulty deriving pleasure from her children, leaving her daughter hungry for affection and having to go to great lengths to extract what she needed. Lois felt that she had to be mother's caretaker. Mother required cheering, and Lois had to suppress her own wish to be cared for and protected. If she were a good baby with a penis, mother might be more interested. Lois' father demanded performance and demeaned her for her interest in girlish pursuits.

One of the areas requiring close examination is countertransference. Powell (1986) expressed concern that her puritanical upbringing was an obstacle. Being aware of one's sexual and voyeuristic impulses is certainly important. In retrospect, my countertransference of shock over sudden outbursts of feelings unconsciously caused me to align with what for her was unmentionable and prevented me from verbalizing what she warded off. I could have interpreted the intense anxiety she experienced more fully. While supervising the psychoanalysis of a woman sexually molested during latency, I was struck by how both the analyst and the patient veered away from emotions connected with sexual feelings, paralleling the play disruption observed in Lois, and my own hesitancy about confronting her feelings.

To deal with the effects of sexual abuse, one must have a fundamental knowledge of the practices of abusers and what this may represent internally to the child. The leads offered by the child should be followed without introducing extraneous material. That Lois might have been threatened by her abuser and was afraid of retaliation is obvious in retrospect. Initially I connected the child's preoccupation with toilets and bathrooms with concern over masturbation. On further reflection, it seemed she might have become the seducer, be involved in sex play with other children, or be revictimized.

The experience with Lois and learning more about sexual abuse heightened my awareness and caused me to detect episodes in other children and adults whom I treated. It made me keenly aware of the need carefully to pursue the facts, circumstances, and guilty secret feelings associated with past sexual seduction and their effect on later development.

The areas warranting further psychoanalytic investigation include the effects of sexual abuse at different stages of development; and the comparison of analyses of instances where sexual abuse has actually taken place with those where seduction was fantasized. As Anna Freud stated (1981), "normal Oedipal development presupposes that these fantasies remain just what they are, namely irrealities. It is their frustration which leads to the working through of the Oedipus complex initiating the entrance into latency with its inestimable benefits for ego advancement, superego formation and personality development" (pp. 33–34). By studying the deviations caused by sexual seductions, much could be learned about the origin and severity of neuroses, the causes for major resistances in analysis and techniques of dealing with them. One must keep in mind too that in addition to the seduction there are also other traumatic aspects triggering off ordinary neurotic conflicts or neuroses that have lain dormant.

In presenting the case of Lois, I wanted to show what can happen under seemingly banal, ordinary circumstances in any family from an unexpected source. The consequent "soul murder" (Shengold, 1979) destroying the core of a human being leaving a "nothing" is difficult to repair and can have intergenerational consequences. I am not suggesting that every event should be viewed with suspicion; one should be alert, but not paranoid. The symptoms are detectable, requiring quiet, unexcited reassuring resolution. This is a clinical example of how a treatment proceeds.

## SUMMARY

Increased public awareness of the high incidence of sexual abuse of children is prompting reexamination of the psychological consequences of childhood sexual seduction. The conspiracy of silence, which insulates adult society against the terrifying discovery that large numbers of children are molested, exploited, and raped, also affects child analysts. Furthermore, many of us have only limited experience with child sexual abuse and may fail to deal with or recognize the signs and symptoms if consulted for other reasons. The case presented illustrates the profound effects of sexual abuse on the development and character structure of a child who functioned relatively well before the traumatic events took place.

## REFERENCES

Adams, P. (1986), Father-daughter incest: Impact on family subsystems. *The Psychiatric Times*, 3:16.
Burland, J. A. (1985), Workshop: Analysis of adults who experienced sexual abuse as children. American Psychoanalytic Association Meetings, New York, December.
Conner, M. (1986), Southern California Psychoanalytic Institute, Child Analysis Faculty Workshop.
DeMause, L. (1974), *The Evolution of Childhood.* New York: Psychohistory Press.
Ferenczi, S. (1933), The passions of adults and their influence on the sexual and character development of children. *Int. Z fur Psa.*, 19:5–15.

Fraiberg, S. (1952), A critical neurosis in a two-and-a-half year old girl. *The Psychoanalytic Study of the Child*, 7:173–215. New York: International Universities Press.

Freud, A. (1981), A psychoanalyst's view of sexual abuse by parents. In: *Sexually Abused Children and Their Families*, ed. P. B. Mrazek & C. H. Kempe. New York: Pergamon Press.

Freud, S. (1918), From the history of an infantile neurosis. *Standard Edition*, 17:3–122. London: Hogarth Press, 1955.

Furman, E. (1956), An ego disturbance in a young child. *The Psychoanalytic Study of the Child*, 11:312–335. New York: International Universities Press.

——— (1984), Panel. The seduction hypothesis. American Psychoanalytic Association Meeting, New York.

Katan, A. (1973), Children who were raped. *The Psychoanalytic Study of the Child*, 28:208–224. New Haven, CT: Yale University Press.

Kaz, B. (1986), The perpetrators of sexual abuse. Southern California Psychoanalytic Institute, Child Analysis Faculty Workshop.

Kramer, S. (1974), Object-coercive doubting: A pathological defense response to maternal incest. In: *The Analyst and the Adolescent at Work*, ed. M. Harley. New York: Quadrangle.

MacFarlane, K., & Jones, B. (1986), *Sexual Abuse of Young Children*. New York: Guilford Publications.

Masson, J. M. (1984), *The Assault on Truth: Freud's Suppression of the Seduction Theory*. New York: Farrar, Strauss & Giroux.

Powell, G. (1986), Southern California Psychoanalytic Institute, Child Analysis Faculty Workshop.

Shengold, L. L. (1979), Child abuse and deprivation: Soul murder. *J. Amer. Psychoanal. Assn.*, 27:533–559.

Steele, B. F. (1986), Some sequelae of sexual maltreatment of children. Vulnerable Child Discussion Group, American Psychoanalytic Association Meetings, Washington, DC.

Summit, R. (1983), Recognition and treatment of child sexual abuse. In: *Coping with Pediatric Illness*, ed. C. Hollingworth. New York: Spectrum Publications, pp. 115–172.

——— (1985, 1986), Southern California Psychoanalytic Institute, Child Analysis Faculty Workshop.

Toff, H. (1986), Southern California Psychoanalytic Institute, Child Analysis Faculty Workshop.

Unidentified Resident of Southern California (January 1984), My little daughter has been molested. *Los Angeles Times*.

Williams, M. (1984), Reconstruction of an early seduction and its aftereffects. *J. Amer. Psychoanal. Assn.*, 35:145–163.

# 13.

# Child Sexual Abuse: Changes in Psychoanalytic Perspective and Countertransference Denial

## KATO VAN LEEUWEN, M.D.

Annie Katan (1973) in her landmark contribution, "Children Who Were Raped," calls attention to the fact that child analysts rarely have the opportunity to analyze children who at a very early age experience sexual molestation by an adult. Katan vividly reconstructs sexual abuse in the lives of two women patients. She convincingly portrays the tragic drama of their childhood traumata. These analysands had done poorly with their male analysts because of their provocative aggression which masked deep underlying anxiety. One of the patients had told Katan that she could not stand being alone with a man especially if he sat behind her. This led the analyst to suspect that the patient had been seduced by a man who approached her from the rear. The woman then recalled exciting games played with her father, when he bit the child on the cheek and upper arms while caressing her, his hands in her underpants, her legs spread apart, and his genitals touching hers. His excitement would mount until he bit her. After he hurt her he would give her a chocolate bar. When Katan inquired about the patient's

The original version was presented at the 20th anniversary of the Workshop on the Vulnerable Child in San Francisco, May 4, 1989, at the meetings of the American Psychoanalytic Association.

feelings, a further memory emerged of being molested by a stranger.

## SHIFTS IN ATTITUDES

Over time attitudes toward the significance of sexual abuse have undergone marked shifts. Freud (Breuer and Freud, 1893–1895) attributed the hysteric symptoms of twelve female and six male patients to sexual molestation in childhood. After he abandoned the seduction theory, literature involving these events became sparse, and were no longer recognized as major factors in emotional illness and character pathology. Ferenczi (1933) was not taken seriously when he reminded the analytic community of the importance of actual sexual seduction. The Kinsey report (Kinsey, Pomeroy, and Martin, 1948), while indicating that 20 to 30 percent of women college students had been raped in childhood, brought about little change in psychiatric concepts of etiology.

Where twenty years ago not much was written on the subject and the public was unaware of the frequency of sexual molestation, we now have a burgeoning interest in the subject. Analysts too have begun to deal with sexual abuse in papers and workshops. The women's movement should be credited with raising our consciousness first to widespread physical abuse of women in childhood, and ten years later to child sexual abuse (Summit, 1983). The public has become aware of the astonishingly widespread frequency of sexual molestation. A door-to-door survey in San Francisco in 1983 of 930 women showed that 28 percent had had sexual encounters before 14 years of age (Russell, 1983). A *Los Angeles Times* poll in 1985 of 2,627 U.S. adults chosen randomly by telephone showed that 27 percent of the women and 16 percent of the men were molested as children. Two-thirds of the abused were girls and 93 percent of their abusers were men. Since we usually assume that sexual abuse is more likely to occur in emotionally neglected children, it is of interest to note that in this survey, victims were only slightly more likely than nonvictims to come from unhappy, broken homes, or not to have been close to their mothers. Fewer than half told a parent or relative within a year of its occurrence. Usually no effective action was taken. Most people did not tell anyone because they were ashamed, afraid, or did not consider the abuse serious.

More credence is given by psychiatrists today to the history of sexual abuse in childhood. However, there remains a frequent failure to explore the relation between the abuse and the presenting pathology. In order to understand and search for these connections one has to be familiar with the practices of the abusers and pursue what the sexual seduction represented internally to the patient at the time it was experienced. A thorough grasp of child development and the effects of sexual abuse at each stage is extremely helpful.

## TRANSFERENCE AND COUNTERTRANSFERENCE

One of the most important aspects in the diagnosis and treatment of child sexual abuse is countertransference denial. The following vignettes are but a small sample of what I have come across in recent years in my practice and in supervising psychiatric residents and psychoanalytic candidates.

In "Resistances in the Treatment of a Sexually Molested 6-Year-Old Girl" (van Leeuwen, this volume, chapter 12, pp. 185–198) I examined the young patient's desperate attempts to cover up what happened and my reactions to this. The frustration I experienced in following up clues with the child, ran parallel to those one of my students encountered with an adult patient.[1]

In spite of repeatedly pointing out what these abrupt changes indicated, the supervisee was not able to connect them with the patient's forbidden oedipal impulses. Later he came to recognize that his countertransference denial was due to the fact that the woman reminded him of his mother and he feared that any mention of sexuality might be taken as a seductive overture.

---

[1] Play activity disruptions in children probably are the equivalent of sudden shifts in the verbal associations of adults.

Thus, a depressed woman patient presented at a Continuous Case Seminar revealed that she had been sexually abused as a child by her father and older brother. Though the therapist accepted what the patient said there was no attempt to connect the symptoms of estrangement, low self-esteem, and fear of completing her career plans, to her feelings about the abuse. Again in this example, the trainee could not make use of my efforts to help him understand why the abuse was important to the dynamics of the case.

Reluctance to explore incestuous fantasies is commonly experienced by those who do therapy with the sexually abused regardless of the age of the patient. One psychiatrist noted that interviewing court-assigned children presented no problem for him, while his approach differed markedly in private practice. In the latter he noted his avoidance of sexually tinged material.

The reluctance to pursue leads is present even in very experienced analysts. At a case conference, the presenter gave a cohesive picture of the analysis of a 3-year-old boy. Data were presented about the child suddenly beginning to expose his genitals and pull down his pants, which made me suspect molestation. The reporting analyst glanced at me but continued the discussion without mentioning the possibility of sexual abuse. After the presentation, the speaker confided to me that he now saw he had unwittingly avoided this exploration.

Five-year-old Helen had been in therapy because of biting and kicking in school. After several months the child began to report nightmares to her mother which, however, she hid from her therapist. At the same time, Helen began to complain of itching and a rash in the rectal area. The pediatrician treated her for pinworm but the complaint persisted and was aggravated each time the child spent the night with her father who lived separately. She pulled down her panties in the waiting room, and in great agitation wanted to bite the therapist's buttocks. Helen had sustained a disfiguring scar on her face at age 2 from a dog who attacked her, and she underwent a number of operations to improve her appearance. A personality change had taken place at that time, and the child turned from being a sweet, compliant little girl into one who angrily attacked her mother. The question arose whether Helen's new symptoms were due to the dog bite or to sexual abuse. The therapist who had been doing excellent work with the child became completely paralyzed when the question of molestation arose. She feared having to report the event to the authorities, as is the law, and thus aggravate the already tenuous relationship between the parents. All manner of rationalizations were utilized such as precipitation of suicide in the mother, psychosis in the father, or that the child already had too much to cope with.

When the rash cleared up spontaneously because Helen no longer slept at her father's house, the therapist relaxed somewhat, convinced now that her supervisor had been wrong. Nevertheless, she felt compelled to inquire further about the possibility of sexual abuse and did so hesitantly. She reported her findings in a high-pitched, childlike voice quite different from her usual confident tone. Upon recalling that she herself had been accosted as a child, and how hysterical and reproachful her mother had become on hearing the story, obstacles to treatment were removed. Over time with great skill the supervisee was able to analyze the many ramifications of the sexual abuse as it was revealed in the child's dramatic play and behavior. The therapist supported the family through many complicated situations including legal involvements.

Awareness of the possibility of child sexual abuse does not necessarily result in analysis of the symptoms, partly because of the strength of the patient's fears. After a brief illness 9-year-old Marilyn developed a sleep phobia which required mother's presence in her bedroom. The child was afraid to spend the night away from home. A clue to her behavior came from a dream reported at the first session in which Marilyn vomited because of "something very disgusting." At the next session obviously afraid to tell more, the dream was denied. Subsequently whenever the dream was mentioned, the child cried. Other themes were worked through without much difficulty, particularly her struggle with an older brother, and her fear of standing up to him. Disgust was displayed in relating an incident where she observed cats being cut up in a laboratory. Ultimately she expressed feelings of loneliness, and identification with a neglected, deserted kitten.

Occasionally she suddenly would speak of a "freaky" thought about seeing a naked man in a tree looking at her. However, as soon as she was asked to elaborate, she warded off the entire matter. Improvement took place in spite of her developing a phobia about therapy. She became more assertive and friendly with her brother, performed better in school, made new friends, and no longer needed mother to stay in her room at night. Throughout treatment the therapist experienced frustration and found it difficult to work with the reluctant child. It seemed that the analyst failed to interpret the defenses against the intense affect experienced, and felt put off by the patient's withdrawal and crying whenever she was confronted.

Difficulties may be present in the analysis of child sexual abuse because the experiences are repressed, acted out, or split off. Thelma G, an efficient professional woman, sought help in dealing with a work situation. The patient expected to be fired because of abrasive behavior. Furthermore her marriage was suffocating. Resentment about being unable to assert herself had led to many affairs to get even with her husband. She was consumed by anger. When Mrs. G was 4½ years old, her father died after a lingering illness. Much to her dismay she was left to the care of her grandparents. Painfully ambivalent toward her longed-for mother, whom she fantasized had murdered father, the distraught little girl decided to repudiate mother by extremely negative behavior. At age 7 she was molested by a handyman.

Mrs. G escaped from home at 16 by marrying a severe, demanding, much older man, about whom she experienced childlike ambivalence. She recalled manipulating her husband into abusing their daughter sexually at the same age that this had happened to her. The daughter never forgave the mother. Interestingly, Mrs. G's son married a woman who had also been molested and this young woman confided in Mrs. G her concern that she might sexually abuse her own infant. Mrs. G ended her first session by relating that her brother had committed suicide several years earlier, and that she too had suicidal fantasies. If she did succeed, her husband would be undone, and on further analysis, so would her therapist.

Based on the unconscious compulsion to repeat, the patient was alternately compliant and rebellious. Mrs. G acted out her childhood experiences of sexual abuse, abandonment, neglect, and anger. She confounded her psychiatrist with numerous upheavals including an extramarital affair followed by a homosexual liaison. The patient displayed pride at being able to voice angry criticism of her homosexual partner without the intense fear experienced with her husband. Upon being followed by a man on a weekend outing, she recalled how as a child she attempted to seduce her uncle, and her dismay when he would not have any part of this. The stormy therapy soon came to an end without much insight being accomplished. Reluctance to intervene after the act paralyzed the psychiatrist and kept her from confronting the patient with her acting out behavior in the transference.

Responding to the media's current interest in childhood sexual abuse, Barbara E wondered if her sudden disgust with a man to whom she had been very attracted could be related to similar events in her own childhood, though she could not recall any such episodes. Her symptomatology included intense self-loathing, gastrointestinal symptoms, premenstrual complaints, and headaches.

Over time the story emerged in bits and pieces. Mrs. E was her father's favorite and was made to feel that she was very important, easily outstripping her mother whom she thought took little interest in her. At the same time the daughter resented her father's "exploitative" attitude, which put her on display. Father often drank to excess, frequently falling down. The child would take care of him as he lay nude on the floor. These episodes were never mentioned in the family, and Mrs. E too acted as if nothing had happened. One of her early childhood memories was of being on a swing, with her panties exposed, while father watched. She concluded that she must have been an oversexed little girl.

In the therapeutic situation Mrs. E dramatized her symptoms while omitting themes which she found too difficult or embarrassing to deal with, seducing the therapist into admiring her tenacity and wish for discovery. Unconsciously Mrs. E submitted to what she thought her psychiatrist expected from her.

She was in a state of perpetual fury over slights and impositions committed by her friends.

Inability to establish the validity of her feelings and the veracity of her memories was a significant feature. As this tendency was interpreted she recalled being molested by a friend of the family. Later in the analysis when it was brought to her attention that she often used swear words, she revealed the pressure of constant sexual images. Pursuit of the specific expressions led to further details.

## DISCUSSION

These vignettes illustrate the vicissitudes of the diagnosis and treatment of sexual abuse. Where in the past I was aware that the children I saw in treatment had been sexually stimulated, I had not necessarily considered the possibility of sexual abuse. However, I did not assume that adult patients telling me of incestuous relationships were fantasizing. Nevertheless I did not thoroughly analyze how the symptoms of anger and distrust of men were related to early sexual violation.

Alertness to the possibility of sexual abuse definitely has enlarged the scope of my inquiry. The experience is frequently central and clearly recalled, though without accompanying affect. Issues of emotional abuse, neglect, or lack of protection by the mother, and other narcissistic hurts, may be present. There are threats of violence, and major demands for secrecy. These patients feel deeply guilty and want their participation kept secret. They experience self-loathing, shame, and unconsciously punish themselves. A thorough analysis should include the uncovering of the most critical fantasies and affects surrounding the traumatic events. If the trauma continues to be denied, repressed, split off, or acted out, then we may never uncover the full extent of the associated unconscious fantasies and thus place the treatment in jeopardy of remaining anemic and speculative.

There are many gradations of abuse from actual penetration to fondling, exposure to nudity of adults, suggestive remarks (Weil, 1989). If it is so omnipresent, we need to examine how the ubiquitous sexual fantasies of parents about their children are either warded off or acted upon. Lowering of defenses against incestuous fantasies are frequent when men are alcoholic, on drugs, or sexually frustrated. Sexual abuse by the previous generation is reenacted with offspring. Basically, children are considered the parents' property to treat the way they see fit. Experiencing them as separate human beings with their own needs and rights is a recent development in the history of mankind.

It is the analyst's function to ferret out as well as possible the effects of exposure to sexual stimulation, including sexual assault. There is much yet to be learned in terms of detection and technique. What is evident is that we are easily thrown off the track, we do not always follow leads, and there are reasons for this.

The differentiation between actual and fantasied seduction is crucial to our understanding and effectively dealing with patients. When actual seduction takes place, the pathology is far more severe, all other factors being equal. Interpretations are only partially effective in overcoming a patient's reality. Differentiating factors include abrupt, sudden motion, or explosive swearing, or sexualized images indicative of the overwhelming quality of the traumatic situation. The unconscious purpose is both to turn passive into active, as well as to shock, frighten, and seek revenge against the abusing parent via verbally attacking the analyst. Some act out considerably and unconsciously manipulate reality crises in the service of resistance purposes. Abrupt premature termination of treatment by the patient is frequent. The features in an analysis which result in successful therapeutic outcome need to be carefully studied.

There is nothing so humbling and instructive as paying close attention to aspects which are difficult to pursue. But to tune into areas in which one feels frustrated, confused, or reluctant, may help us gain access to the patient's unconscious. This is true in the treatment of adults and even more so with children and adolescents with their sudden manifestations of instinctual drives and prohibitions against them. Of course one has to use caution so as not to assault the patient or move too fast in therapy.

All of this becomes much clearer in the supervisory process as the supervisor has more distance from the patient. If one considers the strength of resistance in patients to emergence of their sexual secrets, it becomes easier to understand why there are widespread resistances to discovery in the psychoanalyst as well. This is so partly in response to the patient's transference, and partly originating in the therapist's unconscious conflicts. Some of the difficulties are the result of unfamiliarity with what can happen to an abused child. Though I experienced much frustration early on, more knowledge has resulted in an increased capacity to recognize the special qualities and behaviors within the transference. I don't find myself as lost and am now more able to overcome my own concerns.

Everyone has blind spots and defenses against voyeuristic and incestuous impulses. There is a reluctance to penetrate what the patient is intent on hiding. No one wants to believe that these unmentionable things happen, and patients of every age tend to reveal, and then retract, bits of information leading to exposure of their humiliating plight. Psychiatrists may not be able to follow leads or are thrown off the track, aiding the patient's denial and colluding in their doubts. There is an unconscious fear of being drawn into a projective identification with the patient's panic state, and the extent of their depression. Seductiveness may be difficult to deal with, and the psychiatrist is concerned both about being seduced or being seductive in turn. Questioning or even listening may be experienced as a repetition of the trauma.

To analyze these patients with good results, one needs to be in touch with and overcome one's hesitancy, and be convinced that making connections with feelings about the sexual seduction is helpful. Be alerted by peculiar remarks, idiosyncratic comments, reenactments, repetition in daily life and in the transference, screen memories, etc. When therapists feel frustrated or at a loss they should suspect child sexual abuse. One could speculate that therapists who have themselves been sexually abused are handicapped in special ways in dealing with sexual abuse unless they have worked through these situations. Those who permit themselves to follow up leads may be rewarded with success. I believe this was the reason for Katan's

KATO VAN LEEUWEN

ability to analyze the women patients mentioned in her article where her predecessors fell short. DeWald (1987) successfully analyzed a patient who had been in treatment with four previous therapists. Weinshel (1986) became suspicious of sexual abuse when a patient fantasied that he was masturbating behind her and that she saw his penis. Others may analyze many areas but back away from indications of sexual abuse.

## CONCLUSIONS

Psychoanalysts are prone to the same sexual conflicts and traumas as everyone else. Our defenses against forbidden impulses and fear of incestuous wishes make treatment of the sexually abused more difficult. It is important to follow up on every lead and not be deterred by evasive maneuvers. We can delay our inquiry but return at a propitious time, always dealing with the mechanisms of defense first and getting in touch with the prevalent affect, whether it be anxiety, the wish to be understood and loved, the fear of loss of support, or of threats. A proper balance between the need to provide reparative care and understanding connections is important, as is giving the analytic process sufficient time to work through the traumas.

Failures of therapy can be due to failure to understand the connection between the sexual events and presenting psychopathology, much as in the treatment of Holocaust victims where we experience horror and therefore are hesitant to fully explore. If 20 to 30 percent of the population has been sexually abused, the same statistics must hold true for those involved in doing therapy. The large number of papers now being published and the focusing of interest on the topic of child sexual abuse may bring forth more knowledge for the future.

## REFERENCES

Breuer, J., & Freud, S. (1893–1895), Studies on Hysteria. *Standard Edition*, 2. London: Hogarth Press, 1955.
DeWald, P. (1987), Effects in an adult of incest in childhood—A case report. Paper presented at American Psychoanalytic Association Meetings.
Ferenczi, S. (1933), The passions of adults and their influence on the sexual and character development of children. *Int. Z. fur Psa.*, 19:5–15.

Katan, A. (1973), Children who were raped. *The Psychoanalytic Study of the Child*, 28:208–224. New Haven, CT: Yale University Press.

Kinsey, A. C., Pomeroy, W. B., & Martin, C. E. (1948), *Sexual Behavior in the Human Male*. Philadelphia: W. B. Saunders.

Summit, R. (1983), Recognition and treatment of child sexual abuse. In: *Coping with Pediatric Illness*, ed. C. Hollingworth. New York: Spectrum Publications.

Russell, D. E. H. (1983), The incidence and prevalence of intrafamilial and extrafamilial sexual abuse of female children. *Child Abuse & Neglect*, 7:133–146.

Weil, J. L. (1989), *Instinctual Stimulation of Children: From Common Practice to Child Abuse*, Vols. 1 & 2. Madison, CT: International Universities Press.

Weinshel, E. (1986), The effects of sexual abuse in childhood as observed in the psychoanalysis of adults. Presentation to panel of the American Psychoanalytic Association.

# CONCLUSION

# Children and the Mean-Spirited Times in Which They Live: A Report to the Committee on Social Issues

## THEODORE B. COHEN, M.D.

A wide-ranging, three-year study for the Carnegie Corporation on the status of young American children was released in April 1994, and it confirms some of our worst fears about the most precious and most vulnerable members of our society. Millions of infants and toddlers are so deprived of medical care, loving supervision, and intellectual stimulation that their growth into healthy and responsible adults is threatened. The plight of the nation's youngest and most vulnerable children is a result of many parents being overwhelmed by poverty, teenage pregnancy, divorce, or work. It paints a bleak picture of disintegrating families, persistent poverty, high levels of child abuse, inadequate health care, and child care of such poor quality that it threatens the intellectual and emotional development of a vast number of American youngsters.

The Carnegie Report (*New York Times*, April, 1994) draws a picture of a United States that ranks near the bottom of the industrialized nations in providing such services as universal health care, subsidized child care, and extensive leaves from work for families with children under age 3. This despite the fact that recent scientific evidence, which has been accumulating for decades, demonstrates that these early years are critical in the development of the human brain.

A version of this report to the Committee on Social Issues was presented at the American Psychoanalytic Association, Philadelphia, PA, May 19, 1994.

The Carnegie report recommends:

1. Offering parent education in school and discouraging teenagers from becoming parents;
2. Guaranteeing quality child care through a combination of government and business support;
3. Overhauling the health care system to provide a standard package of services such as immunization for young children and prenatal care;
4. Mobilizing communities to examine the services available locally for young children and to offer those services in one place, as settlement houses did in the early 1900s;
5. Maternity or paternity leaves of four to six months for parents of children under 3 years of age with at least partial payment of the parent's wages.

The report notes that 3 million children, nearly one-fourth of all American infants and toddlers, live in poverty. Divorce rates and the number of births to unmarried women and single-parent households have all soared in the last thirty years. Children in single-parent households, it points out, are more likely to experience behavioral and emotional problems than those in two-parent households. The number of children entering foster care jumped by more than 50 percent between 1981 and 1991, rising from 300,000 to 460,000.

Reports of child abuse are rising, the task force found, with one in every three abused children being a baby less than a year old. (In 1992, reports of abuse and neglect rose 30 percent, to 2.9 million, with 40 percent of the reports substantiated: again, nearly half of the victims were under one year old.) More than half of women with children under a year old are working. Many of their children spend most of each week in such poor child care that it threatens to harm their development. And an increasing number of very young children grow up witnessing stabbings, shootings, and beatings as everyday events, the task force said.

According to a new study by the Harvard Graduate School of Education, working-class parents face some of the worst shortages of preschools in the country. In many cases both parents have to work, but then earn too much money to get subsidies that poor parents receive to pay for preschool programs like Head Start. Four million children now attend one of 80,000 preschools nationwide. There is a long waiting list for preschools in inner cities.

American children are among the least likely in the industrialized world to be immunized.

Fewer than half of the babies in the nation's major cities get all of their vaccinations by the age of 2. Of the areas studied, Boston had the best rate, 58 percent, and Houston had the worst, 11 percent. Immunizing children has become more expensive and complicated in recent years. In 1983, the total cost in the private sector was $28—in 1993, the cost had risen to $247. The National Commission to Prevent Infant Mortality budget request for $460,000 was axed from the 1994 federal budget. The National Commission is credited with helping call attention to the nation's deplorable infant mortality rate, twenty-first among developed countries at nine deaths per one thousand births.

Meanwhile, life does not get any easier as children get older. The health status of adolescents has actually declined instead of getting better. More kids are committing suicide and dying of homicide. The human immunodeficiency virus (HIV) rate in this population is going up at a faster rate than for any other segment of the population. The American Medical Association and other medical groups have proposed guidelines for addressing the health care needs of adolescents. They view teenagers as a distinct group with unique needs, and seek to meet those needs through annual preventive services visits for patients 11 to 21 years old. The goal is to confront health risks before they cause medical problems.

Surgeon General Joycelyn Elders argues that school-based clinics are vital if the health system reform is to make any difference in the lives of adolescents, whom she calls the most medically underserved segment of the population. President Clinton's health care reform legislation would fund the establishment of such clinics nationwide, along with comprehensive school health education programs targeted to low-income communities. A summary of this reform plan prepared by the Surgeon General's Office identified 4.5 million students in 9411 middle, junior high, and high schools nationwide as being at "high risk" due to poverty, smoking, drug abuse, unprotected sexual activity, or violence.

President Clinton's 1995 budget as submitted to Congress included total outlays of $673 billion for the Department of Health and Human Services, a 6.5 percent increase over 1994. Cathy Brady, speaking on behalf of the Mental Health Liaison Group, a coalition of forty-seven national mental health advocacy organizations said: "The President's budget severely under funds neuroscience and behavioral research at the National Institutes of Health." The freeze in funding for most programs raises questions about the administration's commitment to prevention. However, building on a bipartisan consensus that it pays to invest in children, the budget contains significant increases in health, nutrition, and education programs. If past practice is any guide, Congress will follow Clinton's lead, though it may change some of the numbers. As Marian Wright Edelman, president of the Children's Defense Fund, a liberal advocacy group whose Board of Directors Hillary Rodham Clinton once chaired, said: "In a very tough budget context, the administration has worked hard to maintain and improve children's programs."

The budget would raise the allocation for childhood immunizations by 68 percent, with increases of 21 percent for Head Start and 11 percent for the Women, Infants and Children Nutrition Program. The budget would authorize spending $150 million—an increase of $90 million—on a new "family preservation" program aimed at reducing the number of children in foster care. The new Head Start funds would go to bringing more preschool children into the program, as well as addressing quality concerns by raising the pay of teachers and aides and improving facilities and equipment.

Clinton has also called for a 7 percent spending increase for the Education Department. A new School-to-Work program for young people who don't go to college is to get $300 million. Clinton's pet National Service Corps would get $850 million, up 48 percent, to let 33,000 Americans perform public service in exchange for college tuition grants.

The Institute of Medicine in January 1994 recommended $50 million be spent for the fiscal year 1995 for research on interventions aimed at preventing the onset of mental disorders and behavioral problems in infants and children.

In December 1993, the Clinton administration ordered states to begin payment for medical abortions in cases of rape or incest after March 31, 1994, or risk losing billions in Medicaid funding (Medicaid is a joint federal-state program). At least ten states have said they will not comply with the federal order.

In January 1994, the Supreme Court ruled that abortion clinics can invoke federal racketeering laws to sue antiabortion protest groups for damages, thus giving clinics a new weapon with which to combat violent demonstrations at their facilities.

As we can see, there is awareness in government and elsewhere of the need to do everything possible to improve the appalling situation in which so many of our children live. Since House of Representatives Joint Resolution 302 designates 1994 through 1999 as the "Years of the Girl Child," to encourage equality for girls in health care, education, and all phases of family and community life, it is worth taking a look at the current status of working women, who in so many cases are the sole support of their families.

In 1989, American women in general were paid only 66 percent of their male counterpart's earnings, according to Census data. For the previous three decades that level had hovered around 60 percent. In New York City, women who worked full time in 1989 earned 77.5 cents for each dollar earned by men, up from 71 cents on the dollar in 1979. Comparison with men's earnings is considered the most basic measure of women's status in the work force. Clearly, women still have a long way to go to achieve pay equity, and much of the poverty to be found in the population of single-parent families, most headed by women, is due to this imbalance.

Finally, the Children's Defense Fund describes moments in America for children:

Every 30 seconds a baby is born into poverty

Every 59 seconds a baby is born to a teen mother
Every 104 seconds a teenage girl becomes pregnant
Every 2 minutes a baby is born at low birth weight
Every 2 minutes a baby is born to a mother who had late
  or no prenatal care
Every 2 hours a child is murdered
Every 4 hours a child commits suicide
Every night 100,000 children are homeless

As Surgeon General Elders has said: "We've got to do a better job of taking care of the most valuable resource we'll ever have, our children."

# Name Index

Achenbach, T. M., 155, 161
Ackerman, N., 130
Adams, P., 187
Adelson, E., 159
Adler, A., 12*n*, 25, 31
Amighi, J., 48
Anders, T. F., 160
Anthony, E. J., 153
Arlow, J. A., 147
Axelrad, S., 107

Balint, M., 37
Barrett, T. F., xvi, 7, 110, 122–125
Benedek, T., 172
Benjamin, J., 63
Benveniste, E., 27
Beres, D., 18
Bergman, A., 4, 5, 107, 159
Bergmann, M., 36
Berland, J. A., 108
Berliner, B., 172
Bernard, V. W., 130, 132
Biringen, Z., 18, 19
Blos, P., Jr., xiv–xv, xix, 98, 103,
     107–111
Blume, J., 192–193
Bonaparte, M., 32
Borowitz, E., 36
Borwicz, M. M., 41
Brady, C., 216
Brazelton, T. B., 11, 153
Brenner, E., xi, xiv
Brenner, I., xii–xiii, 42
Bretherton, I., 156
Breuer, J., 200
Brody, S., 107
Buchsbaum, H., 156–157
Buie, D. H., 62, 63, 72

Burland, J. A., xi, 125, 185
Burlingham, D., 107, 123

Campbell, K., 116–119
Carey, W., 153
Cassidy, J., 156
Cicchetti, D., 156–157
Clinton, B., 215–217
Clinton, H. R., 107, 216
Clyman, R. B., 18, 19, 30, 156–157
Cohen, D. J., 31, 145
Cohen, T. B., xi, xviii
Compton, A., 11
Conner, M., 195
Culp, A. M., xvii, 154

Dare, C., 18–19
Davis, E., 129, 130–131
de Hirsch, K., 141–142
DeMause, L., 187
DeWald, P., 209
Drexel, J., 38–41

Eberhart-Wright, A., xvii, 154
Edelman, G. M., 28
Edelman, M. W., 216
Elders, J., 215–216, 218
Elise, D., 143
Emde, R. N., 18, 19, 100, 107–108,
     155–157, 159, 164
Erikson, E. H., 134–135
Escalona, S., 98–99
Esman, A., 150
Etchegoyen, R. H., 11
Etezady, M. H., xi–xii, 24–33

Fenichel, O., 99
Ferenczi, S., 193, 194, 200

219

# Subject Index

poverty of, 60–61
unemployment in, 59–60
Infant
  of adolescent mother, 167–180
  AIDS-infected, 167
  CNS of, 134
  developmental psychiatry in inner
      city setting, 129–151
  mortality rate of, xviii
  research and intervention in, 100–
      101
Infant busy box, 77
Infantile aggression, 62–63
Infantile sexual drives, 139–140
"Inhibitions, Symptoms, and
    Anxiety" (Freud), 32
Injury, preoccupation with, 192
Inner city
  developmental psychiatry in, 129–
      151
  neighborhoods, xv–xvi
Institute of Medicine, 217
Internalization, 4, 5
Interpretation, in developmental
    psychiatry, 146
Introjection, 5

Janowski camp, 39–41
Joint Commission on the Mental
    Health of Children, forma-
    tion of, 132–133

Language
  constitutional deficits and deficits
      in, 143–145
  delayed comprehension of, 144–
      145
  dysfunctional, 149
  hostile aggression and, xiii, 51–57
  learned in relationships, 141–142
Language acquisition
  factors in, 52
  psychological risk of delay in, 51
Learning
  disturbances of, 102
  procedural, 19, 30

Libidinal-aggressive imbalance,53–57
Libidinal cathexis, 3–4, 12–13
  of part-objects, 5
  of self, 36
Libidinization, 7–8, 38
Libido
  distribution of, 13
  investment in body parts, 39–40
  movement patterns and, 36–38
  narcissistic, xiii, 36, 38, 42–43, 45
Libido theory, 25
Little Hans case, 31–32
Loss
  aggression and, 59–72
  early catastrophic, xiii–xiv

Manuel children case study, 64–66
Mastery, 147
  narcissism and, 12
Masturbation, concern with, 196
Mauthausen camp, 38–39
Medicaid funding, 217
Medical education, psychoanalysis
    and child development
    concepts in, 97–98
Memory
  declarative, 30
  procedural, 30
Menninger Clinic, 160
Menstruation, concern about, 192–
    193
Mental health care, 120
  child analysis in, xiv–xvi, 97–111
Mental Health Liaison Group, 216
Mental illness, DSM diagnosis
    classification of, 99–100
Mental life, infant, 100–101
Minimal brain dysfunction, 133
Mirroring, 16
Moral development, 155–156
Moral dilemma story, 163–164
Mother
  adolescent, xvi–xvii, 153–165
  awareness of, 4
  effects of lost adolescence on, 167–
      180